MODERN HORROR
WRITERS

Writers of English: Lives and Works

MODERN HORROR WRITERS

Edited and with an Introduction by

Harold Bloom

CHELSEA HOUSE PUBLISHERS
New York   Philadelphia

Jacket illustration: Hand-colored photograph by J. K. Potter (courtesy of J. K. Potter).

CHELSEA HOUSE PUBLISHERS

Editorial Director Richard Rennert
Executive Managing Editor Karyn Gullen Browne
Copy Chief Robin James
Picture Editor Adrian G. Allen
Creative Director Robert Mitchell
Art Director Joan Ferrigno
Production Manager Sallye Scott

Writers of English: Lives and Works

Senior Editor S. T. Joshi
Series Design Rae Grant

Staff for MODERN HORROR WRITERS

Assistant Editor Mary Sisson
Research Peter Cannon, Stefan Dziemianowicz
Picture Researcher Ellen Dudley

First Printing

1 3 5 7 9 8 6 4 2

Library of Congress Cataloging-in-Publication Data

Modern horror writers / edited and with an introduction by Harold Bloom.
    p.   cm.—(Writers of English)
    Includes bibliographical references (p.).
    ISBN 0-7910-2224-2.—ISBN 0-7910-2249-8 (pbk.)
    1. Horror tales, English—History and criticism. 2. Horror tales, American—History and criticism. 3. Horror tales, American—Bio-bibliography. 4. Horror tales, English—Bio-bibliography. I. Bloom, Harold. II. Series.
PR830.T3M65 1994
823'.0873809—dc20   94-5884
[B]   CIP

Contents

◈ User's Guide

THIS VOLUME PROVIDES biographical, critical, and bibliographical information on the twelve most significant horror writers of the first half of the twentieth century. Each chapter consists of three parts: a biography of the author; a selection of brief critical extracts about the author; and a bibliography of the author's published books.

The biography supplies a detailed outline of the important events in the author's life, including his or her major writings. The critical extracts are taken from a wide array of books and periodicals, from the author's lifetime to the present, and range in content from biographical to critical to historical. The extracts are arranged in chronological order by date of writing or publication, and a full bibliographical citation is provided at the end of each extract. Editorial additions or deletions are indicated within carets.

The author bibliographies list every separate publication—including books, pamphlets, broadsides, collaborations, and works edited or translated by the author—for works published in the author's lifetime; selected important posthumous publications are also listed. Titles are those of the first edition; variant titles are supplied within carets. In selected instances dates of revised editions are given where these are significant. Pseudonymous works are listed but not the pseudonyms under which these works were published. Periodicals edited by the author are listed only when the author has written most or all of the contents. Titles enclosed in square brackets are of doubtful authenticity. All works by the author, whether in English or in other languages, have been listed; English translations of foreign-language works are not listed unless the author has done the translation.

The Life of the Author
Harold Bloom

NIETZSCHE, WITH EXULTANT ANGUISH, famously proclaimed that God was dead. Whatever the consequences of this for the ethical life, its ultimate literary effect certainly would have surprised the author Nietzsche. His French disciples, Foucault most prominent among them, developed the Nietzschean proclamation into the dogma that all authors, God included, were dead. The death of the author, which is no more than a Parisian trope, another metaphor for fashion's setting of skirt-lengths, is now accepted as literal truth by most of our current apostles of what should be called French Nietzsche, to distinguish it from the merely original Nietzsche. We also have French Freud or Lacan, which has little to do with the actual thought of Sigmund Freud, and even French Joyce, which interprets *Finnegans Wake* as the major work of Jacques Derrida. But all this is as nothing compared to the final triumph of the doctrine of the death of the author: French Shakespeare. That delicious absurdity is given us by the New Historicism, which blends Foucault and California fruit juice to give us the Word that Renaissance "social energies," and not William Shakespeare, composed *Hamlet* and *King Lear*. It seems a proper moment to murmur "enough" and to return to a study of the life of the author.

Sometimes it troubles me that there are so few masterpieces in the vast ocean of literary biography that stretches between James Boswell's great *Life* of Dr. Samuel Johnson and the late Richard Ellmann's wonderful *Oscar Wilde*. Literary biography is a crucial genre, and clearly a difficult one in which to excel. The actual nature of the lives of the poets seems to have little effect upon the quality of their biographies. Everything happened to Lord Byron and nothing at all to Wallace Stevens, and yet their biographers seem equally daunted by them. But even inadequate biographies of strong writers, or of weak ones, are of immense use. I have never read a literary biography from which I have not profited, a statement I cannot make about any other genre whatsoever. And when it comes to figures who are central to us—Dante, Shakespeare, Cervantes, Montaigne, Goethe, Whitman, Tolstoi, Freud, Joyce, Kafka among them—we reach out eagerly for every scrap that the biographers have gleaned. Concerning Dante and Shakespeare we know much too little, yet when we come to Goethe and Freud, where we seem to know more than everything, we still want to know more. The death of the author, despite our current resentniks, clearly was only a momentary fad. Something vital in every authentic lover of literature responds to Emerson's battle-cry sentence: "There is no history, only biography." Beyond that there is a deeper truth, difficult to come at and requiring a lifetime to understand, which is that there is no literature, only autobiography, however mediated, however veiled, however transformed. The events of Shakespeare's life included the composition of *Hamlet,* and that act of writing was itself a crucial act of living, though we do not yet know altogether how to read so doubled an act. When an author takes up a more overtly autobiographical stance, as so many do in their youth, again we still do not know precisely how to accommodate the vexed relation between life and work. T. S. Eliot, meditating upon James Joyce, made a classic statement as to such accommodation:

> We want to know who are the originals of his characters, and what were
> the origins of his episodes, so that we may unravel the web of memory
> and invention and discover how far and in what ways the crude material
> has been transformed.

When a writer is not even covertly autobiographical, the web of memory and invention is still there, but so subtly woven that we may never unravel it. And yet we want deeply never to stop trying, and not merely because we are curious, but because each of us is caught in her own network of memory and invention. We do not always recall our inventions, and long before we age we cease to be certain of the extent to which we have invented our memories. Perhaps one motive for reading is our need to unravel our own webs. If our masters could make, from their lives, what we read, then we can be moved by them to ask: What have we made or lived in relation to what we have read? The answers may be sad, or confused, but the question is likely, implicitly, to go on being asked as long as we read. In Freudian terms, we are asking: What is it that we have repressed? What have we forgotten, unconsciously but purposively: What is it that we flee? Art, literature necessarily included, is regression in the service of the ego, according to a famous Freudian formula. I doubt the Freudian wisdom here, but indubitably it is profoundly suggestive. When we read, something in us keeps asking the equivalent of the Freudian questions: From what or whom is the author in flight, and to what earlier stages in her life is she returning, and why?

Reading, whether as an art or a pastime, has been damaged by the visual media, television in particular, and might be in some danger of extinction in the age of the computer, except that the psychic need for it continues to endure, presumably because it alone can assuage a central loneliness in elitist society. Despite all sophisticated or resentful denials, the reading of imaginative literature remains a quest to overcome the isolation of the individual consciousness. We can read for information, or entertainment, or for love of the language, but in the end we seek, in the author, the person whom we have not found, whether in ourselves or in others. In that quest, there always are elements at once aggressive and defensive, so that reading, even in childhood, is rarely free of hidden anxieties. And yet it remains one of the few activities not contaminated by an entropy of spirit. We read in hope, because we lack companionship, and the author can become the object of the most idealistic elements in our search for the wit and inventiveness we so desperately require. We read biography, not as a supplement to reading the author, but as a second, fresh attempt to understand what always seems to evade us in the work, our drive towards a kind of identity with the author.

This will-to-identity, though recently much deprecated, is a prime basis for the experience of sublimity in reading. *Hamlet* retains its unique position in the Western canon not because most readers and playgoers identify themselves with the prince, who clearly is beyond them, but rather because they find themselves again in the power of the language that represents him with such immediacy and force. Yet we know that neither language nor social energy created Hamlet. Our curiosity about Shakespeare is endless, and never will be appeased. That curiosity itself is a value, and cannot be separated from the value of *Hamlet* the tragedy, or Hamlet the literary character. It provokes us that Shakespeare the man seems so unknowable, at once everyone and no one as Borges shrewdly observes. Critics keep telling us otherwise, yet something valid in us keeps believing that we would know Hamlet better if Shakespeare's life were as fully known as the lives of Goethe and Freud, Byron and Oscar Wilde, or best of all, Dr. Samuel Johnson. Shakespeare never will have his Boswell, and Dante never will have his Richard Ellmann. How much one would give for a detailed and candid *Life of Dante* by Petrarch, or an outspoken memoir of Shakespeare by Ben Jonson! Or, in the age just past, how superb would be rival studies of one another by Hemingway and Scott Fitzgerald! But the list is endless: think of *Oscar Wilde* by Lord Alfred Douglas, or a joint biography of Shelley by Mary Godwin, Emilia Viviani, and Jane Williams. More than our insatiable desire for scandal would be satisfied. The literary rivals and the lovers of the great writers possessed perspectives we will never enjoy, and without those perspectives we dwell in some poverty in regard to the writers with whom we ourselves never can be done.

There is a sense in which imaginative literature *is* perspectivism, so that the reader is likely to be overwhelmed by the work's difficulty unless its multiple perspectives are mastered. Literary biography matters most because it is a storehouse of perspectives, frequently far surpassing any that are grasped by the particular biographer. There are relations between authors' lives and their works of kinds we have yet to discover, because our analytical instruments are not yet advanced enough to perform the necessary labor. Perhaps a novel, poem, or play is not so much a regression in the service of the ego, as it is an amalgam of *all* the Freudian mechanisms of defense, all working together for the apotheosis of the ego. Freud valued art highly, but thought that the aesthetic enterprise was no rival for psychoanalysis, unlike religion and philosophy. Clearly Freud was mistaken; his own anxieties about his indebtedness to Shakespeare helped produce the weirdness of his joining in the lunacy that argued for the Earl of Oxford as the author of Shakespeare's plays. It was Shakespeare, and not "the poets," who was there before Freud arrived at his depth psychology, and it is Shakespeare who is there still, well out ahead of psychoanalysis. We see what Freud would not see, that psychoanalysis is Shakespeare prosified and systematized. Freud is part of literature, not of "science," and the biography of Freud has the same relations to psychoanalysis as the biography of Shakespeare has to *Hamlet* and *King Lear,* if only we knew more of the life of Shakespeare.

Western literature, particularly since Shakespeare, is marked by the representation of internalized change in its characters. A literature of the ever-growing inner self is in itself a large form of biography, even though this is the biography of imaginary beings, from Hamlet to the sometimes nameless protagonists of Kafka and Beckett. Skeptics might want to argue that all literary biography concerns imaginary beings, since authors make themselves up, and every biographer gives us a creation curiously different from the same author as seen by the writer of a rival *Life*. Boswell's Johnson is not quite anyone else's Johnson, though it is now very difficult for us to disentangle the great Doctor from his gifted Scottish friend and follower. The life of the author is not merely a metaphor or a fiction, as is "the Death of the Author," but it always does contain metaphorical or fictive elements. Those elements are a part of the value of literary biography, but not the largest or the crucial part, which is the separation of the mask from the man or woman who hid behind it. James Joyce and Samuel Beckett, master and sometime disciple, were both of them enigmatic personalities, and their biographers have not, as yet, fully expounded the mystery of these contrasting natures. Beckett seems very nearly to have been a secular saint: personally disinterested, heroic in the French Resistance, as humane a person ever to have composed major fictions and dramas. Joyce, self-obsessed even as Beckett was preternaturally selfless, was the Milton of the twentieth century. Beckett was perhaps the least egoistic post-Joycean, post-Proustian, post-Kafkan of writers. Does that illuminate the problematical nature of his work, or does it simply constitute another problem? Whatever the cause, the question matters. The only death of the author that is other than literal, and that matters, is the fate only of weak writers. The strong, who become canonical, never die, which is what the canon truly is about. To be read forever is the Life of the Author.

◈ Introduction

IT WOULD BE DIFFICULT to argue a strong aesthetic justification for any of the dozen modern horror writers discussed in this volume. Walter de la Mare was more accomplished as a lyric poet than he was as a tale-teller, while the grim imaginings of H. P. Lovecraft were always stronger as myth, however crude, than as narrative prose. There is something marginal about most of the others; simply, they were very uneven writers. The occasional wound they could inflict in a rare triumph of a story too quickly became obscured by formulaic repetitions elsewhere. L. P. Hartley seems to me the largest exception; his most ambitious novels, even *The Go-Between* and *Eustace and Hilda*, have faded, but the best of his horror stories sustain fairly rigorous rereadings. They are economical and vengeance-ridden, a Borges-like combination that is hard to resist. Why we are so taken by tales of vengeance is a dark matter, which I suspect has something to do with our sense of being outraged by the inevitable limits of our existence, whoever we are. That may be why we—all of us—have to resist our tendency weakly to misread *Hamlet*. When the Prince of Denmark declines to cut down his uncle Claudius from behind, while the fratricide is ineffectually praying, we are tempted to become impatient with Shakespeare's most charismatic protagonist. Reflection teaches us that we are wrong to so react; Hamlet is too great a consciousness to be reduced to a mere avenger. Shakespeare, shrewdest of all psychologists, plays upon our impulse to delight in vengeance, a realm after all claimed by Yahweh for himself alone. In a fiction, we are moved to demand rougher equity than we endorse in reality. L. P. Hartley, less a psychologist than an authentic Gothic obsessive, at his best indulges his readers by gratifying some of their darkest impulses. His is a deliciously unhealthy art, and a faint trace of moral guilt at enjoying his elegant savageries only enhances our pleasure.

It is no accident that so many of his best tales are set in Venice, traditionally a city where the English imagination becomes splendidly rancid. Shylock and Iago are the most sublime instances of this tendency, and Hartley wisely declines large malevolences that would risk destructive comparisons with the Shakespearean shadow. The brief story, "Podolo," is a representative instance of Hartley's Gothic excellence at conveying the miasma and menace of Venice and its environs. Supposedly an exposed island four miles from Venice, Podolo (with the hidden sound of sorrow in its name) is stony and reputedly uninhabited, and an unlikely place to anchor near, in a gondola, for a picnic with the warm-hearted young Angela, recently and happily married. The narrator, who with the gondolier constitutes the rest of the party, is a Hartleyan type, empirical and nonjudgmental. His matter-of-factness heightens the horror of the tale, in which Angela, rather too warm-heartedly, resolves that a starveling cat on the island must be rescued by death from what she presumes to be its misery, yet clearly is its rage. Angela eventually slays the cat, against the chorus of the gondolier's warning that in Venice it is extremely unlucky to kill a cat. And Angela is decidedly unlucky; a savage man, who goes on all fours and is the sole inhabitant of Podolo, avenges his cat upon the murderer. In the story's grisly climax, the gondolier tells the narrator that he had to kill the wounded Angela after finding her, at her request, lest she be devoured alive by the savage, who is as hungry and furious as his cat was.

Summarized thus, the story might be called (ironically) distasteful, yet in its own prose and manner of narration it is a small triumph of atmosphere and event, precisely indeed a triumph of horror. Outrageousness, vengeance, and sadomasochism merge, as possibly they must mesh in this genre, if it is to be raised to its proper uncanniness. Angela's quick disposition to relieve the wretched, furious cat of what she judges to be its misery is difficult to distinguish from sadism, despite the narrator's insistence upon her angelic sweetness. The surface of Hartley's story is dark enough, like the surfaces of Venice at its illusory brightest. The British horror tale frequently takes its strength from an abyss beneath all the surfaces, from a primordial sense of how slippery the passage is from pleasure to pain. Hartley disengages most of his narrators from brooding on this passage, and so intensifies the equivocal element in his stories, freeing both himself and his readers for the aesthetic pleasures of sadomasochism.

—H. B.

◈ ◈ ◈

Robert Aickman
1914–1981

ROBERT FORDYCE AICKMAN was born on June 27, 1914, in London, England, the only son of William Arthur and Mabel Violet (Marsh) Aickman and the grandson of the Victorian supernatural writer Richard Marsh. Aickman's upbringing, as recorded in his poignant autobiography *The Attempted Rescue* (1966), was troubled: he lived in terror of his father, had a love-hate relationship with his mother, was frightened by the constant wrangling of his parents, and, as an only child, led a generally solitary and inward-looking existence. He attended the Highgate School in London, but the coming of World War II interrupted his plans for college.

Shortly after the war Aickman became an ardent environmentalist; in 1946 he founded the Inland Waterway Association, which was devoted to preserving England's rivers and canals from pollution and overdevelopment. He later joined such other organizations as the National Council on Inland Transport, the World Wildlife Fund, and the Lower Avon Navigation Trust. Aickman wrote two treatises on the subject, *Know Your Waterways* (1954) and *The Story of Our Inland Waterways* (1955). His second autobiography, *The River Runs Uphill* (1986), also deals extensively with his environmental interests.

Aickman took to writing relatively late in life, although he had attempted some essays and sketches before the war and was for some years a theatre critic for the *Nineteenth Century and After*. In 1951 he and Elizabeth Jane Howard published a volume, *We Are for the Dark*, containing three stories by Aickman and three by Howard. More than a decade would pass before another volume of tales appeared, but beginning with *Dark Entries* (1964) Aickman published some of the most distinguished horror fiction of his generation: *Powers of Darkness* (1966), *Sub Rosa* (1968), *Cold Hand in Mine* (1975), *Tales of Love and Death* (1977), *Painted Devils* (1979), and *Intrusions* (1980).

Aickman maintained that he wrote not ghost stories or horror stories but "strange stories." In many of his tales there is only the faintest touch

1

of the supernatural, and a weird atmosphere is produced solely by sensitive portrayals of disturbed characters, unusual locales (in which Aickman put to good use his wide travels in Great Britain and Europe), and, in many cases, sexual tension between men and women. Aickman believed that stories of this type must tap the reader's subconscious fears and desires, and as a result many of his tales have little regard for outward logic and are frequently confusing or abstruse in their plot development. Nevertheless, his skillful prose style and sensitivity to delicate shades of emotion make his work powerful and disturbing. He won the World Fantasy Award in 1975 for his short story "Pages from a Young Girl's Diary."

Aickman also edited eight volumes of *The Fontana Book of Great Ghost Stories* (1964–72), whose introductions outline his theory of weird fiction. *The Late Breakfasters* (1964), although having a few ghostly touches, is a delicate novel about lesbianism. In later years Aickman served as the director and chairman of the London Opera Society (1954–69) and the chairman of Balmin Productions Ltd. (1963–68), a firm that administered traveling ballets. Robert Aickman died on February 26, 1981. A volume of his uncollected stories, *Night Voices* (1985), a short fairy tale set in tsarist Russia, *The Model* (1987), and an omnibus of his best stories, *The Wine-Dark Sea* (1988), have been published posthumously.

▨ *Critical Extracts*

BRIGID BROPHY   I have never before reviewed a book without reading the whole of it. I trust Mr. Aickman will forgive me for doing so now, because my excuse pays him a compliment. The first of his ghost stories left me cold. The second left me goose-fleshed. I have no intention of reading the remaining four, because I don't enjoy being frightened in this particular way; but I hope those who do will read the same amount of recommendation as usually goes into 'I couldn't put it down' in my solemn declaration about *Dark Entries* that I could never again take it up.

Brigid Brophy, "Great Man," New Statesman, 29 January 1965, p. 170

ROBERT AICKMAN   There are only about thirty or forty first-class ghost stories in the whole of western literature.

The ghost story must be distinguished from the scientific extravaganza on its left, and from the horror story on its right. The writing of science fiction demands primarily the scientific aptitude for imagining the unrealised implications of a known phenomenon. Its composition is akin to the making of an actual scientific discovery, and it is well known that many of the scientific developments first promulgated as fiction, all too soon become fact. The horror story is purely sadistic; it depends entirely upon power to shock. To-day, of course, de Sade has defenders in high places, such as Madame Simone de Beauvoir; and existentialism contends that life itself is properly seen as a sequence of minute-to-minute shocks, inducing "nausea" and "vertigo". The ghost story, however, seems to derive its power from what is most deep and most permanent. It is allied to poetry. ⟨. . .⟩

The ghost itself reminds us that death is the one thing certain and the thing most uncertain; the bourn from which no traveller returns, except this one. The majority of ghost stories, however, have no actual ghost. A better title for the genre might be found, but the absence of the ghost seldom dispels the alarm. It can be almost worse if *someone else* apprehends the ghost, as in ⟨Walter de la Mare's⟩ "Seaton's Aunt"; or if you cannot tell whether it is a ghost or not, as in ⟨Aickman's⟩ "The Trains"; or if you yourself somehow evade the ghost, at least provisionally, as in ⟨Algernon Blackwood's⟩ "The Wendigo"; and as for the ghost that at first seems, like the things in the shops, useful, as in ⟨Elizabeth Jane Howard's⟩ "Three Miles Up" and ⟨D. H. Lawrence's⟩ "The Rocking-Horse Winner", then you can be quite certain that it is you who are being sold, without being able to withdraw, that you will reach, and far sooner than seemed possible, the cliff edge, screaming. For what the ghost story hints to us is that there is a world somewhere, as Coriolanus put it (meaning something rather different, but that is just like a ghost); that as flies to wanton boys are we to the gods; that luck's a chance, but trouble's sure; that achievement and comfort are (like the poor ghosts themselves) immaterial. ⟨. . .⟩

For, of course, the ghost, though not moral, or useful, or adaptable, is assuredly not evil. ⟨Richard Middleton's⟩ "The Ghost Ship" shows how much positive good he can do us, in the right circumstances and for a time; and in ⟨Marjorie Bowen's⟩ "The Crown Derby Plate" he perhaps even manages to do a little good for himself, which is something beyond most of us. The ghost is neutral, and when he thwacks us or gnaws us to death, the doing (not necessarily the fault) is ours. In his true manifestation, the ghost is an intimation of that wider world than custom, which we disregard at our extreme peril, and in which we should at least try to move without clumsiness and neck-breaking, for it, and not the fish-bowl of history, is our real world. Rightly approached, with awe and feeling, the ghosts in this book will help, though less, no doubt, than Keats and Yeats.

Robert Aickman, "Introduction," *The Fontana Book of Great Ghost Stories* (1964; rpt. New York: Beagle Books, 1971), pp. 7–9

T. J. BINYON   No one is better at raising the hairs on the back of the neck, or causing perspiration to run cold, than Robert Aickman. Yet he employs no spectacular effects, there are no excesses of style or emotion, none of the stock in trade of the gothic school. Some of his stories, indeed, are closer to Kafka than to Mrs Radcliffe; they begin with a seemingly ordinary situation transmogrified by degrees into something strange and enigmatic, and preserve throughout a limpid and objective narrative tone. The seven stories in this collection ⟨*Tales of Love and Death*⟩ range in mood from the light to the macabre; the best are the two longest, one of which deals with a mother's attempts to control her peculiarly unruly twin sons, while the other has as its ostensible subject the proceedings of the Open Spaces and Cemeteries Committee of a local council, but the other five are by no means frisson-free.

T. J. Binyon, "Criminal Proceedings," *Times Literary Supplement*, 23 December 1977, p. 1513

JULIA BRIGGS   "Alive" can hardly be the *mot juste* for the ghost story, but it is certainly well and being written by Robert Aickman, whose latest collection *Intrusions* is the best yet, and arguably the best since Walter de la Mare's *A Beginning*, nearly thirty years ago. Its centrepiece, "The Breakthrough", certainly invites comparison with that great (greatest?) master of the form, in its combination of supernatural events with a deeply felt human tragedy that unfolds slowly, subtly, and with unremitting intensity. The horrors—brilliantly described—that come up from the church's broken pavements, are in the end, subordinated to the drama of the inadequate rector, the uncommitted narrator, and the outcast Lizzie.

All the stories in *Intrusions* seem to benefit from a new-found freedom and expansiveness, as well as a cavalier disregard for the conventional formulae. "The Next Glade" and the extraordinary fantasy, "No Time Is Passing" are imaginative inventions of a particularly high order, but there are no makeweights here. Robert Aickman's gifts, always considerable, have now matured to the point where he has unquestionably become the leading writer in the field.

Julia Briggs, "Brief Hauntings," *Times Literary Supplement*, 2 January 1981, p. 19

CHRISTINE PASANEN MORRIS   Robert Aickman's women protagonists are extremely convincingly portrayed. Their multidimensionality, depth and complexities are unlike the women characters, principal or minor, in horror/ghost fiction in general. The most common roles for female characters in the genre have been those of helpless maidens threatened with death (or, more often, with "worse") by various creatures natural and supernatural; beautiful women who serve as ornamentation and who cling to the hero's arm or swoon at strategic times; or witches and sorceresses with powers of black magic at their command. Aickman's heroines are none of these. ⟨. . .⟩

Aickman's heroines, although they may not exhibit it openly—indeed they may not admit it to *themselves*—are always close to the edge of society's boundaries of what is considered normal. They are isolated emotionally; and even if mature, married, entering into middle age with nearly grown children, they are still aware—acutely or vaguely—that their lives contain chinks which no person or role label or system can fill or satisfy.

His heroines are alienated, but scarcely ever openly persecuted as being different. They are outsiders, but only in rare circumstances do they become monstrously so, as in "Pages from a Young Girl's Journal" in which the main character, a somber and moody adolescent, retreats more and more from the world of her family and other mortals to become one of the undead elect, a vampire, who has nothing but distant scorn for mortal values and perspectives. ⟨. . .⟩

Perverse twists of fate abound in these stories, and that is one of their most fascinating tendencies, one of the things that makes all of Aickman's writing so eerie and unsettling. These twists tend to center about change— changes which come unexpectedly or which result from attempts at change

which go wrong—often catastrophically so. Any period of change calls for
the involved individual to be alert and to use all her resources to deal with
this change and, ideally, to affect its course. The twist in these stories,
though, is that all the best traditional resources seem to be of no use at all.
Logic does not work, and all those tools, guides, and means of transportation
and communication which one has come to rely on seem pathetically puny.
Because these changes are not born of logical situations, logic and reason
will not work in dealing with them. In "The Trains", maps are of no
use when the countryside changes underfoot making points of reference
unreliable. The overall effect goes beyond the character's being "lost". The
whole environment has such dreamlike strangeness that the reader gets the
strong impression that an alien, perhaps malevolent, intelligence is causing
the changes and that the individuals are not merely lost physically, but lost
spiritually and psychologically, lost in a chaos of time and fate.

> Christine Pasanen Morris, "The Female 'Outsider' in the Short Fiction of Robert
> Aickman," *Nyctalops* No. 18 (April 1983): 55–56, 58

COLIN GREENLAND   By chance, five of these six stories ⟨in *Night
Voices*⟩ recount ordeals of young people, obscuring the fact that all Aickman's
fiction was that of a man in the last thirty of his sixty-seven years. It is not
about the heroic endeavour to master the chaos of life, but as John Clute
has demonstrated in a definitive essay about the needs described by Jung
in *The Integration of the Personality*: to come to terms with the chaos, and
prepare a whole self for death. In "The Stains" a civil servant recuperating
after the death of his wife begins to notice lichen and fungus sprouting
everywhere. He suddenly abandons home, job and dependent elder brother
to live in a stone cottage on the moors with a mysterious young woman
not altogether human. At the last, the deftly-intensified claustrophobia is
transcended in an expressly operatic gesture. Death is a consummation. It
is the rest of the blemished world that must go on suffering, mouldering.
The extraordinary "Rosamund's Bower" (hitherto unpublished) preserves
the privacy of Alwyn-Scott's experience through a teasing series of enigmatic
emblems and allusions. At the same time it is perfectly clear that, finding
the bower and penetrating the maze, the young man is resolved to accept
the moment of bliss at its heart, a touch, not even that, at the price of
future misery, failure, persecution and debility. Here in the thicket full of

mock-Spenserian monitors, Alwyn-Scott's whole psychic life is simultaneously present, and therefore always is, this sweetness cancelling out the vile before and after. The consolation is an illusion, of course, but an illusion that will sustain a life and permit a reconciliation with death.

Others of Aickman's pilgrims fail and remain stuck inside the nightmare, telling their stories over and over. Here especially, in "the dreaded demesne of the heart", sex and death combine, whether the invitation is seized, as in the grotesque "Mark Ingestre: The Customer's Tale", or shunned, as in the sad and powerfully restrained "Laura", whose lonely victim admits: "But you won't possibly understand what I mean. You would have had to be there. One day perhaps you will be."

Colin Greenland, "Invitations of the Intimate Stranger," Times Literary Supplement,
6 December 1988, p. 1407

GARY WILLIAM CRAWFORD   Aickman's works are unified by a coherent structure which contains metaphor and symbol, and as in a poem, there is an inner tension that is allegorical—as in symbol and metaphor. Aickman is thus certainly unique, but if he resembles any writer, he is closest to Walter de la Mare. The most striking resemblance between the art of de la Mare and that of Aickman lies in their creation of what Peter Penzoldt calls "the inconclusive tale of terror." The technique of such a tale consists in the writer's suggesting "a supernatural danger lurking directly behind our back, or just outside the range of our five senses, but ready at any moment to pounce upon its victim." In such stories as de la Mare's "Seaton's Aunt," "A Recluse," and "Out of the Deep," the supernatural never appears in any outward manifestation. Similarly, in Aickman's fiction, the supernatural possibilities, if not actualities, grow out of character development naturally, and much like the symbolism and metaphor in poetry, carry the meaning of the stories. Rarely does Aickman write about traditional ghost, werewolf, or vampire (the vampire tale "Pages from a Young Girl's Journal" is an exception), but he evokes an uncanny realm of implicit terror, violence, and death, always counterpoised by human love. Aickman, even in his darkest fictions, conceives of a humanity that can achieve insight into its infections of the soul, even though, frequently, it means willful entrance into those realms. As Aickman has written, the supernatural tale is "allied to poetry."

Above all, Aickman's life and works express a reverence for mystery, or what the Germans call *Ehrfurct*: reverence for what one cannot understand. He thus aligns himself with Sigmund Freud, who in his *Civilization and Its Discontents* speaks most clearly of the concerns expressed in Aickman's art. Like Freud, Aickman revered the unknowable; and all of his stories place his characters, and the reader by extension, in touch with the vast realm of the unconscious. Not only do his stories express such a confrontation, but Aickman's entire life may be called poetic. ⟨. . .⟩

Aickman's stories may be somewhat obscure, but they are, like Lovecraft's, assuredly timeless, the true test of great art. One wonders, as one compares Aickman to such a writer as the phenomenally successful Stephen King, which writer will survive the longest. Aickman will very likely survive longer because he creates a timeless world in the reader's mind. Unlike King, Aickman does not pander to popular taste or fashion, and there is nothing crude or vulgar about Aickman. This coherent philosophy, or rather, outlook, this care for detail and timeless awe, or rather, mystery, will allow Aickman to rise above King and the large numbers of horror novelists and short story writers we find at the present time.

> Gary William Crawford, "The Poetics of the Unconscious: The 'Strange Stories' of Robert Aickman," *Discovering Modern Horror Fiction II*, ed. Darrell Schweitzer (Mercer Island, WA: Starmont House, 1988), pp. 43–44, 49

PETER STRAUB   Robert Aickman at his best was this century's most profound writer of what we call horror stories and he, with greater accuracy, preferred to call strange stories. In his work is a vast disparity between the well-mannered tone and the stories' actual emotional content. On the surface of things, if we can extrapolate from the style, diction, and range of allusion in his work, Aickman was a cultivated, sensitive, thoroughly English individual. It's not hard to imagine him as having been something like T. S. Eliot: dry of manner, more kindly than not, High Anglican in dress, capable of surprising finesses of wit. His chief influences were English, the stories of Walter de la Mare and M. R. James (and probably also the subtle, often indirect supernatural stories of Henry James, England's most assimilated American), and his own influence has been primarily on English writers like Ramsey Campbell and, through Campbell, Clive Barker. (I think Aickman would have cherished Barker's story "In the Hills, the Cities.")

In fact, neither Campbell nor Barker is really very much like Aickman. His originality, conscious and instinctive at once, was so entire that although he has provided us with a virtual model of what the "strange story" should be, if anyone tried to write to its specifications, the result would be nothing more than imitative.

Unlike nearly everybody writing supernatural stories now, Aickman rejected the neat, conclusive ending. He was, you might say, Stephen King's opposite. In his work there are no climactic showdowns, in part because his work uses almost none of the conventional imagery of horror. Aickman was sublimely uninterested in monsters, werewolves, worms, rats, bats, and things in bandages. (He did, however, write one great vampire story.) Absent from this list of horror conventions is ghosts, because Aickman *was* interested in ghosts, at least in a way—in the atmosphere a ghost creates, the thrill of unreality which surrounds it. Aickman was a queerly visionary writer, and ghosts, which are both utterly irrational and thoroughly English, would have appealed to him. In this collection a ghost might very well be making telephone calls in "Your Tiny Hand Is Frozen," and a *kind* of ghost, the "old carlie," plays a crucial role in "The Fetch," one of the most explicit and straightforward pieces here. You could stretch a point—stretch it past breaking—and say that "Never Visit Venice" concerns an encounter with a ghost. It does not, of course. What attracted Aickman to ghosts was not the notion of dripping revenants but the feeling—composed in part of mystery, fear, stifled eroticism, hopelessness, nostalgia, and the almost violent freedom granted by a suspension of rational rules—which they evoked in him. Ghosts—or the complex of feelings I've just tried to summarize—gave him a degree of artistic freedom granted to only a very few writers. ⟨. . .⟩

Unconscious forces drive these characters, and Aickman's genius was in finding imaginative ways for the unconscious to manipulate both the narrative events of his tales and the structures in which they occur. Because there are no logical explanations, there can be no resolutions. After the shock of the sheer strangeness fades away, we begin to see how the facts of the stories appear to grow out of the protagonists' fears and desires, and how the illogic and terror surrounding them is their own, far more accurately and disturbingly than in any conventional horror story. "The Trains" is a perfect story of this type, and "The Inner Room" is even better, one of Aickman's most startling and beautiful demonstrations of the power over us of what we do not quite grasp about ourselves and our lives.

Peter Straub, "Introduction," *The Wine-Dark Sea* by Robert Aickman (New York: Arbor House, 1988), pp. 7–9

STEVE RASNIC TEM   *The Wine-Dark Sea* is one of the best of Aickman's collections to see print, in part because it amply demonstrates the scope and power of the author. The stories range from that chilling masterpiece, "The Trains"—in which the author slowly, painstakingly reveals why a woman has waved from a bedroom window to every passing train for twenty years—to "Growing Boys," a rather contemporary piece in which Aickman explores every parent's nightmare with dark-humored exaggeration: the threat of gigantic, animalistic adolescent children who cannot be controlled.

On the surface "The Fetch" would seem to be a more traditional piece about a banshee who haunts the members of a family, but Aickman's extended psychological portrait of the narrator becomes a compelling study of the ways in which memory haunts us, traps us, and eventually governs our destinies. "The Stains," in which a group of lichen, or blemishes, or vague discolorations, travels from rocks to house walls and eventually to the bodies of two young lovers, is virtually a textbook example of how an author can create an atmosphere that shifts from the ordinary to the bizarre with little indication that such a significant transformation is occurring. Its ending encourages a number of possible interpretations. Aickman always seems able to make such ambiguity work for him—obtaining fictional depth where lesser authors achieve only a dissolution of narrative drive.

A transforming landscape figures prominently in most of Aickman's best fiction. Certainly no other contemporary horror writer better understood the connections between the setting of a story and the inner drives and conflicts of its characters. Aickman possessed that rare ability to *show* naturalistic events coaxing and pulling the unconscious out of a character, transforming the world in which that character lives. Thus, Aickman's preference for the term "strange story" over "horror story." He was after something that goes far beyond a simple scare or disruption of sleep. His narratives lead us to question our assumptions about reality itself and show us "strange" landscapes which we soon discover are not so strange after all. They are the landscapes in which we actually live out our lives, which have the most profound influence on our choices and actions. As critic Mike Ashley said, "Aickman's stories . . . are almost always unsettling, not in the visceral sense, but spiritually."

Steve Rasnic Tem, "A Preference for Strange Stories," *Bloomsbury Review* 8, No. 5 (September–October 1988): 13, 18, 22

MICHAEL DIRDA   Aickman's stories often begin in childhood, when something uncanny—a dollhouse with an inaccessible hidden room, the death of a beloved mother at the appearance of a veiled stranger—blights or beguiles the main character. Years pass, and it is only in middle age that these preparatory traumas find their odd yet profoundly right fulfillment.

For Aickman deals less with horror than with peculiar psychic destinies, with how our deepest fears and deepest desires may be one. His characters resemble mental travelers through landscapes of the numinous, the holy and dreadful. Early in "Bind Your Hair," Clarinda meets a mysterious gypsy woman: "Altogether Mrs. Pagani gave an impression of unusual physical power, only partly concealed by her conventional clothes. It was as if suddenly she might arise and tear down the house." So it is with *The Wine-Dark Sea:* Despite their quiet openings, such stories as "Into the Wood" and "The Trains" suddenly do rise up and tear down the house.

In these dark prose-poems of mid-life crisis, dreams bring destruction, nothing good lasts, and the desire for love masks a preparation for death. Never well-known in his lifetime, Aickman may be too bleak even now for readers reared only on Stephen King or Clive Barker. But to those whose taste includes William Golding or J. G. Ballard, *The Wine-Dark Sea* reveals a neglected master, a superb artist "concerned not with appearance and consistency, but with the spirit behind the appearance, the void behind the face of order." In that void, as Conrad's Mr. Kurtz knew, waits the greatest horror of all.

Michael Dirda, "Crossing into Darkness: Robert Aickman's Strange Stories," *Washington Post Book World*, 11 December 1988, p. 9

S. T. JOSHI   Two of Aickman's stories, "Ringing the Changes" and "Meeting Mr Millar", unite many or all of Aickman's important themes in an exceptionally powerful way. In "Ringing the Changes" we have the idea of travel (a pair of newlyweds, Gerald and Phrynne Pascoe, visit an obscure coastal town in England for their honeymoon), frustrated sex (Gerald at least feels increasingly disturbed at the odd milieu into which he has fallen), and nostalgia (the town seems untouched by modernity). The place has a reputation for its church bells; but the volume of the bells on this particular night seems highly anomalous. How can all the churches be practicing their bell-ringing at the same time? The sound continues without cessation, growing louder and louder; the hotel's proprietors are getting drunker and drunker, as if seeking oblivion for the night. Why? What is the meaning of the bells? An old commander who lives in the hotel finally tells the couple: " 'They're ringing to wake the dead.' " Blunt as this sounds, it carries incredible potency after the enormously subtle and gradual build-up. Gerald and the commander discuss this outrageous proposition:

> "I don't believe in the resurrection of the body," said Gerald.
> As the hour grew later, the bells grew louder. "Not of the body."
> "What other kind of resurrection is possible? Everything else is only theory. You can't even imagine it. No one can."

The idea of ringing all the bells in a town on a special night in order to raise the dead is no doubt illogical, but it has that aesthetic logic which I mentioned earlier; it taps our unconscious in the sense that it is a very short step from ringing bells to commemorate the dead to ringing them to raise the dead. Accordingly, this tale satisfies where others of Aickman's do not. It would require a long commentary to trace the seamless way in which Aickman builds up the cumulative suspense in this story; and the spectacular climax—where the dead (if that's who they are) are only *heard*, never seen— is a masterstroke of suggestiveness.

"Meeting Mr Millar" also plays upon many of Aickman's central themes. A starving writer moves into a cheap flat, forced to take a job as editor for a pornography publisher. The large apartment below him seems occupied by a company ("Stallabrass, Hoskins and Cramp. Chartered Accountants"), but it does not seem to engage in much actual business. The writer hears "endless giggling, shouting, and banging of doors"; the employees' conversation, which he occasionally overhears, "was always of unbelievable commonplaceness or banality". Peculiar details accumulate, including a strange encounter with Mr Millar, evidently the head of the company: rarely has such a completely colourless individual inspired so much vague terror. Finally, after a series of strangely disturbing but curiously inconclusive incidents, another tenant makes an odd suggestion:

> "It just struck me for one moment that you might have seen into the future. All these people slavishly doing nothing. It'll be exactly like that one day, you know, if we go on as we are. For a moment it all sounded to me like a vision of 40 years on—if as much."

It is not clear how seriously we are to take this explanation; I do not imagine that Aickman simply wishes to reduce his story to a sociological dystopia. Nevertheless, the tale's odd twists and turns all seem to work, achieving a cumulative power in no way marred by the lack of an explanation. "Meeting Mr Millar" is also one of Aickman's most autobiographical stories, and much could be written on its connexions with passages and sentiments in *The Attempted Rescue*. It may well be his greatest success.

S. T. Joshi, " 'So Little Is Definite,' " *Million* No. 12 (November–December 1992): 21–22

SCOTT D. BRIGGS   As ⟨Aickman⟩ points out in his autobiography, *The Attempted Rescue* (1966), "Travel, the *art* of travel, is the great impersonal passion of my life, though personal also, because I need a perfect companion, and cannot make art without." Avoiding shallow travelogue, Aickman sets out to accomplish something much loftier, making many of his characters' travels the focal point of the tale—even to the point of making the journey more important than the final destination. Elsewhere in *The Attempted Rescue*, Aickman notes that "I still feel that the supernatural, Freud's *Unheimlich*, can give one at least a sensation of knowing oneself and the world that otherwise can be found (equally rarely) only through poetry, music, travel, and love."

In the several stories to be discussed here, Aickman's characters undergo their journeys as a form of self-discovery. Indeed, the discovery is often painful (and sometimes tragic, as in "The Wine-Dark Sea"), but it always involves some vision of a different or higher reality, heretofore hidden from the character. ⟨. . .⟩

For the narrator of "The Swords", the setting is a carnival sideshow that turns into a ghastly sexual awakening. The tale is both one of Aickman's travel stories and a disturbing allegory of a man's first sexual experience. The unnamed narrator tells his story in flashback, describing a youthful period when he worked for his Uncle Elias as a door-to-door salesman. On his travels through the rather dull town of Wolverhampton, the narrator happens upon a curious carnival, with a sideshow entitled simply "The Swords". In a fit of curiosity, he attends the show, populated as usual by a small crowd of leering men. The show itself turns out to be an impossible display of a man plunging several swords into a passive, pretty woman seated in a chair. Whether this is a parlor trick or something more sinister, the narrator is alternately intrigued and repelled by the sight. ⟨. . .⟩

The narrator describes himself as being naive, shy, and self-conscious as a youth. These qualities are not at all rare in a young person, but in the narrator's case they turn out to be fatal flaws. When he mentions "all the girls [were] giggling at me", we are led to believe that he has not yet learned to deal effectively with members of the opposite sex of his own age. And yet, he is quite attracted to the girl in the sideshow, presumably because she seems more exotic and therefore unattainable.

The disturbing climax comes when the young man makes a deal with the sideshow barker to have Madonna, as she is called, appear at his seedy boarding house room for some kind of private show. For a few pounds, she will do as the narrator pleases for several hours. The girl goes through with the bargain, and lets him have his way with her, although the experience is curiously unsatisfying and empty. He describes her as feeling "queer and disappointing—flabby might be almost the word". Elsewhere she is described as pale, suggesting the pallor of the undead, and the narrator also wonders if she has been hypnotized in some way. Finally, the narrator grasps her hand, only to have it detach from her arm.

Words need hardly be wasted on what Aickman intended to be very obvious sexual symbolism. That a fear of the mysteries of sex is at the root of the tale seems clear, but more puzzling is how Aickman unsettles the reader's sense of reality in "The Swords". The earnestness of the narrator's confession, very much like one of Lovecraft's doomed narrators, suggests that his experiences are to be taken seriously, and not as a satire. The *frisson* of terror comes when we realize that the preceding events are meant to be taken as hard fact, and not as a product of the narrator's possible psychosis. The reader, however, may also see the tale as another kind of allegory, more closely related to the prevalent theme of sexual apprehension. Aickman's narrator here explores several worlds simultaneously: the concrete one of his squalid Wolverhampton surroundings; the no less squalid, but more amorphous, territory of the sexual frontier; and finally the mysterious female form itself. The generally drab and nondescript town of Wolverhampton masks something far more bizarre under the surface, a society that makes a great effort to remain nearly asexual.

Scott D. Briggs, "Robert Aickman: Sojourns into the Unknown," *Studies in Weird Fiction* No. 12 (Spring 1993): 7–8

▣ *Bibliography*

We Are for the Dark (with Elizabeth Jane Howard). 1951.

Know Your Waterways. 1954.

The Story of Our Inland Waterways. 1955.

Dark Entries. 1964.

The Late Breakfasters. 1964.

The Fontana Book of Great Ghost Stories (editor). 1964–72. 8 vols.

The Attempted Rescue. 1966.

Powers of Darkness. 1966.

Sub Rosa. 1968.

Cold Hand in Mine. 1975.

Tales of Love and Death. 1977.

Painted Devils. 1979.

Intrusions. 1980.

Night Voices. 1985.

The River Runs Uphill: A Story of Success and Failure. 1986.

The Model. 1987.

The Wine-Dark Sea. 1988.

E. F. Benson
1867–1940

EDWARD FREDERIC BENSON was born on July 24, 1867, at Wellington College, Berkshire, where his father, Edward White Benson, who would later become the archbishop of Canterbury, was headmaster. He was the fifth of six children and one of three, with his older brother Arthur Christopher and younger brother Robert Hugh, who would distinguish themselves in letters. Edward was educated at Marlborough College and King's College, Cambridge, where he graduated with first-place honors in classics in 1891. His interest in archaeology led to a three-year stint with the British School of Archaeology in Athens between 1892 and 1895 and later to work for the Hellenic Society in Cairo. His travels would later take him to Algiers, Italy, and Capri, but he would always remain fond of the Cornwall of his childhood, where his father had been bishop of Truro.

Benson was a worldly man who loved sports and socialized with the upper crust of England. His first novel, *Dodo* (1893), was a social satire and roman à clef of the idle rich that introduced readers to the prototypical pretty but vapid young women who would appear as protagonists in much of his writing, particularly his Mapp and Lucia series, which began with *Queen Lucia* in 1920. The immense popularity of *Dodo* helped him decide to write full-time, starting in 1895.

For the next forty-five years Benson wrote prodigiously, ultimately producing more than 100 books. Three-quarters of his work was fiction and the remainder a varied collection of history, sport, and biographical books, as well as memoirs that included *As We Were: A Victorian Peep-Show* (1930), *As We Are: A Modern Revue* (1932), and his informal autobiography *Final Edition*, completed just before his death in 1940. His single most productive year was 1903, when seven books bearing his name appeared, but it was the rare year in which he did not turn out two or three titles. Although his prolific output deflected serious critical attention from his work, he remained very popular with the reading public.

The Bensons were personally acquainted with Henry James and M. R. James, and it was partly under their influence that all three brothers wrote supernatural fiction. Edward produced four collections of such work, *The Room in the Tower* (1912), *Visible and Invisible* (1923), *Spook Stories* (1928), and *More Spook Stories* (1934); although largely overlooked at the time, these volumes are recognized today as landmarks of weird fiction. The contents of all four books have now been gathered in *The Collected Ghost Stories of E. F. Benson* (1992); Jack Adrian has assembled Benson's uncollected weird tales in *The Flint Knife* (1988). In addition, a number of Benson's novels incorporate supernatural elements to a greater or lesser degree and reflect his lifelong interest in séances and spiritualism, including *The Luck of the Vails* (1901), *The Image in the Sand* (1905), *The Angel of Pain* (1905), *Across the Stream* (1919), *Colin* (1923), *Colin II* (1925), *The Inheritor* (1930), *Ravens' Brood* (1934), and the children's book *David Blaize and the Blue Door* (1918).

From 1934 to 1937 Benson served as mayor of Rye. In 1938 he received an Order of the British Empire and an honorary fellowship from Magdalen College, Cambridge. He never married and died in London on February 29, 1940. Most of his work remains out of print today, although his Mapp and Lucia novels experienced a revival in popularity following their adaptation for television in the 1980s.

▓ *Critical Extracts*

UNSIGNED   In comparison to the well-fortified vintage which may be found in *The Room in the Tower*, that contained in the present volume ⟨*Spook Stories*⟩ is more bland to the palate. Sensitive scalps will prick in a pleasant response to its thrills, but the achievement will be a more gradual process, the fearful ecstasy will be longer in the savouring, and the uneasy impression will be produced that just such an adventure as any one of the dozen detailed might come to be the reader's lot. As a rule it is a pity to try to provide an explanation for a ghost story; an apparition loses its fine cutting edge for effective use if it can be scientifically suggested that it is a psychological record impressed upon the ether which will mechanically reproduce itself regardless of appropriateness until the record be worn away.

Mr. Benson, however, by a touch can produce just sufficient hint of explana-tion—a vast granite slab, an empty niche, a piano—to justify his develop-ment where it is fitting that such justification should be provided. In the case of the plainly inexplicable, he is content to leave it at that, and merely to record the fact that the birds either do not, or do, sing, in conformity with the duration or termination of the manifestation of the unaccountable. He gaily permits some of his characters to talk about clairvoyance or telepa-thy, and then produces a couple of hard-working mediums who, to their grave discomfort, get "messages" from "controls" other than those they have tamed or taught for the purposes of their profession, and find themselves in company with an entirely unwanted corpse which has busily been haunting a disembodied spirit in the hereafter just as corporeal beings in this world are sometimes beset by intangible phantoms. Yet, in one story, one of these phantoms is able to push a conscience-stricken rogue over a cliff, just as the corpse by its offensive substantiality is able to compel the deceased reprobate to make confession from beyond its unexpected grave.

Unsigned, [Review of *Spook Stories*], *Times Literary Supplement*, 29 March 1928, p. 244

E. F. BENSON   One windless summer day two friends, of whom the Vicar of Rye was one, were lunching with me, and afterwards we strolled down to the secret garden. It was a brilliant, broiling day and we seated ourselves in a strip of shade close to the door in the wall which communicated with the other garden. This door was open: two of our chairs, the Vicar's and mine, faced it, the other had its back to it. . . . And I saw the figure of a man walk past this open doorway. He was dressed in black and he wore a cape the right wing of which, as he passed, he threw across his chest, over his left shoulder. His head turned away and I did not see his face. The glimpse I got of him was very short, for two steps took him past the open doorway, and the wall behind the poplars hid him again. Simultaneously the Vicar jumped out of his chair, exclaiming: "Who on earth was that?" It was only a step to the open door, and there, beyond, the garden lay, basking in the sun and empty of any human presence. He told me what he had seen: it was exactly what I had seen, except that our visitor had worn hose, which I had not noticed.

Now the odd feature about this meaningless apparition is that the first time this visitor appeared he was seen simultaneously by two people whose impressions as to his general mien and his gesture with his cloak completely tallied with each other. There was no legend about such an appearance which could have predisposed either of them to have imagined that he saw anything at all, and the broad sunlight certainly did not lend itself to any conjuring up of a black moving figure. Not long afterwards it was seen again in broad daylight by the Vicar at the same spot; just a glimpse and then it vanished. I was with him but I saw nothing. Since then I think I have seen it once in the evening on the lawn near the garden-room, but it was dusk, and I may have construed some fleeting composition of light and shadow into the same figure.

Now ghost stories, which go back into earliest folk-tales, are a branch of literature at which I have often tried my hand. By a selection of disturbing details it is not very difficult to induce in the reader an uneasy frame of mind which, carefully worked up, paves the way for terror. The narrator, I think, must succeed in frightening himself before he can hope to frighten his readers, and, as a matter of fact, this man in black had not occasioned me the smallest qualms. However, I worked myself up and wrote my ghost story, describing how there developed an atmosphere of horror in my secret garden, how when I took Taffy there he cowered whining at my heels, how at night a faint stale luminance hovered over the enclosing walls, and so led up after due preparation for the appearance of the spectre. Then, for explanation, I described how I found in the archives at the Town Hall an account of the execution three hundred years ago of the then owner of that piece of land who had practised nameless infamies there, and how the skeletons of children, hideously maimed, were found below the bed over which Augustus reigned. I took a great deal of trouble over this piece, and having read it through I treated it as I had treated the first draft of *Charlotte Brontë*, and tore it up. What had actually happened (for I have no doubt whatever that the Vicar and I saw something that had no existence in the material world) made a far better ghost story than any embroidered version, and so I have set it down unadorned and unexplained.

E. F. Benson, *Final Edition: Informal Autobiography* (London: Longmans, Green, 1940), pp. 267–69

PETER PENZOLDT   Like ⟨F. Marion⟩ Crawford and Machen, his work is not limited to horror tales, nor to the wider field of short stories of the supernatural. Even in his weird tales he shows an astonishing versatility. They range from true ghost stories like "The Room in the Tower" and "The Face" and orthodox vampire stories like "Mrs. Amworth" to the purely imaginative and entirely original horrors that one finds in "Caterpillars." All these are exceedingly clever tales written with obvious facility, but reading them one gets the impression of artificiality. Benson was not a neurotic, nor a visionary, nor had he any great intuition for subconscious problems. His stories lack the true symbolism which is de la Mare's great strength, and which would have created masterpieces out of Machen's and Crawford's tales, had they not so obviously been unconscious of the true origins of their stories. Benson was an excellent craftsman and his perfect technique did much to conceal the occasional thinness of his themes. In fact technique is of first importance in his tales, and in this respect he somewhat resembles Dr. James on the one hand, and Hartley on the other. But he never quite attained their level. James outrivalled him in the art of construction, and Hartley in dramatic sense, irony, and cynicism.

Yet Benson is certainly among the better ghost-story writers. "Caterpillars," for instance, is a striking and original horror tale about a room in an Italian villa, where a number of people have died of cancer. The narrator repeatedly dreams that he sees huge caterpillars with crab-like pincers crawling over the deathbed. One night they invade the chamber of his friend John Inglis. Inglis had previously discovered a species of vermin very much resembling the creatures of his friend's dreams. In jest he baptised the unknown specimens "Cancer Inglisensis." As one would expect, he falls ill with cancer shortly thereafter. The allegory is dreadful but it remains an allegory. There is no known cancer-complex yet, and the subconscious does not produce crab-like clawing worms as a symbol for the disease that attacks the boy in a horrible manner. Yet it is certainly an original and effective idea to create a main motif out of a pun on the word cancer.

Peter Penzoldt, *The Supernatural in Fiction* (London: Peter Nevill, 1952), p. 178

JACK SULLIVAN   E. F. Benson's numerous ghostly tales fall into two categories: visionary outdoor stories that attempt to communicate a romantic sense of place, and grim, claustrophobic stories that frequently involve supernatural revenge in haunted-house settings. In both categories he is a master of imagery and a consummate craftsman, although his stories have a curious tendency to fall apart at the end ("And No Bird Sings," "The Face," "The Room in the Tower"). His celebrated skill in characterization and social commentary, especially praised by critics in his revived Lucia novels, is always brought to bear in his ghost stories, making them some of the most sophisticated in the genre.

The outdoor stories are in the mystical tradition of Blackwood and Machen: nature, which is both dazzling and sinister, has animistic qualities that suggest supernatural forces. "The Man Who Went Too Far," Benson's most famous tale in this category, unleashed a Pan-like deity similar to Machen's "The Great God Pan." "A Tale of a Deserted House," a more obscure work, has a vast sense of space that recalls Blackwood. Although Benson is less magical and surreal than Machen and less original in his elemental imagery than Blackwood, he has a deft sense of contrast: his stories have a healthy out-of-doors quality, a relentless prettiness, that suddenly becomes stained with the onslaught of vampires ("Mrs. Amworth"), mummies ("Monkeys"), or giant slugs ("Caterpillars," "Negotium Perambulans," "And No Bird Sings"). Although Benson stocks his forests and landscapes with all manner of demons and ghosts, he has a special, charmingly perverse fetish for monstrous slugs and wormlike creatures.

His claustrophobic haunted-house tales are as gray and grim as any in the genre. Especially powerful is "The Bath-Chair," the story of a man haunted by the ghost of a crippled, vengeful father. Others include "Naboth's Vineyard," "The Corner House," and "James Lamp." Even the stories that do not quite come off have a strong sense of cumulative buildup and invariably contain memorable apparition scenes. The control and understatement in Benson give him an affinity with M. R. James, as does his flair for sardonic humor. His collections are uniformly high in quality, despite the critical carpings of August Derleth and Edmund Wilson.

Jack Sullivan, "Psychological, Antiquarian, and Cosmic Horror: 1872–1919," *Horror Literature*, ed. Marshall B. Tymn (New York: R. R. Bowker, 1981), pp. 233–34

GEOFFREY PALMER and NOEL LLOYD   Fred never quite decided whether or not he really believed in ghosts but his agnosticism was tilted toward a desire to believe that something existed after death that conventional religious ideas could not satisfy. Though he realized that many mediums were frauds he was impressed by many of the things he saw and heard at séances, enough to make him refuse to dismiss out of hand the general view that psychic phenomena were all rot. His own experiences of the paranormal were few and not very convincing, but he pursued his quest with enthusiasm.

Fred was a traditionalist when it came to ghost stories. He kept to a well-tried formula, but within the limits he allowed himself he developed an amazing variety of plots and situations. He was especially convincing in his descriptions of locations, and created an atmosphere that exactly matched the occasion. As a result, the emotions he aroused were genuinely menacing, awe-inspiring or portentous. He set his stories in bleak and wintry places, or by a sullen sea, in remote villages or on wild marshlands, and added to the atmosphere by the weather he chose to accompany the tale. Haunted houses, of course, dominate the scene, but no two are alike. Each has its own smell, its own draughts, its own history and its own ghost. He didn't try to find lucid explanations for his ghosts. By a touch he could produce a hint of explanation that would justify his development where it was fitting that it should be provided, but in the case of the plainly inexplicable he was content not to probe too deeply.

Geoffrey Palmer and Noel Lloyd, E. F. Benson: As He Was (Luton, UK: Lennard Publishing, 1988), pp. 147–48

JACK ADRIAN   The critic Michael Sadleir was perhaps being generous when he noted merely that Fred had a "generalized dislike of women." Frankly, however many women he might have known on a social basis, however many titled ladies he might have corresponded with, or hobnobbed with at dinner parties or during long weekends in country houses, the evidence is that, as a breed, he actively detested them. In the comedies they are, almost without exception, fools, fakers, brainless butterflies, useless appendages, social-climbing freaks; or, worse, active destroyers, in one way or another, of brilliant young men. It's significant that when you do come across a "good" female character she exhibits many of the attributes society then deemed desirable in the perfect male. In effect, like many females in the novels of E. M. Forster, Fred's good heroines are men in drag.

In the ghost stories the position is even more clear-cut; indeed, stark; apart from the odd, and usually very shadowy, wife—thrown in, one suspects, to appease the largely female magazine-buying public—his women are thoroughly hateful.

If they are not simply shrews and harpies who drive good men to an early grave, or worse, they are real vampires, soul-suckers, predators, witches, and, in one striking instance, the reincarnation of "the worst being that ever lived," Judas Iscariot.

A. M. Burrage, that much neglected ghost-story writer, had utilized the Judas theme two years before Fred in a story he wrote for *Lloyd's Magazine* called "The Recurring Tragedy." Here, his reincarnated Judas is a British Army general everyone loathes without knowing why. Fred's version (and there is no suggestion that he stole the idea), "The Outcast," concerns a society woman who is charming and witty and good-looking (the epitome, in fact, of all Fred's society women), but from whom dogs turn tail and run and humans shrink in fear and disgust. When she dies, flowers wither on her coffin, the sea casts her up and, in an ugly finale, even the kindly earth rejects her. Only cremation can finish her off. Burrage's "The Recurring Tragedy" is sensitively handled; Fred's story amounts to an act of revenge.

Other revenges on the female sex are to be found throughout his weird fiction. In "How Fear Departed from the Long Gallery" (*The Room in the Tower*) the apparitions are two angelic-looking little toddlers who yet cause stark terror in, and hideous death to, all who see them. Fred relates what happened to three of their victims, two men and a woman. He dismisses the fate of the two men in a couple of brief paragraphs but spends two and a half pages describing in great, and almost gleeful detail how the woman was struck down with a ghastly and decaying leprous growth across her face.

In "Christopher Comes Back" (*More Spook Stories*) there is a dreadful inevitability about the eternal triangle of Old Husband, Young Wife, Other Man. The husband is dying of cancer; the wife gives him an overdose. In essence she is innocent; the husband is cruel, is in pain, cannot be saved; and she and the Other Man have not even kissed. It is all a happy release, and a release for her into happiness—which, naturally, does not happen. The husband returns; the Other Man rejects her; she commits suicide. In "The Dance," which begins with a graphic description of a spider killing a fly, the tragedy is even more intense. Again there is a triangle, but this time the husband is not merely cruel but malevolence personified, the kind of man any sane being would shoot like a dog as soon as look at him. One feels, reading the story, that it is only right and just that he should be done in with the greatest despatch so that heroine and hero can at last enjoy the peace and happiness they so thoroughly deserve. Yet it's clear that Fred took the greatest pleasure in denying them this, and in the most horrifying way.

Jack Adrian, "Introduction," *The Flint Knife: Further Spook Stories* by E. F. Benson (Wellingborough, UK: Equation, 1988), pp. 16–17

BRIAN MASTERS   While all three Bensons wrote ghost stories, Fred's were the most numerous, and the most horrid. He did not shirk the consequences of his vivid prose style, which gloried in descriptions of flies and loose eyeballs, malformations and dismemberments, and knew he could make the reader's flesh creep. In *Final Edition* he more or less said that it presented no great difficulty, so he did not value his horror fiction at all highly. Which is a pity, because nearly all his stories are uncomfortable and powerful, and should be rated alongside the best. "Caterpillars," for example, tells of a vile dream in which millions of the insects are crawling in through keyholes and covering the floor with their writhing mess, which on waking turns out to be a presentiment of cancer. M. R. James, the master of the *genre* and an old family friend, ranked Fred's supernatural writing very high. However, he criticised his "stepping over the line of legitimate horridness," and pointed out that it was was relatively easy to be nauseating.

"Caterpillars" is such a long way from the arch humour of Benson's English village novels that it scarcely seems credible they were written by the same man, but the bridge between them can be crossed at various points where he dwells upon the nature and function of evil. In the horror stories evil is incarnate and terrifying; in the Lucia books it is emasculated by silly women who do not realise the harm they are up to. But they are both, in the end, about the same thing, and demonstrate that E. F. Benson, for all his irresistible light humour, has a serious point to make.

A story called "Lady Massington's Redemption" is one such bridge. It was a story which mattered intensely to Fred, who wrote to his agent several times imploring him to place it well. Lady Massington is dead and buried, but shows up for lunch with her husband and goes out to a concert. She remembers she was buried in her own body, so is certain the coffin cannot be empty. The coffin is disinterred, and within it is found a little body fast asleep, wrapped in a bride's veil. An obligatory clap of thunder accompanies the opening of the coffin. As the tale develops, we discover that Lady

Massington was a selfish woman and consequently, when she died, found herself in Hell where she was visited by God and offered salvation. This little baby is her redemption, for it represents "utter forgetfulness of self . . . a soul had been born to her as well as a child." She tells her husband that either she or the baby must die, and she has chosen to die again herself. "The child is my redemption, for at last I have cared for something not myself," she tells him. Underlining the point, Fred terminates with, "her redemption was accomplished, for she had loved."

Benson's central ideas are contained in this not altogether successful story—that the powers of Good are capable of conquest over Evil; and that salvation is possible through abnegation and love. The original title of the story was "Lady Massington's Resurrection."

Brian Masters, *The Life of E. F. Benson* (London: Chatto & Windus, 1991), pp. 231–32

JOAN AIKEN   The heroes of Benson's ghost stories mostly come in pairs, the narrator and his friend Hugh (or Jack or Fred or Frank or Philip); they are forever renting summer holiday houses in very agreeable and familiar coastal regions of the British Isles. The houses sound perfectly delightful— positively archetypal—with lavender hedges and rose garden and flagged walks and lime alleys. Fred brings along a parlour-maid and Frank a house-maid, and, as soon as they are settled in, the heroes bustle off to play golf and swim and do something called 'loafing' which nobody seems to practise any more. After a while there is some slightly unnerving occurrence, then another, rather worse; events build up to a climax, which often takes place in a thunderstorm, and then, by means of confrontation, exposure, atone-ment, or reconciliation, everything settles down, the old crime is ventilated, disinfected, and laid to rest. Benson's ghost stories, most of them, are tidy and predictable. Most of them, too, relate to events in the past which are not connected with the heroes and narrators, who are merely spectators, bystanders, who merely chance to trigger off a recurrence on the astral plane of some bygone crime or calamity; they are witnesses but not directly involved.—It is almost as if Benson is reassuring himself that life can always be tidied up in the end. Though an exception, 'Pirates', that touching tale, in complete contrast to the other stories, suggests in the writer an unappeasable longing for the lost past, the safety and security of childhood and family life, and the original Edenlike family home. All those desirable houses in his stories, on the surface so welcoming and comfortable, in reality infected by some sinister haunt, appear to represent the vanished state of infancy.

In fact Benson's cheerful and comfortable world is a great deal less cheerful, on a closer look, than it seems at first sight.

'Unattached and middle-aged persons'—the phrase he often uses to describe the narrators of his ghost stories—this phrase may be a pointer. Unattached, Benson certainly was; he never married or contracted any close or long-term relationship with members of either sex. Unattached to people his heroes may be, but for houses they have a positively Freudian passion. In several of the stories the lust to possess a particular house forms the fulcrum of the plot (as in 'Bagnell Terrace') and the unassuaged anger and resentfulness of the dispossessed owner is often within what creates the haunt. 'Reconciliation' and 'Naboth's Vineyard' are two of his most successful stories, especially the latter which has a really blood-curdling climax:

> His body pressed against the wall at the head of the bed and the face was a mask of agonised horror and fruitless entreaty. But the eyes were already glazed in death, and before Francis could reach the bed the body had toppled over and lay inert and lifeless. Even as he looked, he heard a limping step go down the passage outside.

And here we are given an interesting sidelight: Benson's more alarming spectres tend to limp. The angry ghost of 'Naboth's Vineyard' limps; so does the terrifying unseen whistler in 'A Tale of an Empty House'. The dread-inspiring headmaster in Benson's autobiographical novel of schooldays, *David Blaize*, also limps; he was modelled on Benson's own headmaster, Waterfield, and also, I suspect, on Benson's father, the equally terrifying Edward White Benson, first headmaster of Wellington College and subsequently Arch-bishop of Canterbury. Arthur Benson, brother of E. F., once wrote 'I hate Papa' on a piece of paper and buried it in the garden. A father capable of arousing this kind of suppressed resentment and fear in his children seems a fertile source for the grim material of ghost stories.

Joan Aiken, "Foreword," *The Collected Ghost Stories of E. F. Benson*, ed. Richard Dalby (New York: Carroll & Graf, 1992), pp. viii–ix

S. T. JOSHI   The curious thing about Benson is that, almost in spite of himself, he modernised or updated the Jamesian ghost story in several ways. ⟨M. R.⟩ James' tales always hark backward, sometimes into the very distant past, as is perhaps fitting for an authority on mediaeval manuscripts; Benson's tales rarely do so, and are sometimes aggressively set in the present. One of his earliest stories, "The Dust-Cloud", involves the ghost of a motor-car ("Seems almost too up-to-date, doesn't it?" one character remarks). In "The Confession of Charles Linkworth" the ghost of a man who has been executed for murder communicates by telephone to a chaplain, pleading for absolution; "In the Tube" takes place in the London underground. Other stories, in order to introduce the weird subtly and covertly, are written in that archly sophisticated manner found in his society novels, but in so doing they create a "modern" atmosphere precisely analogous to contemporary writers' setting weird tales at rock concerts or nightclubs. The opening pages of "The Shootings of Achnaleish" involve a comic banter and emphasis on the mundane ("Rent only £350!") that suggest anything but the weird, so that the supernatural phenomenon is the more striking and powerful when it finally does emerge.

But there is more to this than merely using the observable tokens of the present in a tale. It must be declared that Benson was a confirmed spiritual-ist—his brief discussion of ghost stories in *Final Edition* is prefaced by a perfectly serious account of an apparition he and a friend claim to have seen—and many of his tales present elaborate pseudo-scientific justifications of ghosts and other weird phenomena on spiritualistic grounds. This also serves to "modernise" his tales, and in two ways: first, Benson is riding a wave of spiritualism that gathered strength after the first world war; and second, Benson's very need to account for his apparitions by means of philosophy or science (or what for him passes for such) betrays his uncon-scious absorption of the positivism of his day, whereby spiritualistic phenom-ena could not be accepted on their own but required a (usually specious) "proof" to overcome the scepticism that had already become ingrained in the majority of intelligent people.

It should be pointed out that Benson is not exactly an occultist, in spite of his passing mention in "The Dust-Cloud" of "occult senses" by which the supernatural can be perceived. But his tales (as well as some of his otherwise mainstream novels) are full of ouija boards, séances, and other paraphernalia of the spiritualism popular in his day, and there is no ques-tion—in spite of the flippancy of some of his treatments of these matters—

that he took the whole subject quite seriously. The canonical spiritualistic/ philosophical "defence" for the weird occurs in "The Other Bed":

> "Everything that happens," he said, "whether it is a step we take, or a thought that crosses our mind, makes some change in its immediate material world. Now the most violent and concentrated emotion we can imagine is the emotion that leads a man to take so extreme a step as killing himself or somebody else. I can easily imagine such a deed so eating into the material scene, the room or the haunted heath, where it happens, that its mark lasts an enormous time. The air rings with the cry of the slain and still drips with his blood. It is not everybody who will perceive it, but sensitives will."

This is all very elegant, even though upon analysis it devolves into mere poetic metaphor instead of science or philosophy. But it neatly accounts for the "haunting" of a given spot (which in nearly all Benson's stories is the product of a crime—usually murder or suicide—committed there) and for why only "sensitives" can perceive it rather than most of us hard-headed materialists. In effect, what Benson is arguing for is (as he says in an another story, "Outside the Door") "how inextricable is the interweaving between mind, soul, life . . . and the purely material part of the created world"—an utterance, incidentally, that betrays the flaw in Benson's thinking at this point in its invalid distinction between "mind, soul, life" and what he fallaciously takes to be "dead" matter. But let that pass; the mere fact that Benson felt the need for such justifications—rather laborious on occasion— is telling. No longer could the weird be presented merely as such, without at least the gesture of rationalisation.

S. T. Joshi, "Spooks and More Spooks," *Necrofile* No. 11 (Winter 1994): 18

▨ *Bibliography*

Dodo: A Detail of the Day. 1893.
Six Common Things. 1893.
The Rubicon. 1894. 2 vols.
A Double Overture. 1894.
The Judgment Books. 1895.
Limitations. 1896.

The Babe, B.A.: Being the Uneventful History of a Young Gentleman at Cambridge University. 1896.

The Vintage: A Romance of the Greek War of Independence. 1898.

The Money Market. 1898.

The Capsina. 1899.

Mammon and Co. 1899.

The Princess Sophia. 1900.

The Luck of the Vails. 1901.

Scarlet and Hyssop. 1902.

Daily Training (with E. H. Miles). 1902.

The Book of Months. 1903.

The Valkyries: A Romance Founded on Wagner's Opera. 1903.

The Relentless City. 1903.

An Act in a Backwater. 1903.

A Book of Golf (editor; with E. H. Miles). 1903.

The Cricket of Abel, Hirst, and Shrewsbury (editor; with E. H. Miles). 1903.

The Mad Annual (editor; with E. H. Miles). 1903.

The Challoners. 1904.

Two Generations. 1904.

Diversions Day by Day (with E. H. Miles). 1905.

The Angel of Pain. 1905.

The Image in the Sand. 1905.

Paul. 1906.

The House of Defence. 1906.

Sheaves. 1907.

The Climber. 1908.

The Blotting Book. 1908.

English Figure Skating: A Guide to the Theory and Practice of Skating in the English Style. 1908.

A Reaping. 1909.

Daisy's Aunt. 1910.

The Osbornes. 1910.

Juggernaut ⟨Margery⟩. 1911.

Account Rendered. 1911.

Mrs. Ames. 1912.

The Room in the Tower and Other Stories. 1912.

Bensoniana. 1912.

The Weaker Vessel. 1913.

Thorley Weir. 1913.

Winter Sports in Switzerland. 1913.

Thoughts from E. F. Benson. Ed. Elsie E. Morton. 1913.

Dodo the Second ⟨Dodo's Daughter⟩. 1914.

Arundel. 1914.

The Oakleyites. 1915.

David Blaize. 1916.

Mike. 1916.

The Freaks of Mayfair. 1916.

An Autumn Sowing. 1917.

Mr. Teddy. 1917.

Thoughts from E. F. Benson. Ed. H. B. Elliot. 1917.

Deutschland über Allah. 1917.

Up and Down. 1918.

Poland and Mittel-Europa. 1918.

The White Eagle of Poland. 1918.

Crescent and Iron Cross. 1918.

David Blaize and the Blue Door. 1918.

Robin Linnet. 1919.

Across the Stream. 1919.

Queen Lucia. 1920.

The Countess of Lowndes Square and Other Stories. 1920.

Our Family Affairs 1867–1896. 1920.

Lovers and Friends. 1921.

Dodo Wonders. 1921.

Miss Mapp. 1922.

Peter. 1922.

Visible and Invisible. 1923.

"And the Dead Spake—" and The Horror-Horn. 1923.

Colin. 1923.

David of King's. 1924.

Alan. 1924.

Expiation and Naboth's Vineyard. 1924.

The Face. 1924.

Spinach and Reconciliation. 1924.

Rex. 1925.

Colin II. 1925.

Mother. 1925.

A Tale of an Empty House and Bagnell Terrace. 1925.

The Temple. 1925.

Mezzanine. 1926.

Pharisees and Publicans. 1926.

Lucia in London. 1927.

Sir Francis Drake. 1927.

The Life of Alcibiades. 1928.

Spook Stories. 1928.

Paying Guests. 1929.

Ferdinand Magellan. 1929.

The Male Impersonator. 1929.

The Inheritor. 1930.

The Step. 1930.

As We Were: A Victorian Peep-Show. 1930.

Letters to A. C. Benson and Auguste Monod by Henry James (editor). 1930.

Mapp and Lucia. 1931.

Secret Lives. 1932.

As We Are: A Modern Revue. 1932.

Charlotte Brontë. 1932.

Travail of Gold. 1933.

King Edward VII: An Appreciation. 1933.

The Outbreak of War 1914. 1933.

Ravens' Brood. 1934.

More Spook Stories. 1934.

Lucia's Progress. 1935.

Queen Victoria. 1935.

The Kaiser and English Relations. 1936.

Old London. 1937. 4 vols.

Queen Victoria's Daughters. 1938.

Trouble for Lucia. 1939.

Final Edition: Informal Autobiography. 1940.

The Horror Horn and Other Stories. Ed. Alexis Lykiard. 1974.

The Flint Knife: Further Spook Stories. Ed. Jack Adrian. 1988.

Desirable Residences and Other Stories. Ed. Jack Adrian. 1991.

Collected Ghost Stories. Ed. Richard Dalby. 1992.

◈ ◈ ◈

Algernon Blackwood
1869–1951

ALGERNON HENRY BLACKWOOD was born in Shooter's Hill, Kent, on March 14, 1869, the son of Sir Stevenson Arthur Blackwood, a clerk in the Treasury and later secretary of the Post Office. In his youth Blackwood absorbed a strict Evangelical upbringing from his father, although early on he showed signs of rebellion by surreptitiously reading the *Bhagavad Gita* and theosophy. Blackwood spent time at a series of private schools, and a year-long stay (1885–86) at the School of the Moravian Brotherhood in Königsfeld, Germany, impressed him profoundly with its military discipline but also its "beautiful spirit of gentleness and merciful justice." He spent the summer of 1887 in Switzerland before being sent by his father to Canada on business. In 1888 Blackwood entered Edinburgh University, but he left the next year.

In May 1890 Blackwood went to Canada again to make his living. He attempted to start a dairy farm, but it failed and Blackwood lost much of his investment. He then engaged in a partnership to run a hotel, but found the work not to his liking and sold his share in it in 1892. After an idyllic summer in the Canadian backwoods he went to New York, where he became a reporter for the *Evening Sun*. Here he fell into the company of Arthur Bigge (disguised as Boyde in his autobiography, *Episodes Before Thirty* [1923]), who as Blackwood's roommate stole much of his money and whom Blackwood finally tracked down and had arrested. Blackwood lived in desperate poverty at this time, although his circumstances improved when he became a reporter for the *New York Times* in 1895 and then a private secretary to the wealthy banker James Speyer in 1897.

By 1899 Blackwood felt the urge to return to England. He became a partner in a dried milk company, although he was little involved in its operations. Over the next several years he took various lengthy trips—to the Danube (the setting of "The Willows"), France, his old school in Germany, and elsewhere. He became interested in paranormal phenomena, joining the Golden Dawn in 1900.

Although a voluminous reporter, Blackwood wrote only a few stories, essays, and poems until his middle thirties. A chance meeting with Angus Hamilton, an old friend from Canada, led Blackwood to submit a collection of his stories to Eveleigh Nash; it was published as *The Empty House* (1906). Blackwood became a writer of stature with the enormously popular *John Silence: Physician Extraordinary* (1908); from then on he devoted his life to writing. From 1908 to 1914 he lived in Böle, Switzerland, where he wrote prolifically. A trip to the Caucasus Mountains in 1910 inspired *The Centaur* (1911), the central work of his oeuvre, and travels in Egypt led to the writing of "Sand" (in *Pan's Garden*, 1912), "A Descent into Egypt" (in *Incredible Adventures*, 1914), and *The Wave* (1916). *A Prisoner in Fairyland* (1913) was later adapted into the play *The Starlight Express,* with music by Elgar.

During World War I Blackwood served as an undercover agent for British military intelligence. After the war he settled in Kent, turning his attention principally to drama. By 1923 Blackwood felt that he had come to the end of his career as a fiction writer, and he began writing articles and reviews. *Tongues of Fire* (1924) and *Shocks* (1935) were his last collections of stories, and the novels of this period are largely children's books or whimsies— *Sambo and Snitch* (1927), *Dudley and Gilderoy* (1929), and *The Fruit Stoners: Being the Adventures of Maria Among the Fruit Stoners* (1934). Blackwood continued to travel extensively in Europe and also visited New York briefly in 1933.

In 1934 Blackwood began a new career reading stories on BBC radio. He was enormously popular, and in 1936 he began to appear regularly on television. In 1940 the house of Blackwood's nephew was destroyed in the Battle of Britain, Blackwood surviving by accident. He retired to Bishop-steighton, Kent, where he continued preparing talks and plays for radio. This work continued after the war, leading to Blackwood's becoming a Commander of the British Empire in 1949. Algernon Blackwood, who never married, died on December 10, 1951.

▨ *Critical Extracts*

ROBB LAWSON   Mr. Blackwood's greatest attempt at stating the faith he holds is contained in that much misunderstood story of his, *Julius*

LeVallon, which devotes itself to a daring exposition of the theme of rebirth. As to its purport I may be permitted to adumbrate somewhat of the ideas that Blackwood has set himself to interpret. In remote times Humanity lived so close to Nature that the elemental activities of Nature were actually shared by them. Nature worship was the communicating chord which the Invisible Brain and reason had not developed. Men *felt* rather than thought. They read Nature like a written script. By *feeling with* the elemental powers they could even share those powers. Such powers might then be regarded as gods. And in the Nature worship of that day they evoked these gods and shared their strength and beauty.

To those who have not made acquaintance with the Blackwood books, perhaps, in naming *Julius LeVallon* I am doing its author an injustice in counseling that this should be their first adventure into the realms of the Unknown. There are fifteen others. Each is alive with a tense spirituality. For Blackwood the true Shekinah is the soul of man, and in pursuit of his subject (his whole material possessions contained in three trunks) he has wandered through Europe, the pantheist pilgrim visiting every possible shrine where Beauty might be. For *The Wave*, his latest volume, Egypt became his resting-place; the idea of the book of strange wonders, *The Centaur*, came to him in the Caucasus Mountains; *A Prisoner in Fairyland*, with all the madness of its dreams and the wild largeness of its outlook, was born in the Alps; *Pan's Garden*, that eerie collection of nature stories, was evolved in the Jura Mountains, to which he again returned in the rushing splendor of *The Human Chord*. I have already spoken of *John Silence*, which owes its atmosphere to his sojourn in the Black Forest, but I have left no space to speak of those wondrously beautiful books in which he guides us adults, tiptoeing fearfully through those realms sacred to the hearts of children, such as *Jimbo* and *The Extra Day*.

The ordinary mystic is well content if his vision may conjure up from the dim shadowland that lies at the Back of Beyond, the pale, ineffectual ghosts of yesterday—ineffectual shapes forever pathetically dumb. There are no vaguely moving shadows in the realms of Blackwood's world—his transcendent imagination rising to the nth sense invests his characters with the contours of living beings. For, above all, he is a practical mystic with a message for this generation. Arnold Bocklin, the Swiss painter, had the same vivid, uncanny imagination, and had these two met I do not doubt they would have joined hands and, wandering together in that ancient

Garden of the World-Soul, have evolved together some immortal work, whose purpose would have been to take away the ache of the World.

Robb Lawson, "Algernon Blackwood," *Bookman* (London) No. 314 (November 1917): 51

H. P. LOVECRAFT   Of the quality of Mr. Blackwood's genius there can be no dispute; for no one has even approached the skill, seriousness, and minute fidelity with which he records the overtones of strangeness in ordinary things and experiences, or the preternatural insight with which he builds up detail by detail the complete sensations and perceptions leading from reality into supernormal life or vision. Without notable command of the poetic witchery of mere words, he is the one absolute and unquestioned master of weird atmosphere; and can evoke what amounts almost to a story from a simple fragment of humourless psychological description. Above all others he understands how fully some sensitive minds dwell forever on the borderland of dream, and how relatively slight is the distinction betwixt those images formed from actual objects and those excited by the play of the imagination.

Mr. Blackwood's lesser work is marred by several defects such as ethical didacticism, occasional insipid whimsicality, the flatness of benignant supernaturalism, and a too free use of the trade jargon of modern "occultism". A fault of his more serious efforts is that diffuseness and long-windedness which results from an excessively elaborate attempt, under the handicap of a somewhat bald and journalistic style devoid of intrinsic magic, colour, and vitality, to visualise precise sensations and nuances of uncanny suggestion. But in spite of all this, the major products of Mr. Blackwood attain a genuinely classic level, and evoke as does nothing else in literature an awed and convinced sense of the immanence of strange spiritual spheres or entities.

The well-nigh endless array of Mr. Blackwood's fiction includes both novels and shorter tales, the latter sometimes independent and sometimes arrayed in series. Foremost of all must be reckoned "The Willows", in which the nameless presences on a desolate Danube island are horribly felt and recognised by a pair of idle voyagers. Here art and restraint in narrative reach their very highest development, and an impression of lasting poignancy is produced without a single strained passage or a single false note. Another amazingly potent though less artistically finished tale is "The Wendigo", where we are confronted by horrible evidences of a vast forest daemon about which North Woods lumbermen whisper at evening. The manner in which certain footprints tell certain unbelievable things is really a marked triumph in craftsmanship. In "An Episode in a Lodging House" we behold frightful presences summoned out of black space by a sorcerer, and "The Listener" tells of the awful psychic residuum creeping about an old house where a leper died. In the volume titled *Incredible Adventures* occur some of the finest tales which the author has yet produced, leading the fancy to wild rites on nocturnal hills, to secret and terrible aspects lurking behind stolid scenes, and to unimaginable vaults of mystery below the sands and pyramids of Egypt; all with a serious finesse and delicacy that convince where a cruder or lighter treatment would merely amuse. Some of these accounts are hardly stories at all, but rather studies in elusive impressions and half-remembered snatches of dream. Plot is everywhere negligible, and atmosphere reigns untrammelled.

> H. P. Lovecraft, "Supernatural Horror in Literature" (1927), *Dagon and Other Macabre Tales*, ed. S. T. Joshi (Sauk City, WI: Arkham House, 1986), pp. 427–29

STUART GILBERT   The secret of Algernon Blackwood's pre-eminence over such of his contemporaries as essay this most difficult and precarious type of fiction is, I think, his absolute sincerity, coupled with an unusual command of language and a feeling for the numinous world. I use the term *sincerity* in something wider than its usual application to works of art. An author is often said to be sincere when he writes with genuine conviction, states his views frankly, or uses his art as a medium for expressing a deeply felt belief. Applied to Mr Blackwood the word "sincerity" involves an ampler connotation. He has, it seems, a power of second sight and a clarity of vision allied—what is more and rarer—with an equal clarity of expression. He neither formulates a belief nor points a moral; all the experiences he describes are particular experiences—neither universal, nor symbolic, but intuitive—and intuition is the 'sincerest' form of knowledge. Yet, as Porphyry said of Homer, "it must not be denied that he has obscurely indicated the images of things of a more divine nature in the fiction of a fable." Our outlook on those diviner things has been occluded by the overgrowth of civilisation and the dark forest of desires, psychic and material, which hems in the modern man; hence the aptness of the word "occult"

to Mr Blackwood's work. And yet the knowledge that we call occult may well be the clearest of all, like the divine *arcana* which an early theologian described as for ever veiled "in the dazzling obscurity of the secret silence, outshining all brilliance with the intensity of their darkness." The paradox of the occult is its transcendent clarity.

It is because Mr Blackwood himself has this gift of clairvoyance—in a word, sincerity—that he can open windows which so many exponents of the occult leave shut, or merely feign to open. "To him philosophy was to be something giving strange swiftness and double sight, divining the sources of springs beneath the earth or of expression beneath the human countenance, clairvoyant of occult gifts in common or uncommon things, in the reed at the brook-side, or the star which draws near to us but once in a century." Pater's description of Leonardo's philosophy is applicable word for word to Mr Blackwood's—if philosophy it can be called, this intuitive knowledge of things unseen. Reading such novels as *The Centaur* and *The Human Chord,* or such an amazing story as 'The Wendigo', we have so keen a sense of an authentic experience, of participated swiftness and double sight, that we seem to see the world invisible, partaking for a fugitive but splendid moment in "the only kind of knowledge that is everlasting."

Stuart Gilbert, "Algernon Blackwood: Novelist and Mystic," *Transition* No. 23 (July 1935): 95–96

ARTHUR COMPTON-RICKETT   Tall, lean and muscular in figure, with vivid blue eyes and low-pitched musical voice. Such is Algernon Blackwood's outward demeanour. Those who from his writings have visualised him as a dark-eyed dreamer cut in the Celtic mould are astonished to come across this virile, breezy personality:

> He on honey-dew hath fed
> And drunk the milk of paradise.

No! The only honey-dew beloved by Blackwood is to be found in Virginian tobacco!

The first impression is that of an open-air man, a traveller and athlete, rather than a writer. The second impression is that of an artist, peculiarly sensitive to sound and colour. Then, just as you have made up your mind that with Blackwood beauty is the one thing worth consideration, as in the *Garden of Survival,* you find a third trait in his personality, the scientific strain. Undoubtedly, he is an artist, but, as with Tennyson, he is also a scientist, and Beauty without Truth is but a meaningless jingle to him.

A psychic experience of his throws considerable light upon his complex personality. Blackwood had taken leave of a middle-aged woman friend to whom he was much attracted. Turning at the doorway, he saw to his amazement that intermingled with the placid kindly figure of his friend was that of a Red Indian squaw. Each was distinct and yet the two figures were strangely blended. Blackwood used to say his dominant feeling was fear, stark fear. He bolted down the stairs and into the street, without another word or gesture. Meeting him the next day, his woman-friend told him, without hearing his story, that when she looked at the doorway the night before, she could not see him, but the figure of a Red Indian. A torrent of words, of which she understood nothing, came from this man, though she felt she was listening to a living language.

Here is a case of synchronous illusion which to those who believe in reincarnation is especially interesting. All who have met Blackwood more than once will feel that this touch about the Red Indian explains much in understanding the man. One has only to read Thoreau's comments on the Red Indian, primitive, uncivilised and curiously detached from the majority of men and women, to realise that what may be called the Red Indian element illustrates an integral part of Blackwood's work.

The Red Indian, like the gypsy, stands apart from the ordinary track of humanity, and Blackwood's deeply ingrained horror of the amiable conventions of ordinary life cannot be explained away by the distaste of the born traveller for accommodating himself to the routine that the majority of us rather welcome than otherwise. The trend of his work is best understood when we realise that most of his tales take their origin from places he has travelled through, from Egypt and the mystery of the desert, Russia, Switzerland and the Black Forest.

Arthur Compton-Rickett, "Algernon Blackwood," *Portraits and Personalities* (London: Selwyn & Blount, 1937), pp. 55–56

ALGERNON BLACKWOOD   To be known as the "ghost man" is almost a derogatory classification, and here I may perhaps refute it. My interest in psychic matters has always been the interest in questions of extended or expanded consciousness. If a ghost is seen, what is it interests

LeVallon, which devotes itself to a daring exposition of the theme of rebirth. As to its purport I may be permitted to adumbrate somewhat of the ideas that Blackwood has set himself to interpret. In remote times Humanity lived so close to Nature that the elemental activities of Nature were actually shared by them. Nature worship was the communicating chord which the Invisible Brain and reason had not developed. Men *felt* rather than thought. They read Nature like a written script. By *feeling with* the elemental powers they could even share those powers. Such powers might then be regarded as gods. And in the Nature worship of that day they evoked these gods and shared their strength and beauty.

To those who have not made acquaintance with the Blackwood books, perhaps, in naming *Julius LeVallon* I am doing its author an injustice in counseling that this should be their first adventure into the realms of the Unknown. There are fifteen others. Each is alive with a tense spirituality. For Blackwood the true Shekinah is the soul of man, and in pursuit of his subject (his whole material possessions contained in three trunks) he has wandered through Europe, the pantheist pilgrim visiting every possible shrine where Beauty might be. For *The Wave*, his latest volume, Egypt became his resting-place; the idea of the book of strange wonders, *The Centaur*, came to him in the Caucasus Mountains; *A Prisoner in Fairyland*, with all the madness of its dreams and the wild largeness of its outlook, was born in the Alps; *Pan's Garden*, that eerie collection of nature stories, was evolved in the Jura Mountains, to which he again returned in the rushing splendor of *The Human Chord*. I have already spoken of *John Silence*, which owes its atmosphere to his sojourn in the Black Forest, but I have left no space to speak of those wondrously beautiful books in which he guides us adults, tiptoeing fearfully through those realms sacred to the hearts of children, such as *Jimbo* and *The Extra Day*.

The ordinary mystic is well content if his vision may conjure up from the dim shadowland that lies at the Back of Beyond, the pale, ineffectual ghosts of yesterday—ineffectual shapes forever pathetically dumb. There are no vaguely moving shadows in the realms of Blackwood's world—his transcendent imagination rising to the nth sense invests his characters with the contours of living beings. For, above all, he is a practical mystic with a message for this generation. Arnold Bocklin, the Swiss painter, had the same vivid, uncanny imagination, and had these two met I do not doubt they would have joined hands and, wandering together in that ancient

extension of consciousness; speculative and imaginative treatment
of possibilities outside our normal range of consciousness.

In another letter, Mr. Blackwood becomes more explicit, and adds:—

> Also, all that happens in our universe is *natural* [sic]; under
> Law [sic]; but an extension of our so limited normal consciousness
> can reveal new, extra-ordinary powers, etc., and the word
> 'supernatural' seems the best word for treating these in fiction. I
> believe it possible for our consciousness to change and grow, and
> that with this change we may become aware of a new universe. A
> 'change' in consciousness, in its type, I mean, is something more
> than a mere extension of what we already possess and know.

Thus it is extension, and even 'change' of consciousness that Mr. Blackwood seeks. His message is of the beauty or possible dangers involved in
this extension of consciousness.

Yet in his work he has no didactic purpose. He detests the idea of teaching
anybody. He has a message, but no dogma. His pleasure lies in dreaming
or living through a new adventure in the other-worldly regions, and as
the travellers of bygone centuries brought home sketch-books from their
journeys, so he brings back the written image of what he has seen. In his
novelette, 'The Damned', he writes: ". . . I cannot explain it, but I can tell
it, I think, exactly as it happened, for it remains vivid in me for ever . . ."

Through his books others may then follow him as far as their imagination
will allow, or, as he repeatedly admits, as far as written words are able to
render his experience. Blackwood beautifully describes the quality of his
message in the following paragraph.

> Any little Dreamer [sic] in his top-floor back, spinning by
> rushlight his web of beauty, was greater than the first critical
> intelligence that ever lived. The one, for all his poor technique,
> was stammering over something God had whispered to him, the
> other merely destroying thoughts invented by the brain of man.

This paragraph from *The Centaur*, and his quotations from the two letters,
not only reveal the quality of Blackwood's message, but also the artistic
form in which it had to be cast. The extension of consciousness and what
it reveals are something sacred, something 'God had whispered' to the author.
Any experience of the 'Dreamer' must therefore be recounted faithfully as
it occurred, nor must it be soiled by critical analysis, for common logic is

the arch-enemy of everything that is 'dreamt'. For all his 'poor technique' the author will therefore try to relate as exactly as possible what he has experienced, and in doing so will feel a reverence akin to that of the author of a holy text.

Peter Penzoldt, "Algernon Blackwood," *The Supernatural in Fiction* (London: Peter Nevill, 1952), pp. 228–30

DEREK HUDSON   His friends agree that he was a happy man and the best of company. If he had a fault, it was one that might have been expected of his temperament—he was easily bored. That he was disappointed by the relative failure of his larger literary ambitions is true, but he consoled himself by the knowledge that he was the accepted expert of the eerie short story. He was an inspiring friend who conveyed, as Sir Clifford Norton put it to me, the idea that one might always meet something unexpected 'just round the corner'.

Blackwood's life remained fundamentally solitary, and determinedly independent. Although many of his friends were women, and although he formed several deep attachments, he avoided marriage. He remained 'Uncle Paul', a nickname derived from his early novel *The Education of Uncle Paul*. He was happy in boarding-houses in the company of strangers, and had a strong distrust of accumulated personal possessions, which he believed to be cramping to the personality. With one or two hampers in storage, he was accustomed to living out of the contents of a suitcase and needed little else except a typewriter. He was once given a handsome clock, which worried him considerably; he was thoroughly relieved when he was able to announce that he found a way of getting rid of it.

When death came to Algernon Blackwood at Sheffield Terrace, Kensington, it is not recorded that a beggar was playing a penny-whistle on the street, as had happened to that other wanderer Terence O'Malley in *The Centaur*; but nothing would have been less surprising. His ashes were scattered at Saanen-Möser in Switzerland, a place that he loved.

Derek Hudson, "A Study of Algernon Blackwood," *Essays and Studies* 14 (1961): 113–14

JACK SULLIVAN   An unforgettable example ⟨of Blackwood's ghost stories⟩ is "The Willows," Blackwood's most frequently anthologized tale. The elusive forces which besiege the campers on a Danube island also besiege the reader; they emerge as a deeply felt experience of "bewildering beauty" and escalating terror. The story has its dull, jargonistic passages, but Blackwood mercifully keeps these to a minimum. In the apparition scenes, Blackwood is a freewheeling pantheist: he envisions nature as an altogether ambiguous divinity, impossible to pin down, both enticing and insidious, spreading out into everything. The deadly willow bushes, the strange sand-funnels, and the otherworldly sounds which vibrate sometimes like gigantic gongs, sometimes like "the whirring of wings" and sometimes like "a swarm of great invisible bees" are not lethal deities in themselves, but satellites of larger unknowable powers. Like symbols in a Symbolist poem, they progressively suggest or evoke each other without defining what they are moving toward.

In this important sense, Blackwood is part of the Le Fanu tradition which opts for suggestion over definition. His best stories ("Confession" and "The Haunted Island" are other notable examples) are the ones which know how to keep a few secrets: "The Willows" moves us precisely because we never quite know what the Willows are. In classic Le Fanu fashion, the story builds intensity through a slow accretion of detail: the willow bushes which each day seem a little closer to the tent; the otter-like creature "turning over and over in the foaming waves" of the Danube; the "flying apparition" which makes the sign of the cross as it glides by; the unexplainable destruction of the canoe; the "nude, fluid shapes" which materialize in the patterns of the trees at night; the multiplying sand-funnels; the otherworldly gongs— all build toward a conclusion that is at once climactic and mysterious. Although interconnections between details gradually clarify themselves, the larger structure of the "unearthly" region remains a mystery.

Jack Sullivan, "The Visionary Ghost Story: Algernon Blackwood," *Elegant Nightmares: The English Ghost Story from Le Fanu to Blackwood* (Athens: Ohio University Press, 1978), pp. 120–21

MIKE ASHLEY   Although Blackwood may originally have claimed he had no desire to be a writer, he clearly did not mean he had no *desire* to write. Once having discovered the freedom of expression writing afforded I am sure he turned to pen and paper if ever the need arose. That creativity may have been curbed to some extent by his periods as a reporter, for writing to a deadline may inspire some people but deanimates others. If his becoming a writer was chance, I have a feeling that the dice were loaded. We are certainly in the debt of Angus Hamilton, who drew the stories to the attention of a publisher, and we must thank Maude ffoulkes as the entranced first reader. By the same token we must be grateful to Eveleigh Nash for gambling on an unknown name, and to Hilaire Belloc for adding further inspiration. Then there is Dr. Withrow, who first paid Blackwood to write, and Sir Thomas Galt, whose daughter introduced Blackwood to Withrow. Above all we must acknowledge the debt owed Blackwood Senior; there is no doubt he inspired in his son a love of nature and a religious fervor that in their natural channels of expression produced a torrent of inspired fiction.

One question remains unanswered. Why ghost stories? Blackwood himself concluded they were a way of release for the built-up horrors experienced in his New York years—but is that all? There is no doubt that someone of Blackwood's sensitive nature, with his intense interest in religious matters, would take the natural step to an interest in the world beyond that which our limited senses perceive. But perhaps we are overlooking one other influence.

During the Canadian visit of 1887 Blackwood's father kept a journal. It has never been published, and I must thank Mrs. Reeves, who now represents the Blackwood estate, for making it available to me. In September the Blackwoods were visiting some officials in Quebec who, though friendly, were not expert in the art of conversation. With some exasperation, Sir Stevenson wrote in his diary:

> I verily believe that if I had not told them ghost stories and every
> imaginable thing I could rake up, we should have sat twiddling
> our thumbs the whole evening. . . .

Blackwood's father, that most ardent of evangelists, telling ghost stories! Yet the ghost story has always been an entertaining way of conveying a moral message, and this could have been the manner in which they were told; nonetheless it reveals an early direct influence on the youthful Algernon. There is further evidence in a letter written to Algernon Blackwood in 1947 by a long-time friend, Percy Radcliffe, which looks back to the summer of 1887, three months before the Canadian trip:

> . . . I wonder if you remember a long night walk we made up
> through the forest by Böle on to the mountain. It was a night in

June 1887, the even of Queen Victoria's Jubilee and we proposed
to celebrate it by climbing the summit of the Tête le Rang to
camp up there and see the sunrise on the Alps.
    If you do recollect it you will remember that we left the Curé's
late in the evening walking through the dark forest road up the
village of Rochefort and then climbed for some hours reaching
the summit of the mountain about midnight. I think you told us
some ghost stories to keep our spirits up.

There we have it—Blackwood telling ghost stories when he was just 18,
a habit almost certainly learned from his father.

So it would seem that Blackwood's life, though he may not have realised
it, was progressively shaped by his father; and in thinking of his son's
achievements we should never forget Stevenson Arthur Blackwood, lover
of nature, disciple of God—and teller of ghost stories.

> Mike Ashley, "The Road to 'The Empty House': The Story of How Algernon Black-
> wood Became a Writer," *Fantasy Commentator* 5, No. 3 (Fall 1985): 173–74

S. T. JOSHI   I am frankly at a loss to explain how exactly Blackwood
produces the effects he does, either in the tales of horror or in the tales of
awe. As I have mentioned before, in many of the "climaxes" in Blackwood's
tales nothing in particular "happens"; and it becomes even more of a quan-
dary when we add Lovecraft's comment that Blackwood labors "under the
handicap of a somewhat bald and journalistic style devoid of intrinsic magic,
colour, and vitality." Without taking quite so dim a view of Blackwood as
a stylist—and without agreeing with the common assertion that Blackwood
is habitually prolix—I must admit that I find Blackwood's style merely
serviceable: it gets the job done—no more. In only a few random works—
like "The Old Man of Visions" (in *The Listener*) or "The Return" (in *Pan's
Garden*)—do we find Blackwood approaching anything that could be called
prose-poetry. And yet Blackwood has some strange power to create an almost
unbearably intense atmosphere of clutching horror or fascination, especially
toward the end of his tales—"Sand," "The Regeneration of Lord Ernie,"
"The Willows," "The Wendigo," "A Descent into Egypt," and "Ancient
Sorceries."

Perhaps "The Wendigo" offers the simplest way to analyze the *indirection*
that is at the heart of Blackwood's horrific technique. It is not merely that

the monster is always kept in the background; it is that the influence of the monster draws progressively closer. The first manifestation of the Wendigo is detected by *smell* ("an odour of something that seemed unfamiliar—utterly unknown"). As the tale builds, the following events occur in sequence:

> 1. Défago, the ultimate victim, begins sobbing in his sleep for no apparent reason.
> 2. The Wendigo calls Défago ("A sort of windy, crying voice," one character says); Défago leaps out of his tent with the cry "Oh! oh! My feet of fire! My burning feet of fire!" and disappears into the wilderness.
> 3. Simpson, his tentmate, pursuing Défago, sees massive footprints which suddenly cease in the snow.
> 4. Examining the tracks more closely, Simpson notices an impression of *burning* around some of them.
> 5. Simpson hears the horrific cry of Défago—"My burning feet of fire!"—*coming from the air.*
> 6. In an interlude, Simpson rejoins the other members of his party, and more information on the Wendigo is supplied.
> 7. As the hunt for Défago resumes, the party encounters him—frightfully altered; Défago makes a loathsome joke: "I'm havin' a reg'lar hell-fire kind of a trip, I am."
> 8. The Wendigo sweeps Défago up again and he is lost forever.

Of course, this bald schematization cannot even begin to convey the excruciatingly gradual buildup Blackwood orchestrates—and without ever requiring the actual presence of the Wendigo. And this analysis brings us no closer to assessing the effectiveness of those tales in which no "monsters" are involved at all. Somehow Blackwood can invest the recreation of appallingly archaic rituals—and this is the core of his greatest tales—with not merely a sense of hypnotic intensity but a dim suggestion that the whole fabric of the universe is involved. And now and again he can pen some imperishable utterance, as in the simple statement toward the end of "Sand" (in *Pan's Garden*): "The Desert stood on end."

> S. T. Joshi, "Algernon Blackwood: The Expansion of Consciousness," *The Weird Tale* (Austin: University of Texas Press, 1990), pp. 119–20

▓ *Bibliography*

The Empty House and Other Ghost Stories. 1906.
The Listener and Other Stories. 1907.

John Silence: Physician Extraordinary. 1908.

Jimbo: A Fantasy. 1909.

The Education of Uncle Paul. 1909.

The Lost Valley and Other Stories. 1910.

The Human Chord. 1910.

The Centaur. 1911.

Pan's Garden: A Volume of Nature Stories. 1912.

A Prisoner in Fairyland (The Book That "Uncle Paul" Wrote). 1913.

Ten Minute Stories. 1914.

Incredible Adventures. 1914.

The Extra Day. 1915.

Julius Le Vallon: An Episode. 1916.

The Wave: An Egyptian Aftermath. 1916.

Day and Night Stories. 1917.

The Promise of Air. 1918.

Karma: A Reincarnation Play (with Violet Pearn). 1918.

The Garden of Survival. 1918.

The Wolves of God and Other Fey Stories (with Wilfred Wilson). 1921.

The Bright Messenger. 1921.

Episodes Before Thirty. 1923.

Tongues of Fire and Other Sketches. 1924.

Through the Crack (with Violet Pearn). 1925.

Ancient Sorceries and Other Tales. 1927.

The Dance of Death and Other Tales. 1927.

Sambo and Snitch. 1927.

Mr. Cupboard. 1928.

Dudley and Gilderoy: A Nonsense. 1929.

Strange Stories. 1929.

Full Circle. 1929.

By Underground. 1930.

[Untitled collection] (in series "Short Stories of To-day & Yesterday"). 1930.

The Parrot and the—Cat. 1931.

The Willows and Other Queer Tales. 1932.

The Italian Conjuror. 1932.

Maria (of England) in the Rain. 1933.

Sergeant Poppett and Policeman James. 1934.

The Fruit Stoners: Being the Adventures of Maria among the Fruit Stoners. 1934.

The Fruit Stoners. 1935.

Shocks. 1935.

How the Circus Came to Tea. 1936.

Tales. 1938.

Selected Tales. 1942.

Selected Short Stories. 1945.

The Doll and One Other. 1946.

Tales of the Uncanny and Supernatural. 1949.

In the Realm of Terror. 1957.

Selected Tales. 1964, 1965 (as *Tales of Terror and the Unknown*).

Tales of the Mysterious and Macabre. 1967.

Ancient Sorceries and Other Stories. 1968.

Best Ghost Stories. Ed. E. F. Bleiler. 1973.

Best Supernatural Stories. 1973.

Tales of Terror and Darkness. 1977.

Tales of the Supernatural. Ed. Mike Ashley. 1983.

The Magic Mirror: Lost Supernatural and Mystery Stories. Ed. Mike Ashley. 1989.

Robert Bloch
1917–1994

ROBERT ALBERT BLOCH was born in Chicago on April 5, 1917, the son of bank cashier Raphael A. Bloch and schoolteacher Stella Loeb. He and his younger sister enjoyed a comfortable middle-class upbringing and were encouraged by their parents to develop interests in reading and the performing arts. In 1926 Bloch's life was changed irrevocably by his viewing of Lon Chaney in *The Phantom of the Opera,* an experience that initiated an early interest in film and a lifelong fascination with the macabre.

Bloch's family moved to Milwaukee in 1927. That same year he discovered the magazine *Weird Tales* and the work of H. P. Lovecraft. A fan letter to Lovecraft in 1933 began a correspondence that would have a major impact on Bloch's future career. Lovecraft encouraged Bloch's efforts as a writer, which hitherto had been devoted to comedy and skits for high school plays. Bloch's first professionally published story, "The Feast in the Abbey," appeared in *Weird Tales* in 1935, heralding a burst of stories that strongly reflected Lovecraft's influence yet displayed a sardonic edge that would become Bloch's trademark. Following Lovecraft's death in 1937 Bloch branched out into other types of writing, yet he remained a strong supporter of Lovecraft's work, contributing to his mentor's mythology over the ensuing decades and eventually writing a Lovecraftian horror novel, *Strange Eons* (1978).

Unable to make a living solely from writing fiction, Bloch wrote political campaign material for a Milwaukee gubernatorial candidate between 1939 and 1944. He married Marion Ruth Holcombe in 1940 and, with the birth of their first daughter imminent, took an advertising copywriting position in 1942. He also began writing prolifically for the science fiction and detective pulps, quickly distinguishing himself as a writer able to blend humor with horror.

Over the years, the cast of Bloch's weird fiction began to change as he turned away from the supernatural to delve more deeply into the psychology of his characters. In 1943 he wrote "Yours Truly, Jack the Ripper," about the reincarnation of the infamous Victorian psychopath in response to modern society's violent tendencies. The story blended an acute inquiry into the criminal mind with deft social criticism and proved a popular and critical success. The following year it was adapted for the first of many times for radio; it launched Bloch's career in nonprint media when he was asked to script thirty-nine episodes for the radio program "Stay Tuned for Terror." His first hardcover story collection, *The Opener of the Way*, was published in 1945.

Bloch's first novel, *The Scarf* (1947), a first-person portrait of a sexual psychopath, established several concepts that came to dominate his crime and suspense writing, among them the miserable lives of his criminals, the banality of their evil, and their society's complicity in either inducing or reinforcing their behavior. Bloch developed these themes over his next four novels and perfected them in his masterpiece *Psycho* (1959), the story of a young man so distraught over his mother's death that a part of his fragmented psyche begins impersonating her. The novel was recognized immediately as a bridge linking the horror and crime-suspense fields, and eventually it was credited with opening up the possibilities of psychological horror fiction.

Interest in *Psycho* as a film property convinced Bloch to move his family to California in 1960 and pursue a career in film and television. Alfred Hitchcock's film of the novel became one of the most famous horror films of all time and a source of bitterness for Bloch, who had sold the rights to his story cheaply. Bad feelings were exacerbated when Bloch's novel *Psycho II* (1982) and script for it were rejected as the source for the film of the same name.

Bloch divorced in 1963 and remarried the following year. Between 1960 and 1975 he wrote scripts for a wide variety of shows including "Alfred Hitchcock Presents," "Night Gallery," "Star Trek," and "Boris Karloff's Thriller." He scripted the remake of *The Cabinet of Dr. Caligari* in 1962 and several films for William Castle. His own stories were adapted for a series of omnibus films throughout the 1960s and 1970s.

All the while he nursed a love-hate relationship with Hollywood, whose business practices he criticized for exploiting the baser tastes of audiences and contributing to the social ills documented in his crime fiction. This became the subject of *The Star Stalker* (1968), his first novel after a hiatus of more than eight years. Bloch returned to writing novels on a regular basis in 1972 with the thriller *Night-World*. His later novels *The Night of the*

Ripper (1984) and *Psycho House* (1990) extend his exploration of the criminal's relation to his society.

Bloch served as president of the Mystery Writers of America in 1970. Among his many awards are the 1959 Hugo Award for best science fiction story and the World Fantasy Convention's first lifetime achievement award in 1975. He died of complications of cancer of the larynx on September 23, 1994.

▨ Critical Extracts

H. P. LOVECRAFT   Well—the three MSS. duly arrived & I have read them with the keenest pleasure & appreciation.   Darned good stuff—all of it! You certainly have the secret of atmosphere & dramatic situation, & your style is improving at a marvellous rate. The tendency toward overcolouring so marked last year is waning rapidly, & your command of effective diction—& of prose rhythm, in the case of the archaic specimens—is becoming more and more dependable. Good work! I wish I could see the output of some of my professional clients improve as fast & as substantially! I have made a few pencil notations, most of which are probably self-explanatory. In other cases, the dictionary will probably indicate the reason for the change—or I'll be glad to explain anything which seems obscure. None of these emendations, of course, is really structural. "The Shambler in the Night" has powerful potentialities, & needs only a little less *definiteness* in the theoretical parts—pp. 4–5 in particular—to be extremely notable. Keep working on this, & in the end even the capricious ⟨Farnsworth⟩ Wright ⟨editor of *Weird Tales*⟩ will be likely to yield to its malign magic. In places your atmospheric tension & imagery are tremendously powerful—for example: "The frozen moon was his eye, & his limbs were streamers of stars. The snow drifted down like drops of white blood from his body." "The Black Lotus" is another powerful specimen. In places this gets to a really poetic level, & the various turns are excellently managed. The rhythm of the prose is delightful, too. I also like "The Grinning Ghoul" exceedingly. Its dark implications & evil suspense are very potent, while the sense of underground horror is such as I tried to convey in "The Nameless City." The climax has the requisite punch—& justifies the title admirably. I must congratulate warmly on all three stories—not only because of their great intrinsic merit, but because of the development in your powers of the narration which they reveal. You have certainly covered a lot of ground in a year or year & a half! Keep it up, & you'll undoubtedly become one of the weird magazine standbys—if not a good deal more!

> H. P. Lovecraft, Letter to Robert Bloch (early to mid-November 1934), *Letters to Robert Bloch*, ed. David E. Schultz and S. T. Joshi (West Warwick, RI: Necronomicon Press, 1993), p. 55

BERNARD AUSTIN DWYER   I have left the best till last. In the present issue, I consider "Slave of the Flames," by Robert Bloch (apart from the Lovecraft story ⟨"The Doom That Came to Sarnath"⟩), the finest and most powerful thing in the magazine, and beyond comparison Bloch's best. Living and wonderful description; the character of Nero perfectly summed as we know it, and all seen through the glow of a fearful, fiery dream. I tell you, I don't know when I have seen words used more effectively. I honestly believe this is one of the best stories you have ever published. Nothing by ⟨Robert E.⟩ Howard ever had more living force. The descriptions of the blazing buildings and of the reactions of the gloating idiot are absolute masterpieces of word imagery. Then the cleverness of combining those elements; the modern degenerate; the ancient lyre with its implications of Nero, who sang poetically while Rome burned—these surpass my present mastery of adjectives. Cheers for Mr. Bloch, on producing such a work!

> Bernard Austin Dwyer, Letter to the Editor, *Weird Tales* 32, No. 3 (September 1938): 379–80

H. R. HAYS   It is rather difficult to review a collection of stories ⟨*The Opener of the Way*⟩ about which both author and publisher are so apologetic. Both are anxious to point out that the tales "are not written for posterity—only for immediate reader reaction." However, a formula is a formula whether it appears in *The Saturday Evening Post* or in *Weird Tales* and over again Bloch makes use of such worn-out devices as the Egyptian curse, vampirism, demonic possession, etc. Moreover, he is constantly trying for surprise endings which don't come off. Even if Bloch's stories did not, in the words of the introduction, "cause the reader to shudder over the style rather than the content," the type of horror which he employs arouses no reaction other than mild discomfort.

The purely physical thrill of sadism or resurrected occultism is a kind of tent-show method of working up terror and depends upon concepts which are outmoded. It is the waxwork macabre of Mrs. Radcliff ⟨sic⟩ and Walpole, and, yes, Poe which still lives on in the tales of Mr. Bloch.

> H. R. Hays, [Review of *The Opener of the Way*], *New York Times Book Review*, 9 December 1945, p. 24

ANTHONY BOUCHER   About a year ago I was complaining in this space that Robert Bloch, as a murder writer, is rarely as effective as he can and should be. Now, in his sixth suspense novel, *Psycho*, he is more chillingly effective than any writer might reasonably be expected to be, and I will have my words with *sauce bearnaise* please.

Here Mr. Bloch demonstrates almost like a male Margaret Millar, that a believable history of mental illness can be more terrifying than all the arcane horrors summoned up by a collaboration of Poe and Lovecraft. The narrative surprises and shocks are so cunningly arrayed that it's unwise even to hint at plot and theme beyond mentioning that they seem suggested by a real-life recent monstrosity in the Middle West. It's a short book, powerfully and speedily told; read it in one gulp on a fine spring day when the bright sun may restore warmth to your Bloch-frozen bloodstream.

> Anthony Boucher, [Review of *Psycho*], *New York Times Book Review*, 19 April 1959, p. 25

SAM MOSKOWITZ   *The Opener of the Way* contained an excellent cross-section of the best of Bloch's work to date, including "The Strange Flight of Richard Clayton"; "Yours Truly, Jack the Ripper"; "The Feast in the Abbey"; "Slaves of the Flames"; and a sampling of his stories in the Lovecraft vein. To fill out the volume, Bloch wrote a new story, "One Way to Mars," a psychiatric fantasy about the antics of a man trying to avoid being sold a one-way ticket to Mars. It had a polish and finesse which

Bloch, writing after hours and at full tilt, rarely bothered to give his work, and betrayed no trace of the Lovecraft "monkey on his back."

As early as 1943, Bloch had switched a major part of his writing to magazines such as *Mammoth Detective*, *New Detective*, *Thrilling Mystery*, and *Dime Mystery*. In 1947, he tried his hand at a full-length mystery, *The Scarf*, published by Dial. Here he wrote in the manner of Raymond Chandler, short, jolting, hard sentences carrying events relentlessly forward. This was the first of seven mystery novels, his own personal favorite being *The Kidnapper*, an original paperback published by Lion Books in 1954. "Nobody, but nobody, liked this little effort, which is a matter-of-fact, straightforward account of a vicious psychopathic kidnapper, told in the first person," he complained. "I think it's my most honest book; there are no 'tricks' and there's no overt 'Look, Ma—I'm writing!' touches. I believe it was disliked just because it *was* realistic, and hence unpleasant."

Bloch had educated himself out of the Lovecraft style, but he would never lose the Lovecraft method. True, now his themes were conveyed with merciless, naked realism, where before the language of a more genteel school of rhetoric partially softened his meaning. But his practice was still the same. To tell all. To hold nothing back. To build towards the ultimate horror with every device at hand and then spring it on the reader in its "hideous totality." The terrors he described had slowly converted from virtually unbelievable mythos to all-too-frightening aberrations of the human mind. But the public wasn't ready for his brand of brutal directness, regardless of its authenticity.

Sam Moskowitz, "Robert Bloch" (1962), *Seekers of Tomorrow: Masters of Modern Science Fiction* (Cleveland: World Publishing Co., 1966), pp. 347–48

GAHAN WILSON   Bloch stories in *Weird Tales* often differed from the others in that they possessed a kind of shocking friskiness and took such an oddly jolly approach to the most godawful subjects. Chatting on about rotting vampires or slavering fiends did not seem to depress him in any way. Indeed, it often appeared that nothing cheered him up more than some new way to sever heads or inflict damage on innocent children, and any ghastly act of sadism which crossed his mind only set him to chortling, so long as he could make a pun on it.

I can offhand only think of one author simultaneously given to sickening horror and drollery, and that would be Ambrose Bierce (who can forget—or forgive—his little chapter heading describing a hideously mutilated corpse: "A Man Though Naked May Be in Rags"?); but Bierce was a bottomless cynic and unrelievedly bitter, whereas Bloch, though owning a really superb appreciation of the brutal ugliness and tacky dismalness which life can and does offer, is essentially an optimist, at least of sorts, and patiently cheerful.

> Gahan Wilson, "Introduction," *Such Stuff as Screams Are Made Of* by Robert Bloch
> (New York: Ballantine/Del Rey, 1979), pp. xi–xii

RANDALL LARSON   *Strange Eons* draws liberally from the rich tradition of the Cthulhu Mythos, containing numerous references to the Lovecraft concepts and themes, including that of miscegenation (as in HPL's "The Dunwich Horror"), terrible self-discovery ("The Outsider"), and monster-concealed-within-human ("The Shadow over Innsmouth"). Bloch utilizes or refers to familiar Lovecraftian elements, such as the towns of Arkham and Innsmouth, characters like Richard Upton Pickman (Lovecraft's mad painter from "Pickman's Model"), the Deep Ones (from "The Shadow over Innsmouth"), the Starry Wisdom Cult and the Shining Trapezohedron (both from "The Haunter of the Dark"), and of course in the specific references to Lovecraft stories in the murders discovered by Albert Keith.

Aside from the underlying legendry, though, the telling of the story is purely Bloch. He plays cat-and-mouse with the reader, introducing main characters only to have them unexpectedly killed off, their loss disturbing because they have been so real to us. Bloch delineates his characters through telling point-of-view commentaries and observations, and they are brought vividly to life.

But the main character of the novel remains the sly, inhuman villain, Nyarlathotep. This is the Cthulhian prophet whom Bloch has dealt with more than any other member of the Mythos pantheon throughout his series fiction. In *Strange Eons*, Nyarlathotep finally accomplishes his intended role—that of instigating, like the false prophet of the Book of Revelations, the return of Cthulhu.

But there is no messianic deliverance for humanity in *Strange Eons,* no victorious savior to thwart Cthulhu's resurrection. There is only the hopeless resignation that embodied Lovecraft's own view of the Mythos and which Bloch effectively adopts for this novel. As one reviewer (Joel Lane) has noted: "This vision is one which Bloch is able to share . . . Most writers in the field of weird fiction see an interplay between darkness and light, sickness and health, death and life; but for Bloch as for Lovecraft, all roads lead to Hell. Thus Bloch is better equipped than most to portray the pessimistic Lovecraftian experience of a journey into the entropic vortex in which there is no 'sane' point of reference. [Colin] Wilson's and [Brian] Lumley's characters come to terms with a limited threat; Bloch's can only succumb to the inevitable doom."

While the whole of Bloch's work is not necessarily as pessimistic as this reviewer implies (indeed, it seems to me far more *optimistic*), his efforts in the Cthulhu Mythos are completely barren of hope. From "The Shambler in the Stars" on through *Strange Eons,* Bloch nowhere gives us any reassurance to cling to amidst the chaos of cosmic doom. Despite occasional respites, Bloch's characters all end up flung down the wriggling gullet of Great Cthulhu. This may not so much be Bloch's world-view as it was Lovecraft's, and Bloch very consciously intended to remain true to HPL's intent as well as to his mythology: "I believe the Mythos is Lovecraft's creation," Bloch said, "and his views on it, which he expressed, should prevail."

Randall Larson, *Robert Bloch* (Mercer Island, WA: Starmont House, 1986), pp. 25–26

DAVID PUNTER   I have (previously) talked mostly about two of Bates's personality fragments, Bates-as-child and Bates-as-mother (in *Psycho*). But Bates has a triple personality; and alongside, or within the continuing child-mother conflict there is also Bates-as-adult, the 'normal' person who continues to feed himself, to run the motel, to gather firewood. And this prompts us to recall a third *différance* in the encounter between Bates and Mary; for we are told she is the first, and thus only, person whom he has ever invited to the house behind the motel.

We may thus hypothesize that this penetration of the inner sanctum is the source both of intense desire and of intense fear: Bates wishes his inner secrets to be probed in at least a single flirtation with the reality principle, but at the unconscious level he also uses this inverted penetration as symbolic evidence of the threat which is continually posed to his fragile personality by the outer world. Mary's presence in the house constitutes the only evidence of a 'normal' interest on Bates's part in the opposite sex; but it is precisely this moment of normality which contributes to placing the long-delayed question about stability at the forefront of his warring psyche.

What is important, I think, about this 'normal' adult within the traumatic structure is that it represents routine; and routine is the sign for a reversible mastery, the adult's mastery of outer events through prediction and reliability, and at the same time the domination of the person by events which will continue to flow in predestined ways despite the individual's attempts at control. We may thus see the 'normal' Bates as representing a midpoint of power: where Bates-as-mother and Bates-as-child stand for unresolved problems about omnipotence and domination, Bates the harmless motel-keeper stands on a conventional edge where power is actually limited and clear.

We are thus returned to the underlying symbolism of Bates's drinking, which again takes on the form of a triple sign. First, as we have seen, it forms a substitute gratification for Bates the thwarted child. Second, it forms a moment of escape from the control of the mother, both in its revolt against social convention and also in its loosening of restraint. Third, it represents, to Bates, 'normal' adult male activity, and in this sense it again returns us to the problems of control, because it stands as the sign for a habit which, so Bates thinks, is under the control of the rational mind when in fact it is vividly demonstrated to us that the mind loses its control under precisely this influence.

Bates the adult needs objects to validate his adult status; but in this respect he is a collector. He gathers firewood; he collects stuffed animals; he collects books of various kinds, including pornography, which can be seen as the motif of the collector *par excellence*. In these attempts at collection, we may see Bates as trying to establish a psychic and physical terrain of his own, away from the omniscience of his mother; we may also think metaphorically about his attempts to 'collect' himself—to get himself, as it were, all in one place at the same time.

In this respect, Bloch's portrayal of Bates is startlingly different from the Anthony Perkins portrait in the Hitchcock film. Where Perkins is dark, moody, halting, Bloch's protagonist is fat, balding, gingery, perhaps even benign. He has, in effect, protective colouring; and it is this ability of the psychotic to sink into the texture of everyday life which repeatedly fascinated Bloch as writer and filmmaker.

David Punter, "Robert Bloch's *Psycho:* Some Pathological Contexts," *American Horror Fiction: From Brockden Brown to Stephen King,* ed. Brian Docherty (London: Macmillan Press, 1990), pp. 98–99

ROBERT BLOCH   Speaking at the then-equivalent World Science Fiction Convention in 1948, I suggested that the time had come to forsake literary voyages through outer space in favor of exploring "inner space"— the mysterious realm of the human mind.

In so doing, I was far from the originator of such a concept. Many members of the literary establishment have employed it in a variety of ways. James Joyce offered stream-of-consciousness stylization, Dostoevsky examined the workings of the mind in what then amounted to clinical detail, and the characters of Shakespeare, Jonson and Marlowe did a lot of thinking out loud.

But with few exceptions science fiction had not followed the example of Robert Louis Stevenson's 1886 masterwork, *The Strange Case of Dr. Jekyll and Mr. Hyde.*

Having turned much of my own efforts to the more mundane fields of mystery and suspense fiction, I was increasingly aware of a similar neglect therein. Though the plots of such genre novels often revolved around the machinations of what were then called "madmen," we seldom were given a glimpse of the world through their eyes.

Nor did we hear their voices. It was the eloquence of the detective which most frequently found favor, or the admiring accounts of a narrator obviously prejudiced on his or her favor. Reading the words of Dr. Watson was all very well, but speaking for myself, I would dearly have loved to see how the same story might flow from the pen of Professor Moriarty.

Incompetent to assume the persona of "The Napoleon of Crime," at times I elected to enter into the minds of less masterly criminals, including a number who suffered from various forms of mental illness. It became increasingly apparent to me that if even something like Lovecraft's concept of cosmic dread actually existed, there was no necessity to track down terrors from beyond the stars; horror might just happen to live next door. It can whisper to you over the phone, it can knock on your door, it can crawl into your bed.

Properly presented amidst commonplace but convincing everyday surroundings, real horrors can be far more frightening than the fantastic. The credible is always a greater menace than the incredible, merely because we know it *can* happen and—even worse—it can happen to *us*.

That's one of the secrets shared in common by every writer whose work appears in this anthology. I reveal it only because it is the sole secret which I myself can understand. Other secrets, the deeper and darker ones pertaining to their sources of inspiration, their ability to create destruction, their talent for terror—well, there are some things man is not meant to know.

But I do know this; our deepest fears lie buried in our imaginations, and are best summoned forth by whispers rather than screams. Nothing exceeds like excess.

> Robert Bloch, "Introduction," *Psycho-Paths*, ed. Robert Bloch (New York: Tor, 1991), pp. xv–xvi

---

STEFAN DZIEMIANOWICZ   The area where Bloch was to achieve his true notoriety ⟨. . .⟩ was in the tale of human psychopathology. In contrast to Lovecraft, for whom human characters were merely foreground figures that helped to put the immense cosmic backdrop into perspective, Bloch (taking a tip from Lovecraft's instructor, Edgar Allan Poe) found a universe of horror in the workings of the twisted human mind. Lovecraft's contribution to horror had been the peeling back of all our secure assumptions about existence to expose the rancid reality they concealed. In the same spirit, Bloch made a career out of showing that the things in life we can be least certain about are ourselves and those around us.

Bloch's earliest effort in this vein was his 1938 story, "Slave of the Flames," a study of the pyromaniac who set the great Chicago fire of 1871 with the help of supernatural agents. He would return to the theme in 1961 in his crime novel *Firebug*, dropping the fire demons and suggesting that pyromania was a perverse, but not entirely unexpected, response to social pressures on the individual.

A similar type of social critique can be found in Bloch's most famous story, "Yours Truly, Jack the Ripper" (1943), which posits numerous reincarnations of the title character since his heyday and suggests that every era, either through inattentiveness or indifference to its own capacity for violence, carves a comfortable niche for the Ripper's avatars. In the fifty years since he wrote this story, Bloch has used other horrifying historical figures as springboards for similar social analysis—most notably the 19th-century American mass murderer H. H. Holmes in the 1974 novel *American Gothic*, and Robert Louis Stevenson's fictional Henry Jekyll in his 1990 collaboration with Andre Norton, *The Jekyll Legacy*—but none have so captivated his imagination as the Ripper. Bloch returned to this character in such stories as "A Toy for Juliette" and "A Most Unusual Murder", and his 1984 novel *Night of the Ripper,* not only because the Ripper's unsolved crimes lend themselves to fictional speculation, but because the Ripper's ability to elude capture suggests how easy it was for this monster to blend in with his society.

"The monster in our midst" is the theme that has dominated Bloch's writing for the past half-century. Starting in 1945 with his story "One Way to Mars," Bloch began dispensing with supernatural agents to concentrate on the horror of seemingly normal persons motivated by distorted psychological orientations and values. Written at the eleventh hour to fill space in his first hardcover collection, *The Opener of the Way,* "One Way to Mars" is a tour-de-force told from the point of view of an alcoholic musician who loses the ability to distinguish between delusions and reality, with predictably disastrous results. Like his 1952 story, "Lucy Comes to Stay", the tale is memorable for its rendering of a psyche fragmenting before the reader's eyes.

Even more disturbing are those stories told in the first person by characters who take the reader into their confidence and only gradually reveal their psychoses. "Enoch" (1946) is a madman's matter-of-fact account of what is responsible for the voices that tell him to kill, and "The Real Bad Friend" (1957) the narrative of a framed murderer who gradually reveals that the perpetrator is really a part of his psyche that he has split off to project the blame on. When Bloch attempted this approach at greater length in his first two novels, *The Scarf* (1947) and *The Kidnapper* (1954), he produced disturbing portraits of persons whose beguiling façade of normalcy conceals psychopathic and sociopathic tendencies as alien as anything the supernatural has to offer.

Stefan Dziemianowicz, "Bloch Magic," *Necronomi-Con Program Booklet* (West Warwick, RI: Necronomicon Press, 1993), pp. 6–7

S. T. JOSHI   ⟨. . .⟩ Bloch's early Lovecraftian tales may be of the greatest interest, at least as far as Bloch's own subsequent career is concerned, for the hints they provide of how he metamorphosed his writing from the florid supernaturalism of his youth to the psychological suspense of his maturity. At first glance, these two modes could not be more different; but in several tales of the late 1930s through the 1950s, Bloch shows how elements from both can be fused to produce a new amalgam.

The first thing Bloch had to do was to gain control of his style. Already by late 1934 Lovecraft is noting that "The tendency toward overcolouring so marked last year is waning rapidly, & your command of effective diction . . . is becoming more & more dependable." One of the stories that elicited this comment was "The Grinning Ghoul", and indeed it is one of the first of Bloch's stories that plays on the distinction between psychological and ontological horror. The protagonist is a "moderately successful practising psychiatrist", one of whose patients is a professor who admits to having bizarre dreams. Naturally, the psychiatrist initially dispenses with the dreams as mere vagaries, but later learns that they have an all too real source.

Still more remarkable, and one of the finest stories of Bloch's early period, is the uncollected tale "Black Bargain" (*Weird Tales*, May 1942). Here both the Lovecraftian idiom and the customary Lovecraftian setting have been abandoned totally, and the subtle incursion of horror in a very mundane environment produces potently chilling effects. A rather cynical and world-weary pharmacist supplies some odd drugs—aconite, belladonna, and the like—to a down-and-outer who comes into his store clutching a large black book in German black-letter. A few days later the customer returns, but he has been transformed: he is spruced up with new clothes and claims that he has been hired by a local chemical supply house. As the man, Fritz Gulther, and the pharmacist celebrate the former's good fortune at a bar, the pharmacist notices something anomalous about the man's shadow: its movements do not seem to coincide with Gulther's. Thinking himself merely drunk, the pharmacist attempts to put the incident out of his mind.

Gulther then offers the pharmacist a job at the chemical company as his assistant. Going there, the pharmacist finds in Gulther's office the book he had been carrying—it is, of course, *De Vermis Mysteriis*. Eventually he worms the truth out of Gulther: Gulther had uttered an incantation, made a sacrifice, and called up the Devil, who had offered him success on one condition: " 'He told me that I'd have only one rival, and that this rival would be a part of myself. It would grow with my success.' " Sure enough,

Gulther's shadow seems both to be growing and to be subsuming Gulther's own life-force. As Gulther begins to panic, the pharmacist suggests that they prepare a counter-incantation to reverse the effect; but when he returns to Gulther's office with chemicals he has brought from his pharmacy, he finds Gulther transformed:

> I sat. Gulther rested on the desk nonchalantly swinging his legs.
>
> "All that nervousness, that strain, has disappeared. But before I forget it, I'd like to apologize for telling you that crazy story about sorcery and my obsession. Matter of fact, I'd feel better about the whole thing in the future if you just forget that all this ever happened."

The pharmacist, dazed, agrees, but he knows something has gone wrong. In fact, the shadow has now totally usurped Gulther.

It is not the use of *De Vermis Mysteriis* that represents the Lovecraftian connexion in this very fine, understated tale; instead, it is Gulther's concluding transformation. In effect, the shadow has taken possession of Gulther's body and ousted his own personality—in exactly the same way that, in "The Thing on the Doorstep" (1933), Asenath Waite ousts the personality of her husband Edward Derby from his body and casts it into her own body. The concluding scene in "Black Bargain" is very similar to a scene in Lovecraft's story where Derby's personality is evicted while he is being driven back to Arkham from Maine by the narrator, Daniel Upton. Asenath (in Derby's body) remarks: " 'I hope you'll forget my attack back there, Upton . . . You know what my nerves are, and I guess you can excuse such things.' "

S. T. Joshi, "A Literary Tutelage: Robert Bloch and H. P. Lovecraft," *Studies in Weird Fiction* No. 16 (Winter 1995): 21–22

▨ *Bibliography*

Sea-Kissed. 1945.

The Opener of the Way. 1945.

The Scarf. 1947, 1966.

The Kidnapper. 1954.

Spiderweb. 1954.

The Will to Kill. 1954.

Shooting Star. 1958.

Terror in the Night and Other Stories. 1958.

Psycho. 1959.

The Dead Beat. 1960.

Pleasant Dreams—Nightmares. 1960.

Firebug. 1961.

Blood Runs Cold. 1961.

The Couch. 1962.

Terror. 1962.

Yours Truly, Jack the Ripper: Tales of Horror ⟨The House of the Hatchet and Other Tales of Horror⟩. 1962.

Atoms and Evil. 1962.

The Eighth Stage of Fandom: Selections from 25 Years of Fan Writing. Ed. Earl Kemp. 1962.

Horror-7. 1963.

Bogey Men. 1963.

Tales in a Jugular Vein. 1965.

The Skull of the Marquis de Sade and Other Stories. 1965.

Chamber of Horrors. 1966.

The Living Demons. 1967.

The Star Stalker. 1968.

Ladies' Day; This Crowded Earth. 1968.

Dragons and Nightmares: Four Short Novels. 1968.

The Todd Dossier. 1969.

Bloch and Bradbury (with Ray Bradbury). 1969.

Fear Today—Gone Tomorrow. 1971.

It's All in Your Mind. 1971.

Sneak Preview. 1971.

Night-World. 1972.

American Gothic. 1974.

Cold Chills. 1977.

The Laughter of a Ghoul: What Every Young Ghoul Should Know. 1977.

The Best of Robert Bloch. Ed. Lester del Rey. 1977.

The King of Terrors: Tales of Madness and Death. 1977.

The Best of Fredric Brown (editor). 1977.

Reunion with Tomorrow. 1978.

Strange Eons. 1978.

There Is a Serpent in Eden. 1979.

Out of the Mouths of Graves. 1979.

Such Stuff as Screams Are Made Of. 1979.

The First World Fantasy Convention: Three Authors Remember (with T. E. D. Klein and Fritz Leiber). 1980.

Mysteries of the Worm. Ed. Lin Carter. 1981, 1993.

Psycho II. 1982.

Twilight Zone: The Movie. 1983.

The Night of the Ripper. 1984.

Out of My Head. 1986.

Unholy Trinity: Three Novels of Suspense ⟨*The Scarf, The Dead Beat, The Couch*⟩. 1986.

Selected Stories. 1987, 1990 (as *Complete Stories*). 3 vols.

Midnight Pleasures. 1987.

Lost in Time and Space with Lefty Feep. Ed. John Stanley. 1987.

Fear and Trembling. 1989.

Screams ⟨*The Will to Kill, Firebug, The Star Stalker*⟩. 1989.

Lori. 1989.

The Robert Bloch Companion: Collected Interviews 1969–1986. Ed. Randall D. Larson. 1989.

Psycho House. 1990.

The Jekyll Legacy (with Andre Norton). 1990.

Psycho-Paths (editor). 1991.

Three Complete Novels ⟨*Psycho, Psycho II, Psycho House*⟩. 1993.

Once Around the Bloch: An Unauthorized Autobiography. 1993.

The Early Fears. 1994.

Walter de la Mare
1873–1956

WALTER JOHN DE LA MARE was born in Charlton, Kent, on April 25, 1873, the son of James Edward and Lucy Sophia (Browning) de la Mare. His father died when de la Mare was four, and he was brought up by his mother. The family eventually moved to London, and de la Mare became a chorister at St. Paul's Cathedral, where he was also educated. In 1890, unable to attend college, he became a bookkeeper at the Anglo-American (Standard) Oil Company, where he worked for nearly twenty years. During his spare time, however, he began to write stories and poems, publishing them in the *Cornhill Magazine*, *Pall Mall Gazette*, and other periodicals. He was, however, so diffident as to the quality of his work that he initially used the pseudonym "Walter Ramal." His *Songs of Childhood* was published in 1902 under this pseudonym, as were several horror tales that were posthumously collected as *Eight Tales* (1971). His first novel, *Henry Brocken*, appeared in 1904 under his own name.

In 1899 he married Constance Elfrida Igpen, with whom he had two sons and two daughters. In 1908 the Asquith government granted de la Mare a Civil List pension, and he was able to leave the Standard Oil Company and become a full-time writer, settling down at a home in Twickenham. Much of his early prose fiction has a decidedly supernatural or weird cast, including the novel *The Return* (1910), which involves psychic possession, and several collections of stories, notably *The Riddle and Other Stories* (1923), *The Connoisseur and Other Stories* (1926), *On the Edge* (1930), and *The Wind Blows Over* (1936). These volumes contain such celebrated horror tales as "Seaton's Aunt," "All Hallows," and "A Recluse" and carry on the tradition of psychological horror derived from Poe; in many instances it is impossible to determine whether the events are supernatural or the imaginings of a diseased mind. Some of de la Mare's poetry also contains touches of the weird, notably the title poem in *The Listeners and Other Poems* (1912). He also wrote an important and lengthy introduction to his son Colin de la Mare's anthology of horror tales, *They Walk Again* (1931), giving his rationale for weird writing.

De la Mare, however, is best known as a writer for children, including such volumes as *The Three Mulla-Mulgars* (1910), *Lispet, Lispett and Vaine* (1923), and *Broomsticks and Other Tales* (1926). *Come Hither* (1923), an anthology of "rhymes and poems for the young of all ages," is regarded as among the best of its kind. Of de la Mare's novels for adults, the best-known are *Memoirs of a Midget* (1921) and *At First Sight* (1928). Some of his many essays and reviews are collected in *Pleasures and Speculations* (1940) and *Private View* (1953).

As a poet de la Mare also attained critical renown, and many volumes of poetry, both for children and for adults, were published during his lifetime; his *Complete Poems* appeared in 1969. De la Mare also compiled several unique anthologies, including *Desert Islands and Robinson Crusoe* (1930), a collection of travel writing, and *Behold, This Dreamer!* (1939), an anthology of "reverie, night, sleep, dream, love-dreams, nightmare, death, the unconscious, the imagination, divination, the artist, and kindred subjects."

In 1948 de la Mare became a Companion of Honour, and in 1953 he received the Order of Merit. He received honorary degrees from many universities, including Oxford, Cambridge, and St. Andrew's. Walter de la Mare died on June 22, 1956.

Critical Extracts

J. B. PRIESTLEY   One fairly common misconception must be brushed aside before we can begin to examine Mr. de la Mare, and that is the notion that he is primarily a creator of pretty fancies for the children. Because he has occasionally produced a volume for children, many persons regard him merely as the latest and most delicate of nursery poets, an artist for the Christmas Tree. Nor is this notion, except in its crudest form, confined to the uncritical, for even at this late hour there is a tendency on the part of many critics to treat Mr. de la Mare as if he were not an artist with a unique vision, a man of strange delights and sorrows, but a rather gentlemanly conjurer they had engaged for their children's party. There is, of course, an element of truth in this view, but at the moment it is hardly worth while disengaging it, though ⟨. . .⟩ this element of truth happens to be of supreme importance. Regarded as a general view this popular misconception is so preposterous that if we go to the other extreme, if we argue that Mr. de la Mare is a writer that no child should be suffered to approach, we shall not be further from the truth. We could point out that his work is really unbalanced, decadent, unhealthy, poisonous fruit for any child's eating. Consider his subjects. *The Return* is the story of a man who is partly possessed by an evil restless ghost, who comes back from a meditation among the tombstones in the local churchyard, wearing the face of a long-dead adventurer—a nightmare. The poetry is filled with madness and despair, wonders, and witchcraft, lit with a sinister moonlight; some crazed Elizabethan fool sitting in a charnel-house might have lilted some of these songs. The *Memoirs of a Midget* is the history of a freak who moves elvishly in the shadow of some monstrous spirit of evil; it is a long dream that never turns to the waking world, but only changes, when it does change, to nightmare. The tales in *The Riddle* are worse; they are chronicles of crazed or evil spirits, Miss Duveen, Seaton's Aunt, and the rest; their world is one of abnormalities, strange cruelties and terrors, monstrous trees and birds and dead men on the prowl; their very sunlight is corrupt, maggot-breeding. And is this, we might ask, the writer of pretty fancies for the children; as well might we introduce Webster, Poe, and Baudelaire into the nursery and schoolroom. Such an account of Mr. de la Mare as an unwholesome decadent is manifestly absurd, but on the whole it is probably less absurd than the more popular opinion of him as a pretty-pretty children's poet.

    J. B. Priestley, "Mr. de la Mare's Imagination," *London Mercury* No. 55 (May 1924): 33–34

P. J. KENNEDY   The first story ⟨in *The Connoisseur and Other Stories*⟩ is called "Mr Kempe," and is about loneliness and terror: it is supposed to be told by a schoolmaster who, on a dangerous piece of cliff, was threatened with the hospitality of a madman. The madman's hobby was the soul; he conducted researches into the question of the soul's existence; and he did so (apparently) by murdering his occasional guests. The schoolmaster tells the story in a public-house, and comic relief is provided by a gentleman with eyes like plums in a pudding. It is easy enough to unravel the technique here; Mr. de la Mare is trying to make his horror more real by putting it cheek by jowl with the commonplace. Unfortunately, he has less than no gift for comic relief, and his bright angelic mind is dreadfully ill at ease with the commonplace. ⟨. . .⟩

Mr. de la Mare, it must be remembered, is making in these stories an extraordinarily high claim. He is not proposing just to pass the time for us. He is assaulting one of the loftiest citadels of art, attempting one of the most sacred retreats of emotion. Just because his stories are difficult to understand—just because, at the precise edge where the ordinary story-teller would be expected to give us definition and conclusion, they fade away into airy fantasy and confound us with the implication of inexplicable meanings— he must succeed *absolutely*, or he fails. The stuff must be sheer beauty, or it is nothing. The thrill must be the thrill that poetry gives us. Well, not all men can have, or can expect to have, all gifts. Mr. de la Mare thrills us all right when he writes poetry in verse: I cannot think it is his line to write poetry in prose.

P. J. Kennedy, "New Novels," *New Statesman*, 3 July 1926, p. 328

FORREST REID   One secret of the story's ⟨"Seaton's Aunt"⟩ power lies in the very absence from it of a visible ghost. I do not mean that the effect of an apparition present objectively need necessarily fall flat, though the stories in which this sudden collapse does *not* occur might be numbered on the fingers of one hand. The ghost story, in truth, if it is not merely to be crude and silly, demands a very special technique quite beyond the reach of the average concoctor of horrors. It is significant that the only successful experiments I can recall exhibit a marked element of beauty—the last quality one would look for in sensational fiction. But in such things as *The Turn of the Screw*, or Meade Falkner's *The Lost Stradivarius*, the drama might very nearly be described as a conflict between beauty and ugliness. At all events, any fond idea that the ghost in itself can constitute interest must result in failure. The mere presence of a ghost, decked in however grisly trappings, can only interest the extremely artless. What may be of the *intensest* interest, on the other hand, is the presentation of a normal mind terrified, or revolted by, or simply struggling against the influence of, such an apparition. It is not the ghost but the person who sees the ghost that matters, therefore the finer the mind shown as reacting to such phenomena the richer will be our impression. *The Turn of the Screw* is the most moving and terrifying ghost story ever written simply because the *human* drama in it is the most poignant; and what would 'Seaton's Aunt' be if the characters were the commonplace puppets of the ordinary 'thriller'?

Forrest Reid, *Walter de la Mare: A Critical Study* (London: Faber & Faber, 1929), pp. 222–23

G. K. CHESTERTON   It is the first paradox about him that we can find the evidence of his faith in his consciousness of evil. It is the second paradox that we can find the spiritual springs of much of his poetry in his prose. If we turn, for instance, to that very powerful and even terrible short story called "Seaton's Aunt," we find we are dealing directly with the diabolic. It does so in a sense quite impossible in all the merely romantic or merely ironic masters of that nonsense that is admittedly illusion. There was no nonsense about Seaton's Aunt. There was no illusion about her concentrated and paralysing malignity; but it was a malignity that had an extension beyond this world. She was a witch; and the realization that witches can occasionally exist is a part of Realism, and a test for anyone claiming a sense of Reality. For we do not especially want them to exist; but they do.

G. K. Chesterton, "Walter de la Mare," *Fortnightly Review* 138, No. 1 (July 1932): 50–51

DYLAN THOMAS   How many of the nasty ghosts, from the other side of the razor's edge, from the wrong room, from the chockablock grave, from the trespassing hereafter, from the sly holes, crawl over and into the seedy waiting-rooms, the creeping railway carriages, the gas-lamped late Victorian teashops the colour of stewed tea, where down-at-soul strangers contrive their tales and, drop by drop, leak out the shadows of their grey or black, forlorn, and vaguely infernal secrets. The ghosts of Mr. de la Mare, though they reek and scamper, and, in old houses at the proper bad hours, are heard sometimes at their infectious business, are not for you to see. But there is no assurance that they do not see you.

And remember, in Mr. de la Mare, the scarecrow that suddenly appears in a cornfield behind a house where lately a man has hanged himself. " 'Does the air round the scarecrow strike you as funny at all?' I asked him. 'Out of the way funny—quivering, in a manner of speaking?' 'That's the heat,' he said, but his lip trembled." And the shocking, hallucinatory mask of face and head lying on Mr. Bloom's pillow (in "A Recluse"). And the polluted, invisible presences that seep through the charnel-house in Seaton's bloated and grave-emptying Aunt. Here in this house, and in all the other drenched, death-storied houses, down whose corridors and staircases the past hisses, and in whose great mirrors you see behind you a corridor of hinted faces, and in whose lofty beds you share your sheets and nightmare with an intangible, shifted fellow or the sibilant echo of a sound you wish had never been made, most things that happen are ordinary, or very nearly ordinary, and vile. These are houses suspended in time; and timelessness erupts in them.

Dylan Thomas, "Walter de la Mare as a Prose Writer" (1946), *Quite Early One Morning* (New York: New Directions, 1954), pp. 149–51

JOHN ATKINS   Few others have managed so efficiently the horror theme. It is this, more than anything else, that brings the two (Poe and de la Mare) together. But it is only the subject that is common, for in its treatment and presentation they are in constant divergence. Poe's horror is visual and extremely objective; de la Mare's can only be sensed by some hidden instrument of the mind and is intensely subjective. This does not mean that he writes impersonally of horror, or tries to analyse states of mind of the horrible or horrified; he is never so explicit as this, but allows a sensation of alarm and apprehension to creep across the reader's mind. Poe's situations are horrible to the least and most sophisticated minds; his devices, the living in the tomb, the pit and the pendulum, are frightening even to the most insensitive. But de la Mare, with his mastery of nuance and suggestion, palms his menace off on to the reader like an expert salesman. His harmless Victorian furniture and harmlessly eccentric old ladies (Seaton's aunt, for example) are objects and people we know and meet almost daily without the smallest shudder, yet he transforms them into dark threats and menacing witches.

John Atkins, *Walter de la Mare: An Exploration* (London: C. & J. Temple, 1947), pp. 15–16

LORD DAVID CECIL   Some of his stories are too obscure for most
readers to grasp their meaning. And he does not always succeed in doing
the same justice to the natural and the supernatural aspects of his world.
This is the problem inevitably facing writers, whose stories move on two
planes of reality. How are they to make both equally convincing? Most
come to grief over the supernatural. We believe in their stories till the
magic begins. If Mr de la Mare does ever err, it is, characteristically, on the
other side. Sometimes his picture of the material world is too ethereal and
bewitched to seem material. But at his best he succeeds triumphantly on
either plane. No one has ever described certain aspects of the English
landscape as well as he: character, especially child character, is drawn with
a wonderfully intimate insight, made warm by countless strokes of tender
and humorous observation. As for his command over the world of dream
and spirit, it is unsurpassed in literature. He has a Coleridge-like faculty for
giving a local habitation and a name to those basic nameless terrors and
ecstasies and bewilderments which lurk far below the level of consciousness.
It does not matter if we do not accept his interpretation of these phenomena.
The rationalist may admire these beautiful enigmatic disquieting stories
simply for the true picture they give of the movements of the subconscious
mind. Understood, as Mr de la Mare intends us to understand them, they
reveal a penetration into the spiritual regions of man's experience deeper
than is to be found in the work of any other contemporary author.

Nor is their force weakened by being expressed in so delicate and decorative a symbolism. On the contrary it is this that gives them aesthetic value;
that turns their truth into beauty. Even at their most dreadful, Mr de la
Mare's horrors are too drenched in the quality of his imagination, to be
merely repulsive. His visions owe their intensity of enchanted loveliness to
the fact that, however unearthly, they are as clear as the colour of a harebell.

Lord David Cecil, "The Prose Tales of Walter de la Mare," *Tribute to Walter de la
Mare on His Seventy-fifth Birthday*, ed. W. R. Bett (London: Faber & Faber, 1948),
pp. 69–70

GRAHAM GREENE   How wrong ⟨. . .⟩ it would be to give the
impression that Mr de la Mare is just another, however accomplished, writer
of ghost stories, yet what is it that divides this world of Mr Kempe and Mr
Bloom and Seaton's Aunt, the dubious fellow-passenger with Lavinia in the

train, the stranger in Crewe waiting room from the world of the late M. R. James's creation—told by the antiquary? M. R. James with admirable skill invented ghosts to make the flesh creep; astutely he used the image which would best convey horror; he was concerned with truth only in the sense that his stories must ring true—while they were being read. But Mr de la Mare is concerned, like his own Mr Bloom, to find out: his stories are true in the sense that the author believes—and conveys his belief—that this is the real world, but only in so far as he has yet discovered it. They are tentative. His use of prose reminds us frequently of a blind man trying to describe an object from the touch only—'the thing is circular, or nearly circular, oddly dinted, too hard to be a ball: it might be, yes it might be, a human skull'. At any moment we expect a complete discovery, but the discovery is delayed. We, as well as the author, are this side of Lethe. When I was a child I used to be horrified by Carroll's poem *The Hunting of the Snark*. The danger that the snark might prove to be a boojum haunted me from the first page, and sometimes reading Mr de la Mare's stories, I fear that the author in his strange fumbling at the invisible curtain may suddenly come on the inescapable boojum truth, and just as quickly vanish away.

Graham Greene, "Walter de la Mare's Short Stories" (1948), *Collected Essays* (New York: Viking Press, 1969), pp. 145–46

EDWARD WAGENKNECHT   That Mr. de la Mare has a never-failing delight in the varied phenomena of earth and sky no reader of his poems can need to be told. But the tales attest the same passion. Nor is it only lovely things that enthrall him—the sight of the stars in "All Hallows" or the beauty of the sleeping child in the verger's house: "He had flung back his bedclothes—as if innocence in this world needed no covering or defence—and lay at ease, the dews of sleep on lip, cheek, and forehead." Look at the zest of the picture of the middle-class kitchen of "The Nap" or the concrete realities of the city street at the beginning of "The Connoisseur." De la Mare has, indeed, the same kind of visualizing imagination that he has attributed to the narrator of "Missing," to whom Mr. Bleet's simple "we—I—suffer from want of a plentiful supply of water" called up "a picture of a gaunt yellow-brick building perched amid sloping fields parched lint-white with a tropical drought, its garden little more than a display of vegetable anatomies." There is pleasure in such conjuring even when the pictures are ugly. What an impressive "property," in the theatrical sense, is Mr. Bleet's obscenely melting "ice"; with what gusto did the Ideal Craftsman first perceive, when his eyes fell upon Jacob's dead body in the cabinet, that the hitherto feared and detested creature was actually a *little* man. But de la Mare knows too the comfort that can be derived from the very unspirituality of material objects. The tortured woman in "Physic," half of her consciousness busy with her children's illness, the rest with her husband's newly discovered defection, finds everything in her familiar bedroom "doing its utmost to reassure her": "*things* stay where they are put" in this world, "do not hide, play false, forsake and abandon us," even if human beings do. This whole side of de la Mare's genius is a ballast to his more dazzling faëry insubstantiality, and though it is less than half the truth about him, it has its own importance.

> Edward Wagenknecht, "Introduction," *The Collected Tales of Walter de la Mare* (New York: Alfred A. Knopf, 1950), p. xv

---

V. S. PRITCHETT   The critics of poetry tell us that de la Mare had remarkable technical virtuosity. Here, in verse and prose, he has his strong resemblance to Poe. He knew that there is no point in a macabre story unless it is made more macabre, and that the final macabre moment is the one that relates it to common and not exceptional experience. The last sentence of "Seaton's Aunt" is an example of a technical and a feeling capacity that gets the last drop out of a situation. The essence of Seaton is that he was a nonentity who never had more than the half-hearted interest of the narrator. He was slowly killed by his old Aunt, the vampire, because he had not the will or the guts to live. He died. He was buried. That is mere horrifying anecdote. What follows is, alas, life:

> There was precious little use in pottering about in the muddy dark merely to discover where he was buried. And yet I felt a little uneasy. My rather horrible thought was that, so far as I was concerned—one of his extremely few friends—he had never been much better than "buried" in my mind.

We are living graveyards of the unwanted. It required an extra refinement of the whole conception of this story to make the macabre tragic.

> V. S. Pritchett, "Walter de la Mare," *New Statesman and Nation*, 30 June 1956, p. 767

RUSSELL BRAIN   Looking out of the window at the people walking in Marble Hill he asked: 'Do you prefer to look at people or solitude? I prefer solitude.' Speaking of some treatment that had been prescribed for him he said: 'Some people seem to think it is your duty to obey the doctor, but I suppose you still have a right to die!'

He recalled a dream he had had. He was dining with the Prince of Wales, and when he left, he found that he had left one shoe behind under the table, and couldn't make up his mind whether to go back for it or not.

He said that madness was a form of arrogance. 'Isn't there a type of lunatic who looks down his nose?' And here he threw his head back and imitated this.

My wife and Miss Saxton came back and joined us. I had not seen the budgerigar, and asked where it was. Miss Saxton said they had lost it. A window-cleaner had left the window slightly open, and no one had noticed this when Tony was let out of her cage, and she had escaped. Miss Saxton had called her outside, but in vain: and the park-keepers had seen nothing of her. They were very sad about it.

The time had come to go. Saying goodbye to W. J. always took a long time, for he would think of some unanswerable question which *had* to be discussed. At last he shook my hand in both of his and said: 'Come again soon!'

But this was to be the last of our talks, for when I next saw him, on 21st June, his own cage-door stood open. He had become very ill during the night, and Miss Saxton telephoned to say that he was asking for me. It was clear that he was dying, and I am sure he knew it. He greeted me with a smile and a joke about his lack of party manners. We spoke a little, and I took his hand. Then, after a pause he said: 'All these onlookers! There are so many of them. I wonder where they come from.' He died a few hours later, in the night following the longest day.

Russell Brain, *Tea with Walter de la Mare* (London: Faber & Faber, 1957), pp. 126–27

JULIA BRIGGS   De la Mare's concern with the nature and meaning of death was not limited to his fiction. In a conversation with Lord Brain, recorded at the end of his life, he remarked *à propos* of a head injury he had sustained, 'It means, doesn't it, that our whole perception depends on our body, so that when we die we lose not only our bodies but our whole apparatus of thought; we leave two vacua.' His restless and enquiring mind could not remain secure in the easy answers of religion (Graham Greene remarked on how odd his world appeared 'to those of us with traditional Christian beliefs'). Yet if he was certain of anything it was of the spiritual nature of life and of the universe, the quality to which G. K. Chesterton paid tribute in calling him a mystic. This certainly gave him a detachment and serenity when writing of the physical aspect of death that provides a striking contrast to the morbidness of Poe, a writer whom he much admired. In 'The House', Mr Asprey, approaching death and chasing away some cockroaches, is 'aware at the same moment of the surmise that his next abode might be frequented by another species of vermin'; yet his attitude is one of realistic acceptance, rather than gloomy self-indulgence. In de la Mare's cupboards there are no decaying corpses or skeletons. The most physical of his ghosts resembles a scarecrow, while most of them prefer to be heard and not seen, confining their activities to voices and perhaps 'a light footfall'. Ugliness is essentially a human attribute, and the dead, if well content, may exert the wholesome influence of a country churchyard on a summer night, such as provides the setting of 'Benighted'.

Julia Briggs, *Night Visitors: The Rise and Fall of the English Ghost Story* (London: Faber & Faber, 1977), pp. 188–89

JOHN BAYLEY   The sinister thing about this wonderfully bland and intricate tale ⟨"A Recluse"⟩, in which the young narrator has an involuntary experience in the house of a Mr Bloom, is that the theme of *The Turn of the Screw* is both exploited and reversed. Mr Bloom, big, sly, ineffectual, copious of speech and manner, is an appalling parody of childhood, and its proper distance from the adult world. He plays a trick on Mr Dash, the brashly unsuggestible narrator, who has been drawn by what seems the deserted beauty of an English country house to do a bit of harmless trespassing. Sitting in his little sports car he contemplates the Palladian porch and the gracious front door, and suddenly there is Mr Bloom, materialized in its opening, contemplating him, and presently inviting him in to see the house. After a few moments of Mr Bloom's overwhelming affability Mr Dash is conscious above all of an equally overwhelming desire to escape. He himself is like the child now who longs to get away from a particular sort of 'grown-up' atmosphere; and this disturbing alternation of roles will

continue throughout the story. The children's trick the old creature plays on his young visitor, and which the latter never for a moment suspects, is to purloin the ignition key of his sports car, and thus to acquire him as an unwilling guest for the night. Company is what Mr Bloom inordinately desires, for the 'company' that attends him in the house, as a result of his psychical research with the planchette and other false childish devices, he has found to be not the kind to be left alone with.

> John Bayley, "The Child in Walter de la Mare," *Children and Their Books: A Celebration of the Work of Iona and Peter Opie*, ed. Gillian Avery and Julia Briggs (Oxford: Clarendon Press, 1989), pp. 337–38

▣ *Bibliography*

Songs of Childhood. 1902.

Henry Brocken. 1904.

Poems. 1906.

M. E. Coleridge: An Appreciation. 1907.

The Return. 1910.

The Three Mulla-Mulgars. 1910.

The Listeners and Other Poems. 1912.

A Child's Day. 1912.

Peacock Pie: A Book of Rhymes. 1913.

The Old Men. 1913.

The Sunken Garden and Other Poems. 1917.

Motley and Other Poems. 1918.

Rupert Brooke and the Intellectual Imagination. 1919.

Flora. 1919.

Poems 1901 to 1918. 1920. 2 vols.

Memoirs of a Midget. 1921.

Story and Rhyme: A Selection from the Writings of Walter de la Mare Chosen by the Author. 1921.

Crossings: A Fairy Play. 1921.

The Veil and Other Poems. 1921.

Down-adown-derry: A Book of Fairy Poems. 1922.

Lispet, Lispett and Vaine. 1923.

The Riddle and Other Stories. 1923.

Come Hither: A Collection of Rhymes and Poems for the Young of All Ages
        (editor). 1923.

Some Thoughts on Reading. 1923.

Ding Dong Bell. 1924.

Before Dawn. 1924.

A Ballad of Christmas. 1924.

The Hostage. 1925.

Two Tales: The Green Room; The Connoisseur. 1925.

Miss Jemima. 1925.

Broomsticks and Other Tales. 1926.

The Connoisseur and Other Stories. 1926.

St. Andrews (with Rudyard Kipling). 1926.

Poems. 1926.

Stuff and Nonsense and So On. 1927.

Lucy. 1927.

Old Joe. 1927.

Alone. 1927.

Told Again: Traditional Tales. 1927.

Seaton's Aunt. 1927.

Selected Poems. 1927.

At First Sight. 1928.

The Captive and Other Poems. 1928.

Self to Self. 1928.

Stories from the Bible. 1929.

A Snowdrop. 1929.

Desert Islands and Robinson Crusoe. 1930.

On the Edge. 1930.

News. 1930.

Poems for Children. 1930.

Silver. 1930.

Christina Rossetti: Poems (editor). 1930.

The Eighteen-Eighties: Essays by Fellows of the Royal Society of Literature (editor).
        1930.

The Dutch Cheese. 1931.

The Sunken Garden and Other Verse. 1931.

The Printing of Poetry. 1931.

Two Poems. 1931.

Tom Tiddler's Ground (editor). 1931. 3 vols.

Seven Short Stories. 1931.

To Lucy. 1931.

Lewis Carroll. 1932.

Old Rhymes and New. 1932.

The Fleeting and Other Poems. 1933.

The Walter de la Mare Omnibus. 1933.

The Lord Fish. 1933.

A Forward Child. 1934.

Early One Morning in the Spring (editor). 1935.

Poems 1919 to 1934. 1935.

Poetry in Prose. 1936.

Letters to Form Three. 1936.

The Nap and Other Stories. 1936.

The Wind Blows Over. 1936.

This Year, Next Year. 1937.

Poems. 1937.

Two Poems (with Arthur Rogers). 1938.

An Introduction to Everyman. 1938.

Stories, Essays, and Poems. Ed. M. M. Bozman. 1938.

Arthur Thompson: A Memoir. 1938.

Memory and Other Poems. 1938.

Behold, This Dreamer! (editor). 1939.

Animal Stories (editor). 1939.

Haunted. 1939.

Pleasures and Speculations. 1940.

Collected Poems. 1941.

The Picnic and Other Stories. 1941.

Bells and Grass: A Book of Rhymes. 1941.

Mr. Bumps and His Monkey. 1942.

Best Stories. 1942.

Time Passes and Other Poems. Ed. Anne Ridler. 1942.

The Old Lion and Other Stories. 1942.

The Almond Tree. 1943.

The Orgy. 1943.

Love (editor). 1943.

The Magic Jacket and Other Stories. 1943.

Collected Rhymes and Verses. 1944.

The Scarecrow and Other Stories. 1945.

The Burning-Glass and Other Poems. 1945.

The Dutch Cheese and Other Stories. 1946.

The Traveller. 1946.

Collected Stories for Children. 1947.

Collected Tales. Ed. Edward Wagenknecht. 1950.

Inward Companion. 1950.

Winged Chariot. 1951.

Jack and the Beanstalk. 1951.

Dick Whittington. 1951.

Snow-White. 1952.

Cinderella. 1952.

Selected Stories and Verses. 1952.

Private View. 1953.

O Lovely England and Other Poems. 1953.

Selected Poems. Ed. R. N. Green-Armytage. 1954.

The Winnowing Dream. 1954.

A Beginning and Other Stories. 1956.

The Morrow. 1956.

Ghost Stories. 1956.

Walter de la Mare: A Selection from His Writings. Ed. Kenneth Hopkins. 1956.

Best Stories. 1957.

A Penny a Day. 1960.

Poems. Ed. Eleanor Graham. 1962.

Walter de la Mare. Ed. John Hatfield. 1962.

Some Stories. 1962.

A Choice of de la Mare's Verse. Ed. W. H. Auden. 1963.

Envoi. 1965.

Walter de la Mare. Ed. Leonard Clark. 1966.

Complete Poems. 1969.

Eight Tales. 1971.

The Warmint. 1976.

The Wee de la Mare. 1976.

Mollie Whuppie. 1983.

⬧ ⬧ ⬧

L. P. Hartley
1895–1972

LESLIE POLES HARTLEY was born in Whittlesea, Cambridgeshire, England, on December 30, 1895, the son of H. B. and Mary Elizabeth (Thompson) Hartley. Hartley's father, a solicitor who later became chairman of a successful brickworks company, raised his three children in an atmosphere of comfort and upper-class gentility, laying the foundations for his son's many novels and stories about the English aristocracy.

Hartley was educated at Harrow and entered Balliol College, Oxford, in 1915. In April 1916 he was conscripted into the army and left for Flanders. Like many of his generation, Hartley was profoundly shaken by the war, and his writing reveals his growing disillusion with modern society. In September 1918 he was given a medical discharge, returned to Balliol, and received the B.A. in 1921. The next year he visited Venice for the first time, and the city so gripped his imagination that he returned there regularly until the outbreak of World War II. Venice serves as the setting of several stories in his first short story collection, *Night Fears and Other Stories* (1924), as well as of his short novel, *Simonetta Perkins* (1925).

Hartley, independently wealthy, settled in London, writing many reviews for the *Spectator, Observer, Time and Tide,* and other periodicals. This activity, as well as his frequent travels, kept him so busy that he did not write any more novel-length fiction until toward the end of World War II; at that time, however, he wrote his most celebrated work, the *Eustace and Hilda* trilogy (*The Shrimp and the Anemone,* 1944; *The Sixth Heaven,* 1946; *Eustace and Hilda,* 1947—winner of the James Tait Black Memorial Prize). These novels, about the life of Eustace Cherrington and his sister Hilda, are a vivid evocation of the Edwardian period as well as a keen psychological portrait. Later novels by Hartley, mostly comic in nature, include *The Boat* (1949), *My Fellow Devils* (1951), *The Go-Between* (1953; winner of the W. H. Heinemann Foundation Prize of the Royal Society of Literature), *A Perfect Woman* (1955), and *The Hireling* (1957).

Hartley's weird work is restricted to his short stories. Each of his major short story collections (which, after *Night Fears*, include *The Killing Bottle*, 1932; *The White Wand and Other Stories*, 1954; *Two for the River*, 1961; and *Mrs. Carteret Receives and Other Stories*, 1971) contain some ghost stories, tales of the supernatural, or tales of psychological horror. Hartley's work, along with that of Walter de la Mare and Oliver Onions, is pivotal in the transformation of the "classic" ghost story of M. R. James into the psychological ghost story, in which it is sometimes impossible to determine whether the "ghostly" phenomena are real or are merely the product of a character's disturbed mental state. Hartley's importance in the field was recognized by August Derleth, who issued *The Travelling Grave and Other Stories* (1948), a selection of all his weird tales written up to that time, with his small press, Arkham House. In 1960 Hartley published a futuristic novel, *Facial Justice*.

In later life Hartley lived alternately in his London flat and in a country house near Bath on the Avon, which was lavishly and idiosyncratically decorated. His later novels include *The Brickfield* (1964), *The Betrayal* (1966), *Poor Clare* (1968), and the posthumously published *The Will and the Way* (1973). Some of his lectures and essays were gathered as *The Novelist's Responsibility* (1967). His *Collected Short Stories* appeared in 1968 and was augmented in 1973 as the *Complete Short Stories*. Hartley was made a Commander of the British Empire in 1956 and a Companion of Literature by the Royal Society of Literature in 1972. L. P. Hartley, who never married, died on December 13, 1972.

▨ *Critical Extracts*

UNSIGNED   In collections of short stories most authors put their best foremost. Mr. Hartley ⟨in *The Killing Bottle*⟩ begins with the worst and ends with a very good story, "Conrad and the Dragon." It is the old story of the young man who went out to fight a dragon and win a princess, and the place and time are in Romance Land; but the author has given the story an odd twist which makes it new and striking. The other seven stories are all in modern Britain. Mr. Hartley describes hotels, dances, country houses and social ambitions very well, but his efforts to make them a setting for something creepy do not always succeed. The three ghost stories are really vampire stories, for the dead persons go about in very solid bodies, and even have to open a window to enter a house. The author does not seem to have made up his mind what the limits and capacities of vampire life are, and the stories have an air of fumbling. Of the other four, "The Travelling Grave" is about a man-eating coffin which the author fails to make plausible. In "The Killing Bottle" Squire Verdew so passionately hated cruelty to animals that he murdered people for it; but the end leaves too much to the imagination. In "A Change of Ownership," a tragedy of a nervous and fanciful man deceived by shadows in the dark, the author shows a real talent for being creepy without being either unnatural or incredible.

Unsigned, [Review of *The Killing Bottle*], *Times Literary Supplement*, 27 October 1932, p. 792

L. P. HARTLEY   Even the most impassioned devotee of the ghost story would admit that the taste for it is slightly abnormal, a survival, perhaps, from adolescence, a disease of deficiency suffered by those whose lives and imaginations do not react satisfactorily to normal experience and require an extra thrill. Detective-story writers give this thrill by exploiting the resources of the *possible*; however improbable the happenings in a detective story, they can and must be explained in terms that satisfy the reason. But in a ghost story, where natural laws are dispensed with, the whole point is that the happenings cannot be so explained. A ghost story that is capable of a rational explanation is as much an anomaly as a detective story that isn't. The one is in revolt against a materialistic conception of the universe, whereas the other depends on it.

The ghost-story writer's task is the more difficult, for not only must he create a world in which reason doesn't hold sway, but he must invent laws for it. Chaos is not enough. Even ghosts must have rules and obey them. In the past they had certain traditional activities; they could squeak and gibber, for instance; they could clank chains. They were generally local, confined to one spot. Now their liberties have been greatly extended; they can go anywhere, they can manifest themselves in scores of ways. Like women and other depressed classes, they have emancipated themselves from their disabilities, and besides being able to do a great many things that human beings can't do, they can now do a great many things that human beings can do. Immaterial as they are or should be, they have been able to avail themselves of the benefits of our materialistic civilisation.

Has this freedom made the ghost-story writer's task any easier? In a way yes, for it has given him a greater variety of plot and treatment. But in another way no, for a stylised ghost is much easier to handle, so to speak, than one whose limitations are uncertain. If he can only squeak or clank a chain, we know where we are with him. If he can only appear as a smell or a current of cold air, we also know. Simple as these effects are, if they are recognised much can be done with them. But if the ghost can be so like an ordinary human being that we can scarcely tell the difference, what is that difference to be? Where is the line to be drawn?

Banquo's ghost could occupy a chair and spoil the dinner-party, but Shakespeare does not let him eat or drink. I can't quote an instance, but I shouldn't be surprised to come across a modern ghost who could do both. Democracy has been extended to the spirit world. Fair shares for all! Why shouldn't a ghost eat or drink, as well as you and me? It isn't right that he shouldn't be allowed to! Yes, but a stop must be put somewhere to the spectre's material progress, or he will simply be—one of ourselves, and that he mustn't be. There must come a point, and it must strike the reader with a shock of surprise and horror, a tingling of the spine, at which we realise that he is *not* one of us.

L. P. Hartley, "Introduction," *The Third Ghost Book*, ed. Lady Cynthia Asquith (1955; rpt. London: Pan, 1957), pp. vii–ix

---

WINFIELD TOWNLEY SCOTT   Another distinguished English novelist—is it chiefly the English who do this?—has projected one more "novel of the future." One feature of *Facial Justice* may give us pause. Whereas in 1931 Aldous Huxley felt it plausible to project his *Brave New World* 600 years away, and in 1949 George Orwell's *1984* cut the time to a mere 35 years, L. P. Hartley unspecifically but with obvious immediacy in the present Anno Domini begins with "In the not very distant future, after the Third World War. . . ." Whatever the validity of the prophecy, we have here yet another novel of the suppression of individuality in a dictatorship-ridden world.

Mr. Hartley, of course, has his variations of prophecy and plotting. They are not of a kind to insure his narrative of either the clinical cynicism of

Huxley or the overwhelming horror of Orwell. Nor of a kind to persuade readers that *Facial Justice* is at all on a par with such subtle studies of human conduct in the past as his beautiful novel, *The Go-Between*. This one is liable to remain a minor fluke in the Hartley canon, to be read only because its author belongs among that small group of novelists of whom one can say that anything they wrote is worth reading. ⟨. . .⟩

Th⟨e⟩ mud-colored world, which Mr. Hartley has imagined, he has described as "featureless and dull." Those qualities infect his book. As Huxley said about this kind of narrative, "a book about the future can interest us only if its prophecies look as though they might conceivably come true." In Orwell's, for example, the fantasy proceeds from real experience of dictated states. But *Facial Justice* takes off so swiftly into a sort of symbolistic dream of fascism that it never seems real and, therefore, never believable.

> Winfield Townley Scott, "Symbolistic Dream of a Future Fascism," *New York Herald Tribune Book Review*, 7 May 1958, p. 3

JOHN ATHOS   I think we can observe in ⟨Hartley's⟩ first works—*Simonetta Perkins* and the stories—the substantial material and inspiration he was to continue to draw on when the time came for the more sustained efforts.

It all centers, I think, in the way he conceives of evil. In one of the cruelest of the short stories, "Podolo," an Englishman, resident in Venice, takes the wife of a friend of his for a picnic lunch to Podolo, a small island in the Venetian lagoon. "Except for perhaps a rat or two it was quite uninhabited." While they were idling pleasantly off the shore the Englishwoman noticed a cat on the island, scrawny, starving, and crying for food. She was shocked at the sight of such suffering, so she went ashore to take the animal some food. She tried to catch hold of it, but the cat snarled at her and ran away. She wanted to rescue it so she pursued it while her friend and the gondolier napped in the boat, and when they woke, near dark, surprisingly Angela was nowhere to be seen. When at last the gondolier found her, she was, we are to suppose, mangled almost beyond recognition, and able in her suffering only to ask him to kill her before "it" came back. "It's starving, too, and it won't wait."

That is all we ever learn of the monstrous creature inhabiting the island. The Englishman and the gondolier return to the city, stunned and silent.

The reader is apparently supposed to be satisfied with the shock and with conjuring up his own horrible invention to account for the catastrophe. As for the pleasure the story is designed to give, it can only be, in addition to the titillation of horror, admiration for the economy and cleverness by which the conclusion takes hold of us.

John Athos, "L. P. Hartley and the Gothic Infatuation," *Twentieth Century Literature* 7, No. 4 (January 1962): 172–73

PETER BIEN   No treatment of the work of L. P. Hartley would be complete without some discussion of the author's use of fantasy. It is not at all surprising that Mr. Hartley, a disciple of Hawthorne and James, should have started out by writing Poe-like tales of mystery. He sees a direct line running from Poe, the inventor of the "detective-story, the treasure-hunt story, the atrocity story, the ghost story in its modern form," to these writers, with Hawthorne as "a kind of link between James and Poe; he shared the latter's interest in mental aberration, almost for its own sake, but like James he related it to the sum of experience." James modelled his early stories with the clay of Hawthorne, delighting, apparently, in the terrible and ferocious; and in his biography of Hawthorne he seems to feel that the New Englander's most original and successful tales are those which include fantastical elements. Mr. Hartley has followed James and Hawthorne in using fantasy, and James in particular, in so far as he always tries to relate the abnormal to the sum of experience. In his novels (not always in the short stories) we are concerned with fantasy as an element, only, of technique, not as a medium in itself. The problem raised is of the proper relationship of the two verisimilitudes—the fantastical and the realistic. ⟨. . .⟩

⟨. . .⟩ Mr. Hartley has absorbed both Hawthorne's delight in the fantastical and James's dictum of discretion. He does not introduce two verisimilitudes; like James he merely threatens the prevailing one. Yet, like Hawthorne this time, he takes especial care to provide not only the moral but also the physical background for the appearance of a ghost. In the ⟨*Eustace and Hilda*⟩ trilogy, the description of the neglected Venetian garden is a case in point. Mr. Hartley explains that this is meant "to change the atmosphere and prepare the reader's mind for Eustace's vision of the 'larva.' " But apart from the garden we also have other fantastical elements which have appeared regularly and "normally"—Venice itself, the Redentore ritual, the haunted

palace which Eustace's day-dream-mind has already mistakenly but significantly called "Palazzo Sfortunato"—elements which, as Mr. Forster so poetically says, evoke "all that is medieval this side of the grave."

The larva appears and then, as though it were cognizant of Henry James's
rule, disappears. The suggestion is made; dropped. Moreover, the vision
appears to a Eustace who has apparently fulfilled the necessary condition—
he has lived to suffer enough. The apparition, appropriately identified with
sfortuna, can be thought of as a projection of Eustace's anguish over his
mixed feelings about the return to Hilda or simply as a prophetic symbol
for Hilda—who has endured misfortune and who will soon cause it. The
vision is not—as the *Times Literary Supplement* asserts—a "false touch." It
is true, of course, that we know of Eustace's suffering without the need of
a ghost to tell us; nor is a ghost required to convey the underlying vein of
horror in Eustace's relations with his sister, since this is done so much more
convincingly in terms of the ruthless biological competition between shrimp
and anemone. In trying these ways to justify the appearance of the larva
we merely overlook the main point that it is its own justification. Fantasy,
whether or not it aids plot, description, or symbolism, seems to add something
extra, something above and beyond the usual machinery of telling a tale;
something quite its own. To say exactly what this something is would be
to limit and therefore to destroy the fantasy, which, by definition, is whimsical and illusory, defying analysis. But, as Mr. Forster says, "Without this,
truth, when translated from life into books, somehow goes wrong . . . slowly."

    Peter Bien, *L. P. Hartley* (University Park: Pennsylvania State University Press,
    1963), pp. 99, 101–3

LORD DAVID CECIL   The author of *The Go-Between* is one of
the most distinguished of modern novelists; and one of the most original.
For the world of his creation is composed of such diverse elements. On the
one hand he is a keen and accurate observer of the processes of human
thought and feeling, especially of its queerer and more whimsical processes:
he is also a sharp-eyed chronicler of the social scene. But his picture of
both is transformed by the light of a Gothic imagination that reveals itself
now in a fanciful reverie, now in the mingled dark and gleam of a mysterious
light and a mysterious darkness. Further, both observation and imagination
are given significance by the fact that they are made the vehicle of an

intense moral vision. It is not a comfortable vision. Man, as seen by Mr. Hartley, is born with a soul that instinctively desires virtue and happiness. But some original sin in himself and in the nature of things is at work to thwart his strivings towards them and brings them, more often than not, to disaster—a disaster he accepts as largely deserved.

Such is the vision of life presented in Mr. Hartley's novels. We find it also in ⟨his⟩ short stories. With a difference however. In the novels the diverse elements are fused into a single whole; in the stories, one or other tends to dominate. In some the 'Gothic' strain in its author's talent gets its head, as it never does in the novels. Like his eighteenth-century forebears, Mr. Hartley goes in for tales of terror. Sometimes the terror is earthly: 'The Island,' 'The Killing Bottle,' 'The Travelling Grave' are stories of crime. More often the terror is unearthly, an affair of the supernatural. But both earthly and unearthly are steeped in the same atmosphere of eerie and sinister evil. Perhaps this atmosphere suits the unearthly stories best; now and again Mr. Hartley's criminals are too like evil spirits to be wholly convincing as human beings. There is no difficulty, however, in believing in his ghosts. They and their stories assault the imagination with the compelling horror of nightmare. Yet like that of nightmare, their horror is founded on waking experience. For though Mr. Hartley's sense of reality plays a subordinate part in these stories, it is effectively there. The nightmare events are more terrifying because they are interspersed with details drawn from their author's exact and humorous observations of the real world. Rumbold, in 'A Visitor from Down Under,' listens to a programme for children on the wireless, ignorant that it will soon be the medium by which he is brought into communication with the ghost of the man he has murdered.

> '. . . A Children's Party,' the voice announced in an even, neutral
> tone, nicely balanced between approval and distaste, between
> enthusiasm and boredom; 'six little girls and six little' (a faint lift
> in the voice, expressive of tolerant surprise) 'boys. The
> Broadcasting Company has invited them to tea, and they are
> anxious that you should share some of their fun.' (At the last
> word the voice became completely colourless.)

After this it is the ghost's turn to take over: and his intervention is all the more macabre by contrast with what has gone before.

Mr. Hartley's moral preoccupations also have their place in his tales of terror. His ghosts are never inexplicable elementals, but spirits of vengeance or manifestations of spiritual evil. This moral element in his tales gives them a disturbing seriousness not to be found in the ordinary ghost story. Like those of Henry James and Walter de la Mare, they are parables of their authors' profounder beliefs.

Lord David Cecil, "Introduction" (1968), *The Complete Short Stories of L. P. Hartley* (London: Hamish Hamilton, 1973), pp. vii–viii

---

KAY DICK   In a brilliant essay on the Eustace trilogy, the late poet and novelist Stevie Smith wrote: 'Do not be deceived by Mr Hartley's smile. This', she adds about the trilogy, 'is a story of murder.' And it is this deceiving Hartley smile that comes through all these stories ⟨in *The Complete Short Stories of L. P. Hartley*⟩, which, basically, are tales of murder. The murder of life, of love, of joy, of sex. With him it is an old theme; the skeleton in his work. Ever conscious of 'to this favour she must come', Hartley was, as it were, prematurely fearful of death, and therefore unable to view the delights life offers without seeing the skeleton at every turn. In all his books (particularly in the ones which brought him fame) his pleasure with the living environment (whether this be a person or a place), his smile as it were, cast its shadow with the dark and dank grave. Not for a moment could he escape from the final catastrophe of dust and dirt. It was all about him, in his work, this paralysis of will, this inability to accept the moment of joy (whether personal or conceptual) without fear of its eventual decay. Possibly his preoccupation with Venice (the *loco citato* of many of these stories), a city of infinite sensual melancholy, slowly crumbling into the sea, is a further instance of Hartley's fetishistic attachment to death, as indeed are those ancient manor houses and those rivers which invite drowning. ⟨. . .⟩

That his stories should mostly concern themselves with hauntings is appropriate to the range of his longer fiction. Those who are haunted and who participate in the hauntings are not so much unrealistic persons as flitting characters, one-dimensional, grouping themselves with elegant skill in a game of charades. They are playing at being alive until one of them dies or disappears, and they all know that an end to living, even to play-acting, is part of the game.

Kay Dick, "Dancing with Death," *Books and Bookmen* 19, No. 5 (February 1974): 60–61

JACK SULLIVAN   Hartley's ghostly tales deal with every conceiv-
able kind of horror, from the unabashedly supernatural ("Feet Foremost")
to the unnaturally natural ("The Killing Bottle"). Part of the enjoyment
of reading Hartley is that we are never sure a ghost is actually going to
appear in a given tale, yet we are nonetheless assured of a superior jolt. The
deftly executed climax of "The Island" (a favorite of Dorothy L. Sayers) is
scarcely less riveting than the climax of "A Visitor from Down Under" (a
favorite of Lovecraft), even though the former involves the manifestation
of an actual corpse rather than a corpse newly returned from the dead. Thus
Hartley, like Elizabeth Bowen in *The Cat Jumps* (a collection of ghost stories
without ghosts), sometimes violates ⟨M. R.⟩ James's dictum that a ghost
story must have a ghost to be worth the telling.

On the other hand, Hartley occasionally sets up expectations of a psychological or material horror story, only to show at the end that the deadly
phenomenon was supernatural after all. In "Night Fears," for example, the
doomed nightwatchman converses with a spectral figure who appears to be
simply himself—a kind of self-destructive alter-ego which Poe called the
Imp of the Perverse. Yet after the nightwatchman commits suicide, the
mysterious figure is still very much alive; it slinks back into a blind alley,
"leaving a track of dark, irregular footprints" and also leaving little doubt
of its otherworldly origins. Similarly, at the end of "The Thought," we know
all too well that the pursuing creature with the icy breath is more than just
a thought.

In all cases, whether or not ghosts are part of the matter, Hartley's stories
thrill and horrify because of their manner. Stylistically, he displays a subtlety
and power surpassed by no other ghostly writer. Onto everyday settings, he
breeds dozens of ominous incremental images which slowly swarm and
overwhelm, like cockroaches. To the familiar Jamesian formula, he adds a
ringing overtone of childlike fantasy and bedazzlement. His celebrated ability
to superimpose a hallucinated childhood world onto the adult world is put
to good use in the ghost story, a form which habitually exploits feelings of
wonder and powerlessness in a threatening universe. In "A Change of
Ownership," the main character speaks of a man who "from a child, had
been so ill at ease in his own home that the most familiar objects, a linen-
press or a waste-paper basket, had been full of menace for him." It is this
ability to see menace in a wastepaper basket that makes Hartley so special.
The travelling grave is, after all, only a box, the killing bottle only a bottle,

the lift (in "Someone in the Lift") only an elevator. But in Hartley's world, these things are also harbingers of thickly enveloping horror.

Jack Sullivan, *Elegant Nightmares: The English Ghost Story from Le Fanu to Blackwood* (Athens: Ohio University Press, 1978), pp. 101–2

EDWARD T. JONES   The macabre tales in Hartley's *Complete Short Stories* represent explorations in fantasy different in kind from the near allegories of "Conrad and the Dragon" and "The Crossways." Hartley here concerns himself less with right and wrong, as he does in the novels, than with evil and its effects. ⟨. . .⟩

Withal, though, Hartley's climaxes in these stories are often predictable, and strangely flat, because they have not been made to matter very much. When Hartley attaches fear to what Freud calls the "uncanny," i.e., "nothing else than a hidden, familiar thing that has undergone repression and then emerged from it," his macabre stories can be genuinely chilling as in "Night Fears" and "A Visitor from Down Under." Otherwise, fear becomes merely decorative.

In "Night Fears," a newly-hired nightwatchman who has been fabricating incidents of trial and stress to impress his wife finds himself sharing his brazier with a stranger. In conversation with the stranger the watchman articulates the anxiety-producing circumstances of his life, as the stranger, Iago-like, stimulates his most submerged fears—of his wife's fidelity, the loss of his children's affection, the real possibility of his own mental breakdown as a result of his inability to sleep during the day. In desperation, the watchman pulls a knife and, in turn, is murdered with it. And the stranger steps over the dead body, disappearing into a blind alley with only a track of dark, irregular footprints left behind. The watchman's previous fictions of peril and threats have become gruesome reality for him. The imagination, of course, has the power to terrify without any external correlative. The watchman could be a victim of his own dark mind. But there was a stranger, uncannily not feeling the cold which grips and finally destroys the watchman. ⟨. . .⟩

In the best and most provocative of these horror stories, Hartley seems to be saying that man, the sick animal, bears within him an appetite for evil, revenge, and retribution which is inexorable. The more familiar masochism of Hartley's novels is transformed here into something closer to sadism. Hartley can be not only cold to life but actively punishing to it. Of course, the figure in Hartley's carpet may well be a Rorschach inkblot of considerable psychological unpleasantness. As a character observes in "Podolo," "We loved her and so we had to kill her." Admittedly, this statement is made in a dream sequence, yet for that very reason its relevance might be greater than a waking insight. Perhaps Hartley is using the horror story as a kind of little theatre of submerged passions, transforming hidden desires for punishment into freedom, play, and pleasure. Playfully Hartley presents the ubiquity of guilt and corruption in tales of elegant literary spookery through the implication that everyone is latently a killer.

Edward T. Jones, *L. P. Hartley* (Boston: Twayne, 1978), pp. 45–48

PETER QUENNELL   I had the privilege of knowing ⟨Hartley⟩, and it would never have occurred to me at a first glance that his was a gloomy, apprehensive spirit. He had a rounded, well-balanced look, usually a gentle smile, a broad, lofty forehead and a small moustache. He was unmarried; and, according to a dictionary of modern authors, 'his private life, at least as far as the public knows, was almost entirely absorbed by his literary life'. Certainly he worked hard. His *Eustace and Hilda* series was concluded in 1947, twenty years after he had begun writing fiction. But I cannot believe that, meanwhile, his personal existence had been completely untroubled. 'Imaginative literature', he once agreed, when he was kind enough to congratulate me on the publication of a new book, 'takes its raw material from private life'; and from his own experiences, I feel sure, he must have very often drawn his themes. Henry James was a master he always revered; and, like James, he was frequently possessed by ideas of guilt and solitude and evil. As a contemporary reviewer remarked, beneath a surface that seems 'almost over-civilized' a 'hollow of horror' sometimes lay hidden.

Both aspects of his talent are fully illustrated by the tales collected ⟨in *The Travelling Grave*⟩. Not only does he portray the exterior of social life with a novelist's sharp eye for detail; but he also explores the underworld of fears and fantasies through which we wander in our ugliest dreams. It is the combination of these two aspects that gives his stories their strength and their peculiar diversity. Subjects range from human crimes to supernatural visitations, or to any event that shakes our stupid reliance on the explicability

of an inexplicable universe. L. P. Hartley was a highly skilled narrator; and
all his tales are admirably told.

Peter Quennell, "Introduction," *The Travelling Grave* by L. P. Hartley (London:
J. M. Dent, 1984), pp. vii–viii

⬣ *Bibliography*

Night Fears and Other Stories. 1924.

Simonetta Perkins. 1925.

The Killing Bottle. 1932.

The Shrimp and the Anemone ⟨*The West Window*⟩. 1944.

The Sixth Heaven. 1946.

Eustace and Hilda. 1947.

The Travelling Grave and Other Stories. 1948, 1984, 1993 (as *Night Fears and
    Other Supernatural Tales*).

The Boat. 1949.

My Fellow Devils. 1951.

The Go-Between. 1953.

The White Wand and Other Stories. 1954.

A Perfect Woman. 1955.

The Hireling. 1957.

Eustace and Hilda: A Trilogy ⟨*The Shrimp and the Anemone, The Sixth Heaven,
    Eustace and Hilda*⟩. 1958.

Facial Justice. 1960.

Two for the River. 1961.

The Brickfield. 1964.

The Betrayal. 1966.

The Novelist's Responsibility. 1967.

Poor Clare. 1968.

Collected Short Stories. 1968.

The Love-Adept: A Variation on a Theme. 1969.

My Sister's Keeper. 1970.

Mrs. Carteret Receives and Other Stories. 1971.

The Harness Room. 1971.

The Collections. 1972.

The Will and the Way. 1973.
Complete Short Stories. 1973.
The Cat: An Essay. 1986.

William Hope Hodgson
1877–1918

WILLIAM HOPE HODGSON was born on November 15, 1877, in Blackmore End, Essex, the son of Samuel Hodgson, an Anglican clergyman. Hodgson attended a boarding school in Margate, Kent, but in 1891 he ran away and, with the aid of an uncle, apprenticed as a seaman in the merchant marine. In 1895 he completed his apprenticeship and qualified as a seaman, but after four years he gave up sea life; he writes of his disillusionment in a later article, "Why I Am Not at Sea" (*Grand Magazine*, September 1905): "I am not at sea because I object to bad treatment, poor food, poor wages, and worse prospects. I am not at sea because very early I discovered that it is a comfortless, weariful and thankless life—a life compact of hardness and sordidness such as shore people can scarcely conceive." Nevertheless, much of Hodgson's work focuses obsessively on the sea.

Hodgson had by this time developed an interest in scientific exercise (then called physical culture), and in 1900 he opened his own School of Physical Culture. Although Hodgson enjoyed some success in this activity— he wrote several articles on the subject, published in *Sandow's Magazine* with photographs of himself, and in 1902 he had a celebrated encounter with the escape artist Harry Houdini—he gave up the school around 1904.

Hodgson published four novels in his lifetime: *The Boats of the "Glen Carrig"* (1907); *The House on the Borderland* (1908); *The Ghost Pirates* (1909); and *The Night Land* (1912). Recently discovered letters by Hodgson establish that these novels were all written between 1902 and 1905, with *The Night Land*—an enormous apocalyptic novel of the far future—being the first. These novels met with repeated rejections, so Hodgson began writing short stories; his first published tale was "The Goddess of Death" (1904). The celebrated story "The Voice in the Night" appeared in 1907. Some of his tales were collected in *Men of the Deep Waters* (1914) and *The Luck of the Strong* (1916).

Hodgson's mother and sister moved to Borth, Wales, in 1904 (his father had died in 1892), and Hodgson joined them there in 1908. He became friendly with Arthur St. John Adcock, editor of the London *Bookman*, and wrote several reviews for the magazine. In 1910 a series of five tales involving the psychic detective Thomas Carnacki appeared in the *Idler*; in 1913 a volume of these tales appeared as *Carnacki, the Ghost-Finder*. Hodgson had earlier published condensed versions of this volume and of other works to protect his copyright in the United States; these volumes have now become among his rarest works.

In 1913 Hodgson married Bessie Farnsworth, taking up residence briefly in Sanary, France. At the outbreak of World War I Hodgson returned to England and was commissioned as a lieutenant in the 171st Battery of the Royal Field Artillery (RFA), but was discharged because of an injury. In 1917 he reenlisted and was commissioned as a temporary second lieutenant in the RFA, seeing his first action at the front in October. He was killed in Flanders by a German shell on April 19, 1918, and his remains are buried in a cemetery at the foot of Mount Kemmel in Belgium.

Hodgson's literary importance rests in his being among the first to write horror novels: although, aside from *The Night Land*, all his novels are short and somewhat episodic, they reveal a largeness of conception requiring an extended narrative for their realization. Hodgson's work fell into obscurity after his death, but H. C. Koenig helped to resurrect it by bringing it to the attention of H. P. Lovecraft, who wrote enthusiastically about Hodgson, and of August Derleth, who republished his novels. Hodgson's place as an important precursor of modern horror fiction is now secure.

◈ *Critical Extracts*

UNSIGNED   There can be no need to recall to the memory two such remarkable works as Mr. Hope Hodgson's *The Boats of the "Glen Carrig"* and *The House on the Borderland*. They are books of the kind that, once read, cannot easily be forgotten. *The Ghost Pirates* forms the last volume of the trilogy, for, as the author points out, "though very different in scope, each of the three books deals with certain conceptions that have an elemental kinship." The next sentence in his preface is a disappointment to us: "With this book the author believes that he closes the door, so far as he is concerned, on a particular phase of constructive thought." We can only hope that Mr. Hodgson may be induced to reconsider his decision, for we know of nothing like the author's previous work in the whole of present-day literature. There is no one at present writing who can thrill and horrify to quite the same effect. *The Ghost Pirates* does not display Mr. Hodgson's wonderful qualities of imagination to such good effect as did *The House on the Borderland*, nor is it so terrifying a book to read. Nevertheless, it is a very remarkable story, told in a matter-of-fact manner that materially increases its "grip." The author particularly excels in the creation of "atmosphere," but he is also possessed of a vigorous style and a wonderful ingenuity in the concoction of terrifying detail. Mr. Hodgson has his faults: his exaggerated treatment of the cockney dialect of one of the minor characters is unsatisfactory, and his punctuation is annoying. But when all is said *The Ghost Pirates* is a book of high literary qualities and a worthy member of a memorable trilogy.

Unsigned, [Review of *The Ghost Pirates*], *Bookman* (London) No. 217 (October 1909): 54

C. K. S.   Life is so full of tragedy just now, and for every home in which there is sorrow there should be sympathy from the stranger. But to the readers of this page a special measure of sympathy must always be given to the man of letters who dies on the field of war. I have long been acquainted with the work of Mr. Hope Hodgson. One or two of his novels had pleased me greatly, and a letter from him to me which I possess indicates that he had received encouragement from something I had written in these columns.

Lieutenant Hope Hodgson was a son of the Rev. Samuel Hodgson, and he has quite recently met his death in France. ⟨. . .⟩ Many of his books were written in a chalet on the Côte d'Azur, but when the war broke out he promptly joined the University of London O.T.C. ⟨Officer Training Corps⟩ and got a commission in the R.F.A. He was gazetted out of the army once as the result of an accident, but made a point of rejoining as soon as possible. He was a popular officer, and his death was greatly lamented. "He has performed 'wonders of gallantry,' " wrote his C.O. "Many knew him," writes a friend, "as a highly-strung, sensitive, rather dreamy idealist, but he threw himself heart and soul into the work that lay to his hand." One at least of his books, *The Night Land*, may eternally secure the interest of the public, which will not be ungrateful to its heroes who were also men of letters.

C. K. S., "A Literary Letter," *Sphere*, 8 June 1918, p. 184

ARTHUR ST. JOHN ADCOCK   I first met Hope Hodgson about
eleven years ago. At that date, his three best novels had been written; two
of them, *The Boats of the Glen Carrig* and *The House on the Borderland*, had
been published, and the third, *The Ghost Pirates*, was in the press. In those
three stories he showed himself a writer of quite exceptional imaginative
gifts, a master of the weird, the eerie, the terrible, whose strange and grim
imaginings were not unworthy of comparison with the bizarre creations of
Poe. He had already given himself so entirely and enthusiastically to a
literary career that the talk at our first meeting was wholly of books and of
his hopes as an author. He aimed high and, taking his art very seriously,
had a frank, unaffected confidence in his powers which was partly the
splendid arrogance of youth and partly the heritage of experience, for he
had tested and proved them.

There was something curiously attractive in his breezy, forceful, eager
personality; his dark eyes were wonderfully alert and alive; he was wonderfully
and restlessly alive and alert in all his mind and body. He was emphatic
and unrestrained in his talk, but would take the sting out of an extravagant
denunciation of some inartistic popular author, or of some pestilent critic,
and the egotism out of some headlong confession of his own belief in himself
with the pleasantest boyish laugh that brushed it all aside as the mere
spray and froth of a passing thought. His dark, handsome features were
extraordinarily expressive; they betrayed his emotions as readily as his lips
gave away whatever happened to rise in his mind. Always he had the courage
of his opinions and no false modesty; it never seemed to occur to him to
practise politic subterfuges; and it was this absolute candour and naturalness
that compelled you to like him and before long strengthened your liking
into a friendly affection.

Only once, and then casually, he mentioned to me that he had been a
sailor, but, though there was nothing in his manner or his trim, sturdy figure
that suggested the seafarer, one might have guessed as much from his books
and from the fact that the ablest of them were all of sailors and the sea.
He was the son of an Essex clergyman, and left home to serve for eight
years aboard ship, roughing it at the ends of the earth in all manner of
picturesque places and voyaging three times round the world. His record as
a sailor includes the story of a daring plunge overboard and the saving of
a life at sea, for which he received the Royal Humane Society's Medal; and
much of the rest of his recollections of those eight years have gone to make
the characters and incidents and scenery of his stories. ⟨. . .⟩

When the war came, he and his wife had for some while been living in the South of France, but he could not remain there in safety, with the folk at home arming for battle, and, though he was then near forty, he returned to England at once and obtained a commission, in 1915, in the 171st Brigade of the Royal Field Artillery. He put aside all literary work and threw himself heart and soul into his new duties. With characteristic simple frankness, he said his only fear was lest he should feel any shrinking when his time came—a fear that nobody who knew him could ever have had for him. In October, 1917, he went to France with his battery, and was soon in the thick of the fighting. Early in April, 1918, he and a brother officer with a few N.C.O.'s successfully stemmed the rush of an overwhelming number of the enemy who had broken through their line right up to the guns; they fought a gallantly stubborn rear-guard action, under a hail of rifle and machine-gun fire, for three miles across country. A week or two later, on the 17th April, 1918, he was killed in action, whilst acting as observation officer.

It is hard to think of him as dead, he was so vigorously and intensely alive. That vigour and intensity of life pulses and burns in everything he has written; and I think he will still be living in, at least, those three of his novels when we who knew and loved him are passed from remembrance. In the world of letters he had only half fulfilled his promise, but in the larger world of men he left no promise unfulfilled and has an abiding place for ever among the heroic company that the seventeenth-century seaman Thomas James commemorated, when he wrote:

> We that survive perchance may end our days
> In some employment meriting no praise,
> And in a dunghill rot, when no man names
> The memory of us but to our shames.
> They have outlived this fear, and their brave ends
> Will ever be an honour to their friends.

Arthur St. John Adcock, "Introduction," *The Calling of the Sea* by William Hope Hodgson (London: Selwyn & Blount, 1920), pp. 3–6

H. P. LOVECRAFT   Mr. H. C. Koenig has conferred a great service on American "fandom" by calling attention to the remarkable work of an author relatively unknown in this country, yet actually forming one of the few who have captured the illusive inmost essence of the weird. Among connoisseurs of phantasy fiction William Hope Hodgson deserves a high and prominent rank; for, triumphing over a sadly uneven stylistic quality, he now and then equals the best masters in his vague suggestions of lurking worlds and beings behind the ordinary surface of life.

Despite a tendency toward conventionally sentimental conceptions of the universe, and of man's relation to it and to his fellows, Mr. Hodgson is perhaps second only to Algernon Blackwood in his serious treatment of unreality. Few can equal him in adumbrating the nearness of nameless forces and monstrous besieging entities through casual hints and significant details, or in conveying feelings of the spectral and the abnormal in connexion with regions or buildings. ⟨. . .⟩

The House on the Borderland (1908)—perhaps the greatest of all Mr. Hodgson's works—tells of a lonely and evilly regarded house in Ireland which forms a focus for hideous other-world forces and sustains a siege by blasphemous hybrid anomalies from a hidden abyss below. The wanderings of the narrator's spirit through limitless light-years of cosmic space and kalpas of eternity, and its witnessing of the solar system's final destruction, constitute something almost unique in standard literature. And everywhere there is manifest the author's power to suggest vague, ambushed horrors in natural scenery. But for a few touches of commonplace sentimentality this book would be a classic of the first water. ⟨. . .⟩

The Night Land (1912) is a long-extended (538 pp.) tale of the infinite future—billions and billions of years ahead, after the death of the sun. It is told in a rather clumsy fashion, as the dreams of a man in the seventeenth century, whose mind merges with its own future incarnation; and is seriously marred by painful verboseness, repetitiousness, artificial and nauseously sticky romantic sentimentality, and an attempt at archaic language even more grotesque and absurd than that in ⟨*The Boats of the*⟩ *Glen Carrig*.

Allowing for all its faults, it is yet one of the most potent pieces of macabre imagination ever written, and it is said to have been the author's favourite among his works. The picture of a night-black, dead planet, with the remains of the human race concentrated in a stupendously vast metal pyramid and besieged by monstrous, hybrid, and altogether unknown forces of the darkness, is something that no reader can ever forget. Shapes and entities of an altogether non-human and inconceivable sort—the prowlers of the black, man-forsaken world outside the pyramid—are *suggested* and *partly* described with ineffable potency; while the night-bound landscape with its chasms and slopes and dying volcanism takes on an almost sentient horror beneath the author's touch.

Midway in the book the central figure ventures outside the pyramid on a quest through death-haunted realms untrod by man for millions of years—and in his slow, minutely described, day-by-day progress over unthinkable leagues of immemorial blackness there is a sense of cosmic alienage, breathless mystery, and terrified expectancy unrivalled in the whole range of literature. The last quarter of the book drags woefully, but fails to spoil the tremendous power of the whole.

H. P. Lovecraft, "The Weird Work of William Hope Hodgson," *Phantagraph* 5, No. 5 (February 1937): 5–7

UNSIGNED   "I wants," said Mr. Pickwick's Fat Boy, "to make your flesh creep," and this cheerful ambition was that of William Hope Hodgson, whose works in their day—early in the twentieth century—were more than moderately popular. Thrillers, well beyond Grub Street formulas, they showed a thoughtful, even philosophic mind, brooding over present possibilities of horror unguessed by the happy, in a world whose future could envisage the death of the solar system. Yet in this omnibus of four full-length novels ⟨*The House on the Borderland and Other Novels*⟩—beside the title romance, there are *The Ghost Pirates*, *The Boats of the Glen Carrig*, and a long novel of a sunless future, *The Night Land*—his quiet manner and skill in straight narrative remove sensationalism and let what is told produce authentic gooseflesh.

That they are thus revived—though all the novels were copyrighted in the United States they are published here for the first time in this volume—is due to fascination with one of Hodgson's shorter stories that led H. C. Koenig to unearth and cherish all that this writer had produced. This process he describes in an introduction. The novels readily prove their right to a place in the literature of the weird, especially as this involves authentic atmosphere of the sea.

Unsigned, "Real Gooseflesh," *New York Herald Tribune Weekly Book Review*, 29 September 1946, p. 12

PETER CHRISTENSEN   The nine stories in *Carnacki the Ghost-Finder* fall into several distinct categories, and there appears at first to be a major problem in the collection's overall uncertainty of intent. One major step toward the solution of this difficulty is the discovery that only the first six stories were collected in the first edition (1913); the last three were first included, long after Hodgson's death, in the 1947 American edition. They can then be regarded as having been tacked on to a work which the author considered as complete. ⟨. . .⟩

The center of the book's interest for the purpose of this essay are those six stories in which Thomas Carnacki, ghost-finder extraordinaire, is called upon to investigate certain ambiguous phenomena which may or may not ultimately prove to be manifestations of supernatural activity. I maintain that these six stories constitute a coherent and meaningful whole, that they are an organized, cumulative work, one story building upon another; they are not simply a random collection. This structure is the product of a carefully contrived interplay between the world of supernatural horror and the world of logical explanation. ⟨. . .⟩

Although the intensity of Hodgson's writing leaves little doubt that the horrors of which he wrote were real to him in some way, these stories also acknowledge the possibility that supernatural appearances may be explained rationally. When he begins one of these stories, the reader cannot know what type of ending will be given. Anything is possible, and thus an ambiguity or tension is created. This interplay of anxiety and security exists even though the detective story is traditionally the celebration of man's rational powers, its essence being the rational explanation. Hodgson is one of the few who try to have it both ways, and one of an even smaller minority who succeed in doing so. Most readers would probably agree that in comparison to such near-masterpieces as *The House on the Borderland* and *The Night Land* the Carnacki stories are slightly pallid, that the sustained horror of the full-length novels has an impact which, for a number of reasons, is denied to this set of stories. Ambiguity can be a powerful force, however, and as I hope I have demonstrated, when one removes the last three stories and considers the work as it was first devised, *Carnacki the Ghost-Finder* stands revealed as a coherent, cumulative, and chilling work which is worth any reader's close attention.

> Peter Christensen, "William Hope Hodgson: *Carnacki the Ghost-Finder*," *Armchair Detective* 12, No. 2 (Spring 1979): 122–24

GARY K. WOLFE   Hodgson viewed *The House on the Borderland* as the centerpiece of a trilogy which began with his first novel, *The Boats of* the "Glen Carrig" (1907), and continued with The Ghost Pirates (1909). Although these novels differ greatly in scope, he wrote, "each of the three books deals with certain conceptions that have an elemental kinship." Central among such conceptions, apparently, is the notion that the Earth may be coinhabited by beings of other dimensions, with certain regions serving as "portals" which permit humans to encounter these beings. The Boats of the "Glen Carrig" concerns survivors of a shipwreck who, first on a mysterious island and later in the Sargasso Sea, encounter a multitude of strange beings, from tree-people to intelligent giant slugs. In The Ghost Pirates, a ship is cut off from "normal" reality and caught between dimensions, encountering strange ghostly beings from another time. In The House on the Borderland, the house of the title provides the portal between realities.

What these differing realities may mean to Hodgson is problematic, but he nowhere explores them more fully than in The House on the Borderland. More than any of his other works (with the possible exception of The Night Land) it suggests that he sought to imbue his supernaturalism with a metaphorical weight that far transcends its function as a mechanism for generating terror. To be sure, terror is the dominant tone of the bulk of the narrative. It seems to reside in the very landscape around the house, and is felt by the sportsmen who discover the manuscript years later after the unspecified cataclysm that destroyed the old recluse and his house. Most of the recluse's manuscript concerns his continuing struggle to protect himself and his sister from hideous swine-faced creatures who emerge from an immense pit beneath the house and seek to gain access to it, and the narrative ends on a note of unparalleled terror as the recluse is weakened by a glowing greenish infection brought on by contact with a dog who was wounded by one of the monsters. Deformity caused by infection seems to be a characteristic fear for Hodgson, apparent in much of his short fiction; and as this infection slowly spreads to the entire side of the narrator's body, some monstrous presence makes its way up from the pit beneath the house and opens the door to his room as the manuscript trails off. The narrative by itself would serve to place the tale firmly in the tradition of terror tales that stretches from Edgar Allan Poe to Lovecraft, but through the interpolation of two remarkable episodes, Hodgson seeks to place this sensational tale in the context of a more fully realized myth. ⟨. . .⟩

The central opposition in Hodgson's work may well be that between flesh and spirit. His portals, his Sargasso Seas, his borderlands, appear to be regions where that line is erased. The House on the Borderland itself clearly exists in both a physical and a spiritual plane, and the rapport of the two houses suggests that what happens in one plane also happens in the other. When the narrator lost his one love, he lost contact with the creative force in his spiritual life, and the forces of decay moved in—first as the swine-things, and finally as the consuming greenish infection that consumes him physically as his grief had consumed him spiritually. What little love he had left to feel seemed directed at the dog Pepper, and when Pepper died, his last real defense was gone. After being offered a vision of the paradise he had lost, he succumbed to the forces from the hellish pit below.

This may seem an excessively allegorical reading of the story, but Hodgson himself contended that the novel embodied a vision of Heaven and Hell, and the novel's internal patterns of allusion and imagery suggest a more complex ideational scheme than the surface tale of horror would suggest. Yet Hodgson also promised "certain thrills, merely taking the story as a story," and even the most purely sensation-seeking reader would be hard put to deny that he accomplished that. Generic critics may quibble about whether *The House on the Borderland* belongs more properly to the sphere of visionary fantasy than to that of supernatural horror—or even to science fiction, given the astronomical details that accompany the space-time visions—but few would deny that the novel stands as a remarkable imaginative feat.

Gary K. Wolfe, "The House on the Borderland," Survey of Modern Fantasy Literature, ed. Frank N. Magill (Englewood Cliffs, NJ: Salem Press, 1983), Vol. 2, pp. 744–45, 747–48

BRIAN STABLEFORD   As a writer, Hodgson was a remarkable amalgam of hard-headed professional and inwardly driven amateur. Historians of speculative fiction usually regard him as a writer of horrific fantasy and not as a writer of scientific romance, but this is to neglect certain important elements of kinship which link his work to that of Wells, Shiel and John Beresford. There is nothing in his work which is authentically supernatural; his metaphysics is just as thoroughly dis-enchanted as Wells's, though it is certainly baroque. What distinguishes him from the other three writers just named is that they all built their new metaphysical systems around ideas derived from evolutionary philosophy. Their cosmic schemes, whether optimistic or pessimistic, dealt with possibilities of change in the human species. Hodgson was *not* an evolutionist, and did not think in such terms at all. His model of change was taken entirely from the life-history of the individual, and his macrocosmic visions embody the Renaissance principle of 'As above, so below'. His idea of the fundamental, impersonal Force that must stand in for God is therefore very different from that formed by Shiel. In Shiel's view, that basic Force imported a progressive *élan vital* into the history of life and the career of mankind; in Hodgson's view the Force that must ultimately win was the force of decay—ashes to ashes, dust to dust—and the individual's battle was to win an essentially temporary and partial victory. Had he been familiar with the concept of entropy, and had he known how the order of life on Earth is dependent on the influx of energy from the sun to mount its temporary defiance of the entropic decay of the universe, he would surely have made much more use of scientific language in his work, rather than borrowing ideas and images from Hindu mythology. His self-education was too selective to make such ideative resources available to him, and this limited his mode of expression, but his limitations should not obscure the spirit of his endeavours.

Brian Stableford, "William Hope Hodgson," *Scientific Romance in Britain 1890–1950* (London: Fourth Estate, 1985), pp. 101–2

MARK VALENTINE   ⟨. . .⟩ I think it is unfair of Lovecraft to typify Carnacki as the "infallible detective" type. For one thing, the description is not literally true; Carnacki fails in the case of "The Haunted *Jarvee*". Furthermore, the character has a good deal more humanity and credibility than the aloof, supremely cerebral, figures that had so far dominated detective fiction, notably John Silence, J. Sheridan Le Fanu's Dr Hesselius and M. P. Shiel's Prince Zaleski. Whatever, Carnacki certainly knows his work. He is deeply read in spiritualist and occult literature, and he is ready to use both traditional magical protection (candles, herbs, sacred water, charged symbols) and more modern techniques, demonstrating a familiarity with photographic and electrical equipment. He is a practical, methodical individual and has no pretence to superhuman powers, otherworldly intuition or the almost archangelic omniscience of his predecessors. Although he is appropriately unpaid, he is not an amateur in that very English sense of the dabbler or genteel dilettante; he is profoundly and energetically committed to his vocation.

Yet, despite (or more probably because of) this pragmatic, hard-headed side of Carnacki, his encounters with the raw supernatural are amongst the most compellingly authentic in weird fiction. In the four 'pure' occult cases, where the Ab-Normal element is the sole or uppermost feature, we can feel Carnacki's isolation and vulnerability as the wild, disturbed, grotesque forces push at the boundaries of this world: 'There came a sense as of dust falling continually and monotonously and I knew that my life hung uncertain and suspended for a flash in the brief, reeling vertigo of unseeable things' ("The Whistling Room"); 'I had for a moment that feeling of spiritual sickness as if some delicate, beautiful, inward grace had suffered' ("The Gateway of the Monster"). Against these soul-sucking entities seething with implacable power, Carnacki has only his own resourcefulness and his respect for his craft. His mortal fear, which he freely acknowledges, is suppressed only by his sheer determination, as he seeks to resist the prolonged psychic and physical incursions in an atmosphere of ominous intensity. It was doubtless these episodes Lovecraft had in mind when he acknowledged some 'undeniable power' in the Carnacki stories.

> Mark Valentine, "Against the Abyss: Carnacki the Ghost-Finder," *William Hope Hodgson: Voyages and Visions*, ed. Ian Bell (Oxford: Ian Bell, 1987), pp. 25–26

IAN BELL   To the modern reader, the most notable aspect of *The Night Land* is (without doubt) Hodgson's superbly visualised dying Earth, 'a nightmarish landscape that would have taxed the pictorial artistry of Hieronymous Bosch to equal' ⟨Lin Carter⟩. Although he was probably unfamiliar with the concept of entropy, Hodgson nevertheless presents in *The Night Land* an 'entropic romance' of the very highest order—one of the most vivid and compelling visions of a world in terminal decay in the realms of fantastic literature. This is not to suggest, of course, that Hodgson was the first writer to deal with the last days of a far-future Earth, but *The Night Land* is certainly one of the earliest and most striking extended treatments of 'mankind's struggle against a bleak and hostile nature in the endtime' ⟨W. Warren Wagar⟩.

In the future of Hodgson's imagination, countless billions of years from the present, the fate of what remains of Mankind is indeed a dire and dismal one. Not only do the last representatives of Man live in a world enshrouded in total darkness, but they are also forced to remain forever in the pyramid which is their only protection against the malignant creatures and spirits of the Night Land. Even so, the Last Redoubt is only a temporary bastion against the forces of darkness/entropy; in time, the Earth-Current which powers the Electric Circle will fail, the defences of the pyramid will be breached and Man will be no more. However, Hodgson's vision—as one would expect given the courage which he displayed in his own life—is by no means one of unrelieved gloom and despondency. Man as a race may, ultimately, be doomed to extinction, but individuals still have the power of free will and personal victories remain to be won. Indeed, it is on just such an individual triumph that *The Night Land* is centred and, moreover, on which the novel ends.

Ian Bell, "The Restoration of *The Night Land*," *William Hope Hodgson: Voyages and Visions*, ed. Ian Bell (Oxford: Ian Bell, 1987), pp. 38–39

SAM GAFFORD   Hodgson was a "working man's" writer. He approached the task like any other job and was extremely concerned with selling his writing. In the letter dated November 17, 1905, Hodgson states that he has received a total of 427 rejections since starting his writing career. His letters are filled with references to trying to sell his work "to fill his belly". Hodgson was keenly aware of the relationship between selling his material and eating, and this obviously affected his decision on what and how to write. So, in effect, Hodgson tempers his imagination after *The Night Land* and *The House on the Borderland* and begins to concentrate on more salable work. It is interesting to note, then, that he moves away from work that is purely imaginative and begins to focus on the sea, a topic he had known only too well in his youth. Finding publishers unreceptive to his "flights of fancy", Hodgson buckles down to the more "normal" concepts of *The Ghost Pirates* and *The Boats of the "Glen Carrig"*. It was a natural transition for him, as the sea was one area he could write about with authority and passion.

Which brings us to another conclusion about Hodgson's writing style. It is now obvious that *The House on the Borderland* was not a harbinger of *The Night Land* but that their relationship is actually completely opposite. Hodgson is not using *The House on the Borderland* as an experiment toward perfecting the style for *The Night Land* but is actually trying to get *away* from that style. Still unable to abandon completely the seventeenth-century style, he modifies it into the "affected" eighteenth-century style which makes the novel still clumsy but more accessible than *The Night Land*. In *The Ghost Pirates*, he uses the language and lore of the sea to give the novel a "realistic" feel and shows more control of his language and style. It is still a potentially annoying style, but a definite step away from that of *The Night Land* and *The House on the Borderland*. When he finishes the group with *The Boats of the "Glen Carrig"*, Hodgson has managed to rid himself of these affectations of style and produces a book written in a flat but serviceable tone. With each book, Hodgson learns better control of language and more writing savvy and eventually develops his own voice.

This revelation enables us the better to understand Hodgson's growth as a writer. We can more easily chart his development through this order of composition than we were able to under the publishing order. Still, it manages to raise several interesting questions of its own. Most notable is why, if Hodgson finished all four novels by 1905, he never wrote another before his death in 1918. It is possible that he concentrated more on his short story sales, as they gave him much more financial compensation than the novels ever did. It could also be that, drifting more and more into salable "straight" adventure and genre stories, he felt that another novel would not satisfy his desire to be original. He had placed all his hopes on *The Night Land*, and when that became a critical success but a financial failure, he may have been too depressed to consider doing another. Answers to such questions as these are not available now, but could be discovered if more Hodgson letters materialize. Until then, we can only wonder what wonderfully imaginative excesses like *The Night Land* may have been lost because of an unappreciative public.

Sam Gafford, "Writing Backwards: The Novels of William Hope Hodgson," *Studies in Weird Fiction* No. 11 (Spring 1992): 14–15

⊞ *Bibliography*

The Boats of the "Glen Carrig." 1907.
The House on the Borderland. 1908.
The Ghost Pirates. 1909.

The Ghost Pirates, A Chaunty, and Another Story. 1909.
Carnacki, the Ghost Finder and a Poem. 1910.
The Captain of the Onion Boat. 1911.
The Night Land: A Love Tale. 1912.
"Poems" and "The Dream of X." 1912.
Carnacki, the Ghost-Finder. 1913, 1947.
Men of the Deep Waters. 1914.
Cargunka and Poems and Anecdotes. 1914.
The Luck of the Strong. 1916.
Captain Gault: Being the Exceedingly Private Log of a Sea-Captain. 1917.
The Calling of the Sea. 1920.
The Voice of the Ocean. 1921.
The House on the Borderland and Other Novels. 1946.
Deep Waters. 1967.
Out of the Storm: Uncollected Fantasies. Ed. Sam Moskowitz. 1975.
Poems of the Sea. 1977.
William Hope Hodgson: A Centenary Tribute. 1977.
Spectral Manifestations. Ed. Ian Bell. 1984.
Tales of Land and Sea. 1984.
The Baumoff Explosive. 1988.
Fifty Dead Chinamen All in a Row. 1988.
From the Tideless Sea. 1988.
The Goddess of Death. 1988.
The Heaving of the Log. 1988.
Homeward Bound. 1988.
The Mystery of the Ship in the Night. 1988.
Old Golly. 1988.
The Phantom Ship. 1988.
The Riven Night. 1988.
The Room of Fear. 1988.
Sea-Horses. 1988.
The Terrible Derelict. 1988.
The Valley of Lost Children. 1988.
The Ways of the Heathen. 1988.
The Room of Fear and Other Grues. 1988.
The Haunted "Pampero." Ed. Sam Moskowitz. 1991.
Demons of the Sea. Ed. Sam Gafford. 1992.
At Sea. Ed. Sam Gafford. 1993.
Terrors of the Sea. Ed. Sam Moskowitz. 1995.

⊞ ⊞ ⊞

Shirley Jackson
1916–1965

SHIRLEY JACKSON was born in San Francisco on December 14, 1916. (In later years she claimed to have been born in 1919 so as to appear younger than her husband.) In 1933 her family moved to Rochester, New York, and Jackson soon after began attendance at the University of Rochester. Severe depression forced her to leave after only a year. She later enrolled at Syracuse University, where she received a B.A. in 1940. While at Syracuse she met a fellow student, Stanley Edgar Hyman, later to become a prominent author and critic; they married in 1940. Together she and Hyman worked on literary magazines at Syracuse.

After her graduation Jackson and Hyman moved to New York, where she held a clerical job. Her years as a clerk were later recounted in the sketch "My Life with R. H. Macy." After the birth of her first two children (she eventually was the mother of four), Jackson and Hyman moved to North Bennington, Vermont, where Hyman taught at Bennington College while Jackson wrote. On June 26, 1948, her famous short story "The Lottery" was published in the *New Yorker*. The story, which focuses on the modern reenactment of ancient scapegoat rituals, prompted more reader mail—most of it outraged—than any single item previously published in the magazine. Jackson later wrote an essay about the writing of and response to the tale, "Biography of a Story" (1960).

Also in 1948 Jackson's first novel, *The Road through the Wall*, was published; it is a story of adolescents in a suburban town, Burlingame, California, where Jackson had spent her childhood. The celebrity of "The Lottery" caused her publishers to issue a collection of her tales and sketches, *The Lottery; or, The Adventures of James Harris* (1949), which contains several items that—like much of her work—border on the weird or supernatural. *Hangsaman* (1951), her second novel, is about a young woman's coming of age.

Jackson's third novel, *The Bird's Nest* (1954), approaches the realm of psychological horror in its account of a woman afflicted with multiple personalities. Her next three novels are still closer to the weird tradition. *The Sundial* (1958) is a bizarre apocalyptic tale of a family whose members believe that the rest of the human race will be destroyed and that they will be the only survivors. *The Haunting of Hill House* (1959), her most highly regarded novel, tells of four individuals who explore paranormal phenomena in a haunted house; it was made into the successful and accomplished film *The Haunting* (1963), directed by Robert Wise and starring Julie Harris and Clare Bloom. *We Have Always Lived in the Castle* (1962) is a bitterly misanthropic work about two sisters who are ostracized from their community after one of them is accused of murdering the rest of the family.

Throughout her career Jackson wrote many short stories that can be said to belong to the domains of supernatural and psychological horror. One story, "Louisa, Please," won the Edgar Allan Poe Award from the Mystery Writers of America in 1961. But Jackson made no effort to gather these tales in any volume subsequent to *The Lottery*, and the posthumous collection *Come Along with Me* (1968) includes only a small sampling of her short fiction.

Although Jackson's marriage was occasionally troubled by the repeated philandering of her husband, she generated considerable income for her creative writing with a series of humorous sketches about her family, published in *Good Housekeeping*, *Woman's Home Companion*, and other women's magazines of the day. Some were gathered and reshaped into a unified narrative in two books, *Life among the Savages* (1953) and *Raising Demons* (1957), but others remain uncollected. Jackson also wrote several works for children, including *The Witchcraft of Salem Village* (1956) and a play, *The Bad Children* (1959).

Shirley Jackson died at her Vermont home on August 8, 1965. She left unfinished a novel, *Come Along with Me*, that may have involved supernaturalism; the fragment was published as the title work in the posthumous collection assembled by her husband, who also compiled an omnibus volume, *The Magic of Shirley Jackson* (1966).

▨ *Critical Extracts*

JAMES HILTON   The whole collection ⟨*The Lottery*⟩ will enhance Miss Jackson's reputation as a writer not quite like any other of her generation. Indeed, she sees life, in her own style, as devastatingly as Dali paints it, and like Dali also, she has a sound technique in her own art. There is a beguilingness in the way she leads her readers to the precise point at which the crucial shock can be administered.

The stories are of varying length and quality, but there is in nearly all of them a single note of alarm which reminds one of the elemental terrors of childhood—as when the pages of a book are unsuspectingly turned upon a frightening picture, or a shadow moves into sudden shape upon a wall. The story called "The Lottery," for instance, opens with a quietly detailed description of how lots are cast one summer morning in an American village (we are not told where or when), the occasion being evidently one that takes place every year by traditional sanction. Not till the end do we discover its terrible purpose. The effect is in the calm narration culminating, almost casually, in dreadfulness—a method that has often been employed for macabre humor, as in *Arsenic and Old Lace,* or in the immortal disclosure that "Deep into the well / Which the plumber built her / Aunt Maria fell / We must buy a filter." But Miss Jackson plays it not for a laugh but for the unprofitable question of what exactly does she mean—as unprofitable as to puzzle over some night-horror that fades into incomprehensibility a moment after waking.

James Hilton, "The Focus of a Dream," *New York Herald Tribune Weekly Book Review,* 1 May 1949, p. 4

SHIRLEY JACKSON   I can, in the last analysis, talk only about my own work; it is not that I am so entirely vain, but because there is really one writer I know well enough to say these things about; I would not dare discuss intimately anyone else. So I would like to show you a little of how my own fiction comes directly from experience.

I have recently finished a novel about a haunted house ⟨*The Haunting of Hill House*⟩. I was [working] on a novel about a haunted house because I happened by chance to read a book about a group of people, nineteenth-century psychic researchers, who rented a haunted house and recorded their impressions of the things they saw and heard and felt in order to contribute a learned paper to the Society for Psychic Research. They thought that they were being terribly scientific and proving all kinds of things, and yet the story that kept coming through their dry reports was not at all the story of a haunted house, it was the story of several earnest, I believe misguided, certainly determined people, with their differing motivations and backgrounds. I found it so exciting that I wanted more than anything else to set up my own haunted house, and put my own people in it, and see what I could make happen. As so often happens, the minute I started thinking about ghosts and haunted houses, all kinds of things turned up to enforce my intentions, or perhaps I was thinking so entirely about my new book that everything I saw turned to it; I can't say, although I *can* say that I could do without some of the manifestations I met. ⟨. . .⟩

Well, as I say, fiction comes from experience. I had not the remotest desire to see a ghost. I was absolutely willing to go on the rest of my life without ever seeing even the slightest supernatural manifestation. I wanted to write a book about ghosts, but I was perfectly prepared—I cannot emphasize this too strongly—I was perfectly prepared to keep those ghosts wholly imaginary. I was already doing a lot of splendid research reading all the books about ghosts I could get hold of, and particularly true ghost stories— so much so that it became necessary for me to read a chapter of *Little Women* every night before I turned out the light—and at the same time I was collecting pictures of houses, particularly odd houses, to see what I could find to make into a suitable haunted house. I read books of architecture and clipped pictures out of magazines and newspapers and learned about cornices and secret stairways and valances and turrets and flying buttresses and gargoyles and all kinds of things that people have done to inoffensive houses, and then I came across a picture in a magazine which really looked right. It was the picture of a house which reminded me vividly of ⟨a⟩ hideous building in New York; it had the same air of disease and decay, and if ever a house looked like a candidate for a ghost, it was this one. All that I had to identify it was the name of a California town, so I wrote to my mother, who has lived in California all her life, and sent her the picture, asking if she had any idea where I could get information about this ugly house. She wrote back in some surprise. Yes, she knew about the house, although she had not supposed that there were any pictures of it still around. My great-grandfather built it. It had stood empty and deserted for some years before it finally caught fire, and it was generally believed that that was because the people of the town got together one night and burned it down.

By then it was abundantly clear to me that I had no choice; the ghosts were after me. In case I *had* any doubts, however, I came downstairs a few mornings later and found a sheet of copy paper moved to the center of my desk, set neatly away from the general clutter. On the sheet of paper was written DEAD DEAD in my own handwriting. I am accustomed to making notes for books, but not in my sleep; I decided that I had better write the book awake, which I got to work and did.

Shirley Jackson, "Experience and Fiction" (1958), *Come Along with Me*, ed. Stanley Edgar Hyman (New York: Viking Press, 1968), pp. 200–203

UNSIGNED   In *The Haunting of Hill House* Miss Shirley Jackson's considerable talents are exercised on the ghost story—a genre which suffers from over-cultivation at the hands of cheap sensationalists. She skips adroitly over all the pitfalls. Nowhere is there any whiff of pointless eerie-weerie detectable; at no point do the stock ghost story characters make an entrance with their hollow, booming voices and the faraway look in their eyes. Instead we have what we ought always to have in ghost stories but so rarely get; a brooding, claustrophobic atmosphere which thickens overpoweringly as we go along.

This atmosphere is partly generated by an excellent Otranto-ish house in which the characters congregate. It is genuinely Gothick and ghastly, and has been built by the Victorian Hugh Crain, who is horrifyingly evoked in a scrapbook composed by himself for the edification—or, perhaps better, corruption—of his daughters. The atmosphere is also generated by a subtle and satisfying understanding on the part of the author of what constitutes fear and of what goes to its making, and by a vivid demonstration of the truth that the mind is its own place and of itself can make a heaven of hell and a hell of Hill House.

Unsigned, "Honest Ghosts," *Times Literary Supplement*, 16 September 1960, p. 597

IHAB HASSAN   I have always felt that some writers should be read and never reviewed. Their talent is haunting and utterly oblique, their mastery of craft seems complete. Even before reading Shirley Jackson's latest novel ⟨*We Have Always Lived in the Castle*⟩, I would have thought her case to be clear: she is of that company. And now Miss Jackson has made it even more difficult for a reviewer to seem pertinent; all he can do is bestow praise. ⟨. . .⟩

We Have Always Lived in the Castle is not as eerie as some of Miss Jackson's other works, but it is every bit as deviate and gripping. There are three people who live in the ancestral home of the Blackwoods, up on a hill. Their life is a hermetic one, shut against the fearful and railing villagers below, and overcast by the memory of a mass murder, by arsenic, of most of the Blackwood family. The three are Constance Blackwood, who cooks and cares lovingly for the others, acquitted somehow of the murder; Uncle Julian, a survivor of that grim event, now an invalid, and Constance's younger sister, Mary Katherine, better known as "Merricat," who is still in her teens. Merricat is the shy, wild narrator of the story; the significance of that literary fact is one of the grisly discoveries that every reader must make for himself.

Yet the effect on the book does not only depend on mystery or suspense; nor on the casual intimations of evil that Miss Jackson can put in a phrase like "the falseness of spring." The effect depends rather on her ability to specify a real world which is at once more sane and more mad than the world we see.

Ihab Hassan, "Three Hermits on a Hill," *New York Times Book Review*, 23 September 1962, p. 5

HELEN E. NEBEKER   Numerous critics have carefully discussed Shirley Jackson's "The Lottery" in terms of the scapegoat traditions of anthropology and literature, pointing out its obvious comment on the innate savagery of man lurking beneath his civilized trappings. Most acknowledge the power of the story, admitting that the psychological shock of the ritual murder in an atmosphere of modern, small-town normality cannot be easily forgotten. Nevertheless, beneath the praise of these critics frequently runs a current of uneasiness, a sense of having been defrauded in some way by the development of the story as a whole.

Virgil Scott, for example, writes that ". . . the story leaves one uneasy because of the author's use of incidental symbolism. . . . the black box, the forgotten tuneless chant, the ritual salute—indeed the entire reconstruction of the mechanics of the lottery—fail to serve the story as they might have." Robert Heilman discovers similar technical difficulties. While approving the "deadpan narrative style" which screens us from the "horrifying nightmare" to come, he nevertheless believes that the unexpected shock of the ending "crowds out" the impact of Jackson's thematic revelation. He suggests that the "symbolic intention" should be evidenced earlier in the story because, while "to set us immediately on the track of the symbolism" might reduce the shock, it might, on the other hand, "result in a more durable story." ⟨Cleanth⟩ Brooks and ⟨Robert Penn⟩ Warren praise the story for its "web of observations about human nature" and the "all-too-human tendency to seize upon a scapegoat," visiting upon it "cruelties that most of us seem to have dammed up within us." But then they indicate structural weakness by asserting that Jackson has "preferred to give no key to her parable but to leave its meaning to our inference," allowing "a good deal of flexibility in our interpretation," while yet insisting that "everything in the story has been devised to let us know how we are to 'take' the final events in the story."

Perhaps the critical ambivalence illustrated above stems from failure to perceive that "The Lottery" really fuses two stories and themes into one fictional vehicle. The overt, easily discovered story appears in the literal facts, wherein members of a small rural town meet to determine by lot who will be the victim of the yearly savagery. At this level one feels the horror, senses clearly the "dichotomy in all human nature" ⟨Virgil Scott⟩, the "doubleness of the human spirit" ⟨Brooks and Warren⟩, and recoils in horror. This narrative level produces immediate emotional impact. Only after that initial shock do disturbing questions and nuances begin to assert themselves.

It is at this secondary point that the reader begins to suspect that a second story lies beneath the first and that Miss Jackson's "symbolic intentions" are not "incidental" but, indeed, paramount. Then one discovers that the author's careful structure and consistent symbolism work to present not only a symbolic summary of man's past but a prognosis for his future which is far more devastating than the mere reminder that man has savage potential. Ultimately one finds that the ritual of the lottery, beyond providing a channel to release repressed cruelties, actually serves to *generate* a cruelty not rooted in man's inherent emotional needs at all. Man is not at the mercy of a murky, savage id; he is the victim of unexamined and unchanging traditions which he could easily change if he only realized their implications. Herein is horror.

Helen E. Nebeker, " 'The Lottery': Symbolic Tour de Force," *American Literature* 46, No. 1 (March 1974): 100–102

RICHARD PASCAL   In story after story the small town or neigh-borhood is depicted as a nexus of sanctioned intrigue against whatever is individual, different, or alien, and in which the ties that bind may also strangle. In "The Lottery," even the individualism of valuing one's own life is ritualistically and horrifyingly exorcised by the community. In "The Summer People," two vacationers from the city who stay on in a small resort community past the traditional Labor Day leavetaking discover that that tradition is to the townsfolk a taboo, the breaking of which entails forfeiture of normal services and amenities and leads, ultimately, to dark hostility. Sometimes the communal group is simply the family, oppressively nuclear. Elsa Dayton in "A Day in the Jungle" leaves her home and husband because they represent a life of stifling quotidian regularity; marriage has been for her a succession of "hideous unprivate months." Catharine Vincent in "I Know Who I Love," leaving home as a young woman, ceases immediately to think about her nagging parents, and does so only "dutifully" after they have died. The sense of duty, inspired not by love or deep moral awareness, but by anxiety and insecurity, is to the family in Jackson's fiction what custom is to the small community: a bonding mechanism whose primary function is to ensure cohesiveness.

Opposed to the regulated world of the small group is the realm of freedom and self-centeredness represented, usually, by the city. To those in recoil from the confines of the small group, the city stands as a glistening dream of freedom in which communally inculcated patterns of self-abnegating behavior do not hold. Thus Elsa, during her day in the "jungle" of the downtown area to which she has fled from her suburban home, is "very much aware of the fact that for the first time she moved knowingly and of choice through a free world." Such freedom, not merely to do what one likes, but to create a life and a self of one's own, is the promise which the city seems to hold. Yet the inverse of the freedom to create a new self is the destruction of the old, which the city also seems to portend. In "Pillar of Salt," the impression of things crumbling is continually with Margaret during her visit to New York, and she suspects that the disintegrating buildings, streets, and vehicles are symptomatic of the city's effect on people: it is the place where they "come apart." At the end of the story she is utterly panicked by the swarming anonymity of the crowds on the streets outside, and at not being noticed familiarly. Similarly, Elsa Dayton's fears of accidental injury during her day downtown really amount to an insecurity about her ability to hold the jungle of an unfamiliar world at bay. Without the constant external verification of identity which the small community provides, the self may seem to lose its reality and the world may crumble crazily.

These, then, are the two realms between which many of Shirley Jackson's heroines gravitate. In the family or town or neighborhood the ties may chafe, but they do hold you together; in the city there are no ties, and *you* must hold you together—assuming there is a "you" which can exist independently, out of familiar context. Some of the most interesting moments in Jackson's fiction are those in which the flight from familiarity to the realm of strangeness and freedom causes a character's sense of identity to weaken and even vanish. Such experiences of fundamental tremors in the self's sense of who it is aren't easily explicable as schizoid disturbances or breakdowns, a line of analysis which assumes a preexistent central self to feel disturbed or break down. What seems to fascinate Shirley Jackson most is the possibility that behind the self which we ordinarily assume to be irrevocably engrained, if not preordained, there is nothing immutably necessary which we can call our own: it is, for her, an idea which is both frightening *and* alluring.

> Richard Pascal, " 'Farther Than Samarkand': The Escape Theme in Shirley Jackson's 'The Tooth,' " *Studies in Short Fiction* 19, No. 2 (Spring 1982): 134–35

JACK SULLIVAN   In a eulogy to Leonard Brown, her college English teacher, Shirley Jackson wrote that his invaluable gift to her was the insight that "the aim of writing was to get down what you wanted to say, not to gesticulate or impress." Jackson followed this credo throughout her career. A master of the plain style, she was a supremely economical artist whose angular, clear diction gave the American Gothic tale a precision not to be found in Edgar Allan Poe, Nathaniel Hawthorne, or her other predecessors. What she "wanted to say"—that human cruelty and the precariousness of life are the only certainties in our otherwise enigmatic lives—was harsh, and she got it down honestly, without fuss. "The Lottery," one of the most widely anthologized stories in English, expresses the objective, social side of her vision; practically everything else in her serious fiction, from the bleak attenuations of the short stories to the strange rapture of *We Have Always Lived in the Castle*, expresses the inner side, the sense that the human psyche is as treacherous as human behavior.

Yet one of the most striking qualities of Shirley Jackson is her offbeat charm. Her content is severe, but her bright, quirky sense of humor and her sheer oddness soften the blow. Furthermore, no matter how bizarre her characters are—and she consistently creates some of the most bizarre people in fiction—she displays compassion and an almost frightening empathy. Her maddest, most dangerous character, Merricat Blackwood in *We Have Always Lived in the Castle*, is sketched with startling tenderness. Not since Poe has there been a more passionate poet of the freakish and abnormal, the "grotesque and arabesque," but Jackson goes further than Poe; rather than being tragically destroyed, Merricat is "happy" in her final lunacy— indeed, the only character to come out happy in all of Jackson's serious fiction.

In the evolution of the supernatural tale, Jackson's was a distinctly original voice, but her methods were too personal and idiosyncratic to attract disciples or imitators. Her version of the genre took ambiguity to its furthest extremity, beyond Henry James, Walter de la Mare, or her favorite ghost story writer, Elizabeth Bowen. She wrote what are simultaneously some of the most exasperatingly confusing and peculiarly satisfying tales in the genre.

Jackson slyly referred to herself as the only practicing witch in New England, a joke that had an undercurrent of truth. She did dabble in magic, with a Ouija board and tarot cards, and she had a library of some five hundred occult books. Yet most of her comments on the subject—such as her delightful description of how the supernatural, which had never previously harassed her life, suddenly turned up everywhere when she started work on *The Haunting of Hill House*—are laced with irony and gentle self-deprecation. Surprisingly, her fiction contains little sense of spirituality: the supernatural, both real and imagined, lurks as one of life's nasty little surprises rather than as a subject for mystical contemplation.

Jack Sullivan, "Shirley Jackson," *Supernatural Fiction Writers*, ed. E. F. Bleiler (New York: Charles Scribner's Sons, 1985), Vol. 2, p. 1031

JAMES EGAN   *The Sundial* offers an absurdist, satiric, horrific treatment of the domestic. All the while that the outlandish "family" assembled in the Halloran mansion believes in the prophecies of a madwoman, Aunt Fanny Halloran, that the mansion will be their sanctuary during an apocalyptic time of reckoning, Jackson systematically undermines that belief. She illustrates the many ways in which the Halloran entourage inverts the values of the domestic and familial. Orianna Halloran's son has recently died under mysterious circumstances and she has assumed control of the family. Orianna admits early on that she married her crippled, senile husband, Richard, for his money and property. She is a materialist who loves the house rather than its inhabitants, and her fascination with wealth and power are the opposite of the values eulogized in the family chronicles ⟨*Life among the Savages* and *Raising Demons*⟩. Other versions of the anti-familial which surface early are sexual—sexual escapades are clearly excluded from Jackson's domestic vision. The hint that Essex, hired to catalogue the mansion's library, may be Orianna's lover appears, and the narrator makes clear that Aunt Fanny has been pursuing Essex. Even the apparently sexless Miss Ogilvie apparently had a possibly romantic note-writing episode with Richard Halloran before he was confined to a wheelchair. The moral code of the mansion seems ambiguous at best.

Familial distortions extend into the basic power and social structure of the mansion as well. Two matriarchs, Orianna and Fanny, compete for supremacy. In treating Fanny's erratic behavior, Jackson takes *The Sundial's* domestic motifs into the absurdly farcical. Fanny's visions of her father, who warns of impending catastrophe, are given credibility by the Gothic manifestations which occur after she reports on a sighting. As soon as she has narrated her first vision, a snake appears, peering at the assembled family from a fireplace. After another revelation occurs, the glass in the "great picture window" in the drawing room shatters "soundlessly from top to bottom". Somewhat taken aback by these peculiar developments, the rest of the group, despite their doubts, refrains from stopping Fanny's incredible scheme of preparation for apocalypse. Fanny resembles a demented mother-figure frantically stockpiling food for her family, ordering provisions of all sorts by the truckload. Her collection of materials borders on the idiotic, including as it does a carton of tennis balls, suntan lotion, instant coffee, and salted nuts in cans. She creates storage space by throwing away and burning the family library. Fanny sees herself as a sort of maternal priestess whose home will be a shrine for future generations, another ludicrous inversion of Jackson's domestic vision. Predictably, her work speeds the transformation of the already eccentric mansion into a "monumental lunatic asylum". She is absurdly appropriate as the deranged provider for a deluded family, the "first" family of the post-apocalyptic world. ⟨. . .⟩

Unlike the atmosphere of the chronicles, the one prevailing at the Halloran estate is total distrust, cynicism, and paranoia, a psychologically distorted environment. Several more intense forms of horror take their cue from reversals and perversions of the domestic as well. Fancy Halloran, Orianna's granddaughter, could fairly be described as a monstrous child. Suspecting Orianna of killing her father, Fancy asks her mother, Maryjane, if she should push Orianna down the stairs. Later Orianna finds her picture with a hatpin stuck in the throat and again Fancy would appear a likely suspect, as she does when a doll full of pins is found on the sundial in the yard. To confirm the reader's suspicions, after the others find Orianna dead at the foot of the stairs, Fancy dons the crown her grandmother was wearing the previous night. Aunt Fanny's remembrance rooms stand out as another horrific inversion of the domestic, a mockery of the normal growth to maturity portrayed in the chronicles. Fanny has preserved in elaborate detail a dead world in an attic of the mansion, a fully detailed world which includes a reconstruction of her childhood bedroom. She takes Fancy to the reconstructed doll house and tries to get the child to play dolls. This monstrous-child to mad-adult situation parodies the mother-daughter relationships detailed in the chronicles, echoing in reverse the narrator's play with her children in *Life among the Savages* and *Raising Demons*. Orianna's dream of the fable of the witch with the candy house in the forest includes her more fully in the pattern of the horrifically inverted familial. In the dream world of the Gothic nightmare, Orianna's true nature as a monstrous parody of the nurturing mother stands out. A cannibalistic witch in the dream, she wants to eat the children who threaten her material property. Together with Fanny's ghostly visions of her father, the mysterious snake in the library, and the splitting of the great parlor window, these dark recreations of the familial begin to establish the Gothic motifs Jackson will refine in her last and finest novels, *The Haunting of Hill House* and *We Have Always Lived in the Castle*.

James Egan, "Sanctuary: Shirley Jackson's Domestic and Fantastic Parables," *Studies in Weird Fiction* No. 6 (Fall 1989): 18–20

JOAN WYLIE HALL   Although Jackson is frequently categorized as a Gothic writer, "A Visit" is among her few short stories to adhere closely to such conventions as the haunted mansion. A stone faun by the front door and bronze fauns in the hall woodwork introduce a fanciful decorating scheme worthy of Poe. A prominent feature is the series of tapestries that rival any of the rich wall hangings in his stories. Tapestries in the gold room are edged in gilded frames and portray the house in sunlight; silver-framed tapestries of the house in moonlight hang in the silver room. The Gothic obsession with doubles is even more extravagantly incorporated into a mirrored room where Carla and Margaret watch themselves "diminishing and reflecting" in an endless succession of doorways. A nest of tables supports a nest of wooden bowls, and tapestries picture the house reflected in the lake, "and the tapestries themselves were reflected, in and out, among the mirrors on the wall, with the house in the tapestries reflected in the lake." The confusion of inside and outside, reflection and substance, so overcomes Margaret that she withdraws in fright.

Strangest of all the pairings in the house are the alternate versions of Margaret. When she meets the old woman in the tower, the girl searches for an appropriate response to the coincidence of names, then smiles "uncertainly" and makes no comment. The narrator does not record Margaret's reaction when she eagerly reads an inscription in the room of tiles beneath a portrait of a pretty girl who stares "blindly from the floor": " 'Here was Margaret,' it said, 'who died for love.' " Mrs. Rhodes and Carla, who have a special affection for the picture, seem intent on observing its effect on Margaret: " 'I was wondering what Margaret would say when she saw it,' said Carla, smiling also [like her mother]." Near the end of the story, Carla's brother reports that, among new signs of decay, a tile is missing from this portrait. (The signs also include a "crack in the solid stone" over the conservatory window, a likely allusion to Poe's ominous fissure in "The Fall of the House of Usher.") Young Margaret hurries to the room of tiles to verify the loss and discovers "the broken spot looked like a tear."

After Paul and the captain leave, Mrs. Rhodes ignores Margaret's reference to the end of her own visit and turns to her embroidery to create a final Margaret; she asks the girl to sit with Carla on the lawn near the river so she can fill in the foreground and complete the latest tapestry of the house. "We shall be models of stillness," Carla laughs as she invites Margaret to join her outside. Earlier that same day Margaret speculated that the figures in the dining room tapestries "might remember, secretly, an imagined process of dressing themselves and coming with laughter and light voices to sit on the lawn where they were woven." When Margaret arrived at the Rhodeses' house, she felt she had "come home"; the conclusion suggests she is so linked with the substance of the mansion she will never leave, and may always have been there. The house claims her, not as violently as Hill House claims Eleanor Vance at the end of *The Haunting of Hill House*, but just as surely.

Joan Wylie Hall, *Shirley Jackson: A Study of the Short Fiction* (New York: Twayne, 1993), pp. 65–66

S. T. JOSHI   "Nothing has the power to hurt which doesn't have the power to frighten": this single utterance by Shirley Jackson may be all the justification we need to consider some of her darkest and most vicious work, otherwise wholly non-supernatural, as anomalous contributions to the weird tale. Maurice Lévy remarked of Ambrose Bierce that "One is almost tempted to believe that one day he decided to instill fear into his contemporaries *by hatred*, to gain revenge on them", and Jackson seems very frequently inspired by the same motivation. 〈. . .〉

It is interesting that *The Sundial* seems to have been singled out by reviewers for its misanthropy. Harvey Swados snorted: "While Miss Jackson is an intelligent and clever writer, there rises from her pages the cold fishy gleam of a calculated and carefully expressed contempt for the human race." There are two problems with this utterance: one, the whole of Jackson's work is refreshingly misanthropic; two, the assumption here (as I have noted in connexion with Bierce) is that there is something necessarily wrong with misanthropy. I do not know that Jackson anywhere offers an explicit philosophical defence of misanthropy, but perhaps she need not have done so: her work makes it obvious that she had little patience for the stupid, the arrogant, the pompous, the complacently bourgeois, the narrow-minded, and the spiteful—in other words, she hates all those people whom there is every good reason to hate. Since, therefore, I do not acknowledge any prejudice against misanthropy, I can only relish the exquisite nastiness with which Jackson ordinarily displays it. Such a tale as "Strangers in Town" is to be criticised not because it is misanthropic but because in this instance Jackson's blind hatred has resulted in a failure of that artistry and subtlety uniformly evident in the rest of her work. 〈. . .〉

I think we might discuss the celebrated "One Ordinary Day, with Peanuts" here. This spectacularly nasty story has, in its quiet way, some stupendous implications. A man leaves home in the morning and seems intent on accomplishing nothing but good: he keeps an eye on a boy while his mother runs an errand; he advises a man looking for an apartment as to the availability of one he has just seen; he actually gives a cab driver money and advice for betting on horses. Most remarkably of all, he intentionally stops a young man and a young woman on the street, introduces them to each other, and gives them money to take the day off and have a good time. He is benevolence itself. He comes home, meets his wife, and tells her how his day went. She tells him about hers:

> "I had a little nap this afternoon, took it easy most of the day. Went into a department store this morning and accused the woman next to me of shoplifting, and had the store detective pick her up. Sent three dogs to the pound—*you* know, the usual thing."

They plan the next day:

> "Fine," said Mr. Johnson. "But you do look tired. Want to change over tomorrow?"
> "I *would* like to," she said. "I could do with a change."
> "Right," said Mr. Johnson.

With such ease can people be sadistically mean and superhumanly philanthropic in turn! The one seems as good a way of passing the time as the other. But the true message of the story, beyond the implication that misanthropy and benevolence can be sloughed off and put on like a cloak, is the idea of manipulation: both misanthropy and benevolence involve a fascistic manipulation of human beings as if they were puppets; and perhaps Jackson's real misanthropy is directed here not at the couple but at the spineless and stupid people who allow the couple to do their dirty or good work with such insouciance.

S. T. Joshi, "Shirley Jackson: Domestic Horror," *Studies in Weird Fiction* No. 14 (Winter 1994): 23–24

▨ Bibliography

The Road through the Wall. 1948.
The Lottery; or, The Adventures of James Harris. 1949.

Hangsaman. 1951.
Life among the Savages. 1953.
The Bird's Nest. 1954.
The Witchcraft of Salem Village. 1956.
Raising Demons. 1957.
The Sundial. 1958.
The Haunting of Hill House. 1959.
The Bad Children: A Play in One Act for Bad Children. 1959.
Special Delivery: A Useful Book for Brand-New Mothers (with others). 1960.
We Have Always Lived in the Castle. 1962.
9 Magic Wishes. 1963.
The Magic of Shirley Jackson (short stories, *The Bird's Nest*, *Life among the Savages*, *Raising Demons*). Ed. Stanley Edgar Hyman. 1966.
Famous Sally. 1966.
Come Along with Me: Part of a Novel, Sixteen Stories, and Three Lectures. Ed. Stanley Edgar Hyman. 1968.

M. R. James
1862–1936

MONTAGUE RHODES JAMES, the son of an Anglican priest, was born on August 1, 1862, in Goodnestone, Suffolk. Though high-spirited and lively, he exhibited precocious antiquarian interests while at Temple Grove Preparatory School and Eton, immersing himself in the study of medieval manuscripts and Biblical apocrypha. He entered King's College, Cambridge, in 1882, and after graduating stayed on to become a fellow in 1887. In his illustrious career he rose to be provost of King's (1905–18) and vice-chancellor of the University (1913–15), but took greater pride in his function as director of the Fitzwilliam Museum from 1893 to 1908 and in his service on the University Press and Library Syndicates. Though he never married, he played a leading role in Cambridge literary and convivial societies, and in the vacations enjoyed cycling tours with friends in Britain and France.

In 1918 James was appointed provost of Eton, and in later years he served on several royal commissions and was appointed a trustee of the British Museum. He was made a Commander of the Order of Leopold for his aid to Belgian refugees in World War I and received the Order of Merit in 1930.

James's scholarly work gained him great respect, especially in the fields of codicology, Christian art, and Biblical research. He catalogued many manuscript collections, including those of the Fitzwilliam Museum, most of the Cambridge colleges, and Canterbury, and was well known particularly for his version of *The Apocryphal New Testament* (1924).

He reached a wider audience as a master of the ghost story in his volumes *Ghost-Stories of an Antiquary* (1904), *More Ghost Stories of an Antiquary* (1911), *A Thin Ghost and Others* (1919), and *A Warning to the Curious* (1925). His children's novel, *The Five Jars* (1922), also has fantastic elements. His *Collected Ghost Stories* appeared in 1931. James's tales are the culmination of the nineteenth-century British ghost story tradition, and in some of his essays and occasional writings (now gathered in *M. R. James's Book of the Supernatural*, 1979) he laid down clear principles for the writing of this type of work. His stories are characterized by a deceptively casual style, careful building up of mundane details, settings in cathedrals, libraries, and other locales where his scholarly erudition can establish verisimilitude, and skill in the achievement of a dramatic climax. James's work inspired many imitators, including A. N. L. Munby, E. G. Swain, R. L. Malden, and Frederick Cowles.

James published his memoirs, *Eton and King's*, in 1926. He continued as provost of Eton until his death on June 12, 1936.

▓ *Critical Extracts*

M. R. JAMES   Some years ago I promised to publish a second volume of ghost stories when a sufficient number of them should have been accumulated. That time has arrived, and here is the volume. It is, perhaps, unnecessary to warn the critic that in evolving the stories I have not been possessed by that austere sense of the responsibility of authorship which is demanded of the writer of fiction in this generation; or that I have not sought to embody in them any well-considered theme of 'psychical' theory. To be sure, I have my ideas as to how a ghost story ought to be laid out if it is to be effective. I think that, as a rule, the setting should be fairly familiar and the majority of the characters and their talk such as you may meet or hear any day. A ghost story of which the scene is laid in the twelfth or thirteenth century may succeed in being romantic or poetical: it will never put the reader into the position of saying to himself, 'If I'm not very careful, something of this kind may happen to me!' Another requisite, in my opinion, is that the ghost should be malevolent or odious: amiable or helpful apparitions are all very well in fairy tales or in local legends, but I have no use for them in a fictitious ghost story. Again, I feel that the technical terms of 'occultism', if they are not very carefully handled, tend to put the ghost story (which is all that I am attempting) upon a quasi-scientific plane, and to call into play faculties quite other than the imaginative. I am well aware that mine is a nineteenth- (and not a twentieth-) century conception of this class of tale, but were not the prototypes of all the best ghost stories written in the sixties and seventies?

> M. R. James, "Preface," *More Ghost Stories of an Antiquary* (London: Edward Arnold, 1911), pp. v–vi

H. P. LOVECRAFT   Dr. James ⟨. . .⟩ approaches his themes in a
light and often conversational way. Creating the illusion of every-day events,
he introduces his abnormal phenomena cautiously and gradually; relieved
at every turn by touches of homely and prosaic detail, and sometimes spiced
with a snatch or two of antiquarian scholarship. Conscious of the close
relation between present weirdness and accumulated tradition, he generally
provides remote historical antecedents of his incidents; thus being able to
utilise very aptly his exhaustive knowledge of the past, and his ready and
convincing command of archaic diction and colouring. A favourite scene
for a James tale is some centuried cathedral, which the author can describe
with all the familiar minuteness of a specialist in that field.

Sly humorous vignettes and bits of lifelike genre portraiture and character-
isation are often to be found in Dr. James's narratives, and serve in his
skilled hands to augment the general effect rather than to spoil it, as the
same qualities would tend to do with a lesser craftsman. In inventing a new
type of ghost, he has departed considerably from the conventional Gothic
tradition; for where the older stock ghosts were pale and stately, and appre-
hended chiefly through the sense of sight, the average James ghost is lean,
dwarfish, and hairy—a sluggish, hellish night-abomination midway betwixt
beast and man—and usually *touched* before it is *seen*. Sometimes the spectre
is of still more eccentric composition; a roll of flannel with spidery eyes, or
an invisible entity which moulds itself in bedding and shows *a face of crumpled
linen*. Dr. James has, it is clear, an intelligent and scientific knowledge of
human nerves and feelings; and knows just how to apportion statement,
imagery, and subtle suggestion in order to secure the best results with his
readers. He is an artist in incident and arrangement rather than in atmosphere, and reaches the emotions more often through the intellect than
directly. This method, of course, with its occasional absences of sharp climax,
has its drawbacks as well as its advantages; and many will miss the thorough
atmospheric tension which writers like Machen are careful to build up with
words and scenes. But only a few of the tales are open to the charge of
tameness. Generally the laconic unfolding of abnormal events in adroit
order is amply sufficient to produce the desired effect of cumulative horror.

H. P. Lovecraft, "Supernatural Horror in Literature" (1927), *Dagon and Other Macabre
Tales*, ed. S. T. Joshi (Sauk City, WI: Arkham House, 1986), pp. 432–33.

PETER FLEMING   Dr. James, whose four volumes of ghost stories
are now issued for the first time under one cover, has long been an acknowl-

edged master of his craft: unrivalled at his best, for consistent merit never approached. "There is no receipt for success in this form of fiction," he says in his preface. And to be sure you cannot cabin horror in a formula; the raising of hair, unlike the raising of chickens, salaries, and hearty laughs, cannot be taught through a correspondence course. But although Dr. James' subtle methods hardly lend themselves to analysis, some of the foundations of his pre-eminence do become apparent from a study of this book, its monument.

His first secret is tact. I say tact rather than restraint because he can and does pile on the agony when his sense of the dramatic tells him to. (You remember, I dare say, what happened to Anders Bjornsen's face? . . . "the flesh of it was sucked away off the bones.") It is tact, a guileless and deadly tact, that gauges so nicely the force of half-definitions, adjusting the balance between reticence and the explicit so that our imaginations are ever ready to meet his purpose half-way. The best story in this book is " 'Oh, Whistle, and I'll Come to You, My Lad' "; we never know what it was that answered Mr. Parkins' whistle, but we are not likely to forget that when it attacked him, substituting bed clothes from an empty bed for the essential vesture of creation, it revealed "a horrible, an intensely horrible, face *of crumpled linen.*" That is the stuff of nightmares.

There are other constant ingredients in Dr. James' most potent magic. One, inevitably, is the background of learning to his stories. Though in his preface he makes light of his "ostensible erudition," his knowledge of the Unknown is, if I may say so, sufficiently well-simulated to lend an air of authenticity and, sometimes, to serve the purposes of innuendo. His narrative always has a kind of dry naturalism which lends perspective to the action. He shows at times something of the same imaginative adaptability, the same power of suddenly bringing home the implications of an abnormal situation by reference to the trivial, which Swift showed when he made Gulliver notice the Brobdingnagian pores. Add to all this an eye for, rather than a preoccupation with, character—particularly well-developed in the case of what our less democratic ancestors persisted in calling the "low characters"— and you will have excused, if not wholly explained, your surrender to the fascination of these stories.

When Dr. James errs, it is always on the side of reticence. "Casting the Runes," for instance, should carry a stronger climax after its delicate overture of horror, which is one of the best things in the book. But this is backhanded criticism and premises praise. Overstatement has been the besetting sin of the ghost story since the statue at Otranto began to bleed at the nose, and Dr. James will have nothing to do with it, even in its emasculated modern form, which spells thing with a capital T and has a great camp following of dots.

I detect in his later stories a certain leniency, a tendency to let the reader off lightly. There are certain signs that he finds it increasingly hard to take the creatures of his fancy seriously; like Prospero, he retires more and more into the benevolent showman. In such a master this is perhaps a venal fault. Far less easy to forgive is his answer to the self-imposed question: "Am I going to write any more ghost stories?" Who ever heard of Prospero breaking his staff after only four acts? I think Dr. James will find that his laconic "Probably not" has turned all his readers, for once, into critics.

> Peter Fleming, "The Stuff of Nightmares," *Spectator*, 18 April 1933, p. 633

MARY BUTTS   It is the writer's belief that if Dr. James had chosen to write stories about any other subject under the sun, he would be considered the greatest classic short story writer of our time. Yet, in his case, it is more than usually silly—so completely fused with one another are his style and his subject—to suggest such a thing. It is impossible to think of him as writing about anything else than what is rather foolishly called "The Unseen." Idiotically, in his case. "Unseen," indeed! When the essence of his art is a sudden, appalling shock of visibility. The intangible becomes more than tangible, unspeakably real, solid, *present*. He is not a writer—say like Mr. Algernon Blackwood—who relies on suggestion, a strengthening atmosphere in which very little ever happens; or rather one is not sure whether it has happened or not. It is what his people *see* that Doctor James is busy with; not how it affects them. After it has happened they either die, or leave home or go to bed; or, years after, tell it to him, with permission to make a story out of it. It sounds simple. It is not. It is matter-of-fact. A very different thing. Yet in its unpretentiousness, in its absence of worked-up atmosphere, its lack of hints, it carries the driest, clearest kind of conviction. If his stories were about anything else (which heaven forbid) Doctor James would be praised for something of the same qualities for which we praise Horace and Catullus and Villon, for something terse and poignant and durable, and looked at with both eyes wide open. While, in our day at least, writing on the 'Occult'—another inadequate, loosely-used word—is felt to be a bastard of the Muses; a kind of entertainment, a kind of trick. Not quite respectable. The implication being that our emotions are stirred by situations which are essentially impossible: by a lie. That, as letters are more than a game, it is not quite fair.

> Mary Butts, "The Art of Montagu ⟨sic⟩ James," *London Mercury* No. 172 (February 1934): 307

S. G. LUBBOCK On 28 Oct. 1893 there was an historic meeting of the Chitchat Society, a literary society founded in 1860 which had for its object 'the promotion of rational conversation'. It met on Sunday evenings, when papers were read and discussed; Church Portals, Sheridan le Fanu ⟨sic⟩, and Breton Ballads are among the subjects on which Monty himself read papers. The 550th meeting was celebrated by a dinner, after which 'Mr Leathes proposed the health of the society and Mr James. Mr James refused to respond.' The last recorded meeting was on 8 May 1897, and the last entry in the Minute Book, in Monty's hand, ends as follows: '. . . the Club, though never formally wound up, may be said to have expired of inanition due, I fear, to the failure of the Secretary to summon meetings, and to the apathy of the members.'

'The 601st meeting was held in Mr James' room on Oct. 28th 1893. *Present:*

    Mr James
    " W. G. Headlam
    " E. F. Benson
    " V. W. Yorke
    " Barran
    " Shearme
    " R. C. Bosanquet
    " A. B. Ramsay
    " F. H. Cornish
    Dr Waldstein
    Mr E. W. Talbot

'Mr James read "Two Ghost Stories" '

There the minute ends. Lord Fredric Hamilton, editor of the *Pall Mall Magazine*, who was often at Cambridge, secured one of these stories, 'Lost Hearts', and published it with illustrations in the *Pall Mall Magazine*. The other, 'Canon Alberic's Scrapbook', was published by Leo Maxse in the *National Review*.

So the Ghost Stories began; and they were continued at the urgent request of a small party that was used to gather at King's just before Christmas. Some pressure was needed; and on the appointed evening the party met and waited till at last, about 11 p.m. as a rule, Monty appeared with the ink still wet on the last page. All lights except one were turned out and the story was read. Afterwards, when he was Provost, the same ritual was preserved; but by then the small party had grown, and when the Punch and Judy story was read there was a large gathering in the big drawing room of the Lodge. On that occasion the silence which fell when the grim story ended was broken by the voice of Luxmoore: 'Were there envelopes in those days?' and Monty of course was easily able to prove that there were.

> S. G. Lubbock, "Memoir," *A Memoir of Montague Rhodes James* (Cambridge: Cambridge University Press, 1939), pp. 37–39

PETER PENZOLDT   There are many reasons for James' extraordinary success. One is certainly that he is the most orthodox ghost-story writer among his contemporaries. His stories are straightforward tales of terror and the supernatural utterly devoid of any deeper meaning. They are what the orally-told ghost stories originally were: tales that are meant to frighten and nothing more. They contain no study of human nature as do those by W. F. Harvey, Walter de la Mare, Robert Hichens, Conrad Aiken and others of his contemporaries, and no moral lessons as do Dickens' and Stevenson's tales. They have none of Kipling's poetry. In this respect James can only be compared with F. M. Crawford, though the two authors differ fundamentally in taste, style, technique and the atmosphere of their stories. It can therefore be said with truth that James is at once an orthodox and original writer. Orthodox, because he chose for his tales a form that is older than fiction itself; original, because he alone in the 20th century still believed that the simple ghost story could be thrilling if only it were well enough told.

It seems that his ideas were as much in favour with many readers as they were out of favour with most of his colleagues. A great part of the public still wanted simply emotion and terror. They did not want their ghosts analysed or explained. They desired something lighter than those psychological ghost stories that have to be read with a hand-book on psychiatry close by, which they found afforded them little relation and sometimes came just a little too close to reality to be really entertaining.

Naturally, such tales as James chose to write demand a far more elaborate form than most types of ghost story. A horror with a natural explanation, e.g. an illusion caused by mental disease, appears to the reader as being at least possible. Such a story can be presented in a very direct fashion. But when a manifestation of the supernatural forms the climax of the story, and no natural explanation is vouchsafed, the tale becomes far less acceptable to the reader, who because he does not, as he once did, believe in the supernatural, has to be approached with care and brought gradually into a state in which his disbelief is suspended. James' success proves both that he has perfected the technique of 'make believe' and that a large public prefers his kind of story to those with a natural explanation.

Peter Penzoldt, "Dr. M. R. James (1862–1936)," *The Supernatural in Fiction* (London: Peter Nevill, 1952), pp. 191–92

AUSTIN WARREN   In James's stories, owls, bats, and rats and spiders, the traditionally ominous creatures of the night are frequent. But more terrifying than the literal creatures are their properties, operating of themselves: multiple tentacles, for example, which reach out and entwine themselves stranglingly about the human intruder.

Hair is invoked in double signification: often the creatures are described as having their arms or what pass for their bodies covered with gray or grisly hair; a hairy man is a primitive like the Ainus of Japan; he recalls our anthropoid ancestry. But then there is another, opposite but equally repellant, signification of hair: the effeminate long hair of Sir Everard Charlett, the long hair of Absalom, the King's son, who was caught by his hair as he rode horseback through the forest, who was hanged by his own hair. The wallpaper made from a stuff pattern of Sir Everard's hair, the rippling lines, the almost curling waves of tresses, have their serpentine terror, their menace of entanglement. These are the rival fears of the primitive and the decadent.

More characteristic of James's terrors is the terror of the amorphous. In "Whistle and I'll Come to You, My Lad," the only tale which incorporates one of James's own dreams, the presumed figure of a Knight Templar, perhaps of the fourteenth century, materializes itself out of "the bed-clothes of which it had made itself a body": the living spectator's face; and as he looks, he sees the face of the other, "an intensely horrible face of *crumpled linen*." So, analogously, comes, at the end of "The Uncommon Prayer-Book," a roll of white flannel, four or five feet high, with a kind of face in the upper end of it, the face earth-covered, the eyes, "much as if there were two big spiders' bodies in the holes." It falls from a safe where the venomous prayer book has been stored; and, falling, it inflicts a serpent-like bite which kills the dealer who had stolen it from a seventeenth century chapel dedicated to a Royalist's sole object of passion—the hatred of Oliver Cromwell.

Ghosts, as commonly conceived of—white, visual images—rarely appear, and then at some distance. More frequently they are heard in cries, moans, or (more disturbing yet) whispers and murmurs; or their presence in a room, or a landscape, is felt. When, however, the evil dead are menaced, they come close and grow heavy. James rarely used the word 'nightmare,' and then not with technical accuracy, yet his chiefest horror is some version of the incubus—something partly human, partly animal, partly *thing* which presses down, grasps and grips, threatens to strangle or suffocate, a heavy weight of palpable materiality—not 'psychic' but sensually gross—a recall not of shroud but of corpse, of a living dead or death.

Thus, the Abbot Thomas, at the bottom of the well, guarding his treasure bags, is an *it* as well as a *he*. "It hung for an instant on the edge of the hole, then slipped forward on to my chest, and *put its arms around my neck* . . . I was conscious of a most horrible smell of mold, and of a cold kind of face pressed against my own, and moving slowly over it, and of several—I don't know how many—legs or arms or tentacles or something clinging to my body." That night, the creature of darkness—its sounds and its odor—pervaded the narrator's hotel; and it was relief indeed, when daybreak came and he and his servant were able to put the slab of stone back over the well and what inhabited it.

Austin Warren, "The Marvels of M. R. James," *Connections* (Ann Arbor: University of Michigan Press, 1970), pp. 103–4

JULIA BRIGGS   What has been said of James's minor characters also applies to the central figure, the hero who dominates the situation and acts as the focus of the supernatural events. These characters have a transparent simplicity, transparent, because we are required to look *through* them at the unfolding plot, where the emphasis is placed. The reader sees not merely what *is* happening, but also what is going to happen, anticipating, if only vaguely, the disaster that is on the point of overtaking the hero, and is filled with a corresponding sympathy and alarm on his behalf. These transparent, anonymous heroes, often distinctively twentieth-century in their practical, sceptical appproaches to life, are frequently academics of some kind, if their professions are referred to at all. They have a selfless enthusiasm for knowledge (or perhaps a fatal curiosity) which ironically leads them on 'where angels fear to tread', as old Cooper warns Mrs. Humphreys. From one angle the hero is thus a reflection of his sceptical and detached creator; from another he is the clear window through which the reader perceives the plot unfolding, unfolding far faster than the hero himself realizes. For this hero unknowingly inhabits an animistic world where anything might happen, a world into which only the minor characters are given intuitive glimpses so that they may warn the protagonist of what impends. But the hero's materialism, his doubt, prevents him from giving due weight to the warnings he receives.

Such a warning is usually provided in the early stages of the tale, partly in order to increase the sense of suspense and imminent danger, but also to provide an element of dramatic justice. In everyday terms, the hero is mildly culpable in that he wilfully rejects, because of his scepticism perhaps, the advice of older or wiser men. In metaphysical terms, his refusal to be warned is symptomatic of a wider rejection of unproven forces and inexplicable powers, and hence is duly revenged by these powers, when they are conceived as emerging from an outer darkness or an inner id. Nearly all of the stories provide this warning element in some form or another: in 'Canon Alberic's Scrapbook', there is not only the excessive anxiety of the sacristan and his daughter, but even the sight of the fearful drawing itself; in 'The Ash-Tree', the Bishop of Kilmore warns Sir Richard with his allusion to Irish peasant beliefs. The Colonel fulfills this function in ' "Oh, Whistle" '. 'The Treasure of Abbot Thomas' provides a caveat at the end of the coded message, 'Gare à qui la touche'. Thus the hero has to some extent wilfully placed himself 'on the edge'. In the rare cases where visitations fall on the totally innocent, as in 'Casting the Runes', the victim is provided with helpful friends, as Dunning is with Henry Harrington, whose advice he is only too eager to adopt.

Julia Briggs, "No Mere Antiquary: M. R. James," *Night Visitors: The Rise and Fall of the English Ghost Story* (London: Faber & Faber, 1977), pp. 136–37

JACK SULLIVAN   In an odd sense, "Count Magnus" is more in the Le Fanu manner than Le Fanu. James's use of innuendo and indirection is so rigorous that it hides more than it reveals. Le Fanu creates a balance between uneasy vagueness and grisly clarity. But James tilts the balance in favor of the unseen. Tiny, unsettling flashes of clarity emerge from obscurity, but usually in an indirect context. We are allowed to see the protruding tentacle of one of the robed pursuers, for example—but only in the engraving, not in the actual pursuit. In the most literal sense, these are nameless horrors.

James also follows Le Fanu's example in his use of narrative distance, again transcending his model. Le Fanu separates himself from his material through the use of elaborate, sometimes awkward prologues and epilogues which filter the stories through a series of editors and narrators. Sometimes, as in "Mr. Justice Harbottle," the network of tales within tales results in a narrative fabric of considerable complexity. In "Count Magnus," the narrator is an anonymous editor who has access to the papers Mr. Wraxall was compiling for a travelogue. The story consists of paraphrases and direct quotations from these papers, a device which gives the narrative a strong aura of authenticity. The transitions from one document to the other, occurring organically within the text, are smooth and unobtrusive. They are also strangely impersonal, as if the teller in no way wishes to commit himself to his tale.

James's reticence probably relates as much to personal temperament as to the aesthetic problem of how to write a proper ghost story. It is commonly accepted, largely because of the work of James and Le Fanu, that indirection, ambiguity, and narrative distance are appropriate techniques for ghostly fiction. (Material horror tales, such as Wells' "The Cone" and Alexander Woollcott's "Moonlight Sonata," are another matter.) Supernatural horror is usually more convincing when suggested or evoked than when explicitly documented. But James's understated subtlety is so obsessive, so paradoxically unrestrained that it feels like an inversion of the hyperbole of Poe or Maturin. I find his late work increasingly ambiguous and puzzling, sometimes to the point of almost total mystification. It is as if James is increasingly unwilling to deal with the implications of his stories. What begins as a way of making supernatural horror more potent becomes a way of repressing or avoiding it. Often he appears to be doing both at once, creating a unique chill and tension.

Jack Sullivan, "The Antiquarian Ghost Story: Montague Rhodes James," *Elegant Nightmares: The English Ghost Story from Le Fanu to Blackwood* (Athens: Ohio University Press, 1978), pp. 70–71.

DEVENDRA P. VARMA   The structure of the weird tale follows its own norms: a casual opening, the sudden build up of tension and the use of double climax. This skill at construction remains the secret of James's stories. He frames them in a definite period and setting; they contain clear, unobtrusive, normal realistic details, but the climax is often mantled in darkness and mystery.

His characters are normal human beings living a matter-of-fact existence, interested in most ordinary things. As a story-teller he opens in a low key with authentic touches of realism and actuality, and then brings out the most distinctive quality in an exquisite gradation of factual horror. He seems to prove that a sense of malevolence and terror can be created without the glare of evil faces or 'the stony grin of unearthly malice'; the pursuing forms in darkness can be more frightening than 'long drawn, distant screams', and very effective can be a tiny drop of blood seen in half-light. James frightens us with a crumpled handkerchief, or a fold in the linen. He shows us fear in a handful of dust.

> Devendra P. Varma, "The Ghost Stories of M. R. James: Artistic Exponent of the Victorian Macabre," *Indian Journal of English Studies* n.s. 4 (1983): 74–75

S. T. JOSHI   ⟨. . .⟩ perhaps James is rather more interesting as a critic and theorist of the form. We are now concerned with three documents: the preface to *More Ghost Stories of an Antiquary* (1911), the introduction to *Ghosts and Marvels* (1924), and the lengthy essay "Some Remarks on Ghost Stories" (1929). The first two are principally theoretical, and impeccable as far as they go; they prove that James had clear principles for ghost-story writing (⟨Jack⟩ Sullivan makes much too much of James's apparent coyness and indefiniteness in this regard) and that he followed them closely enough ⟨. . .⟩ The final essay is a fascinating history of the ghost story—fascinating precisely because it is so bizarre. Admittedly, James seems to be narrowly restricting himself to the avowed "ghost story" so that perhaps it is under-standable that such figures as Machen or Dunsany have no place in his account. But James's highly ambiguous stance toward Poe is of interest. The editor of *Ghosts and Marvels* had selected Poe's "Ligeia" for inclusion, and James was forced to comment upon it. His cautious remark, "Evidently in many people's judgments it ranks as a classic," scarcely conceals his distaste. "Some Remarks on Ghost Stories" is more ambivalent, as he speaks of "some Americans" (i.e., the pulp writers) who fancy that they "tread . . . in the steps of Edgar Allan Poe and Ambrose Bierce (himself sometimes unpardonable)," but the hint of disapproval is strong. What offended James so much? Clearly it was the concentration on what he felt was the merely physically gruesome, as can be inferred in his slap at Bierce and also in his comment on E. F. Benson: "He sins occasionally by stepping over the line of legitimate horridness." Certainly he has nothing good to say about the American pulp writers: "The[y] are merely nauseating, and it is very easy to be nauseating." This is really an unprovoked attack, since the pulp writers never considered themselves "ghost-story writers" and should therefore not even have been mentioned in James's essay. I think James's squeamishness prevented him from appreciating the fact that there is a lot more to the work of Poe, Bierce, Machen, and Lovecraft than merely loathsome physical horror; James's idol LeFanu can be just as revolting, but evidently his indirection appealed to James.

S. T. Joshi, "M. R. James: The Limitations of the Ghost Story," *The Weird Tale* (Austin: University of Texas Press, 1990), pp. 141–42

Bibliography

Psalms of the Pharisees (translator; with H. E. Ryle). 1891.

The Testament of Abraham (editor). 1892.

Apocrypha Anecdota (editor). 1893. 13 vols.

The Sculptures in the Lady Chapel at Ely. 1895.

On the Abbey of St. Edmund at Bury. 1895.

The Will of Henry VI (editor; with J. W. Clark). 1896.

Life and Miracles of St. William of Norwich by Thomas of Monmouth (editor; with A. Jessopp). 1896.

Apocrypha Anecdota: Second Series (editor). 1897.

Guide to the Windows of King's College Chapel, Cambridge. 1899.

The Ancient Libraries of Canterbury and Dover (editor). 1903.

Ghost-Stories of an Antiquary. 1904.

Notes on the Glass in Ashridge Chapel. 1906.

The Sculptured Bosses in the Roof of the Bauchun Chapel, Norwich Cathedral. 1908.

The Manuscripts of Westminster Abbey (with J. A. Robinson). 1909.

More Ghost Stories of an Antiquary. 1911.
The Sculptured Bosses in the Cloisters of Norwich Cathedral. 1911.
The Second Epistle General of Peter and The General Epistle of Jude (editor).
    1912.
Old Testament Legends. 1913.
The Chaundler Manuscripts (editor). 1916.
The Biblical Antiquities of Philo (translator). 1917.
A Thin Ghost and Others. 1919.
The Founder's Pageant and Play of St. Nicholas (with A. B. Ramsay). 1919.
The Wanderings and Homes of Manuscripts. 1919.
Henry the Sixth by Joannes Blacman (translator). 1919.
The Lost Apocrypha of the Old Testament (translator). 1920.
The Five Jars. 1922.
Eton College Chapel: The Wall Paintings. 1923.
Bibliotheca Pepysiana: Part 3. 1923.
Madam Crowl's Ghost and Other Tales of Mystery by Joseph Sheridan LeFanu
    (editor). 1923.
De Nugis Curialium by Walter Map (translator). 1923.
An Apocryphal New Testament (translator). 1924.
A Warning to the Curious and Other Ghost Stories. 1925.
Abbeys (with A. H. Thompson). 1925.
Eton and King's: Recollections, Mostly Trivial, 1875–1925. 1926.
Latin Infancy Gospels: A New Text (editor). 1927.
Excluded Books of the New Testament (translator; with others). 1927.
Wailing Well. 1928.
Letters of H. E. Luxmoore (editor; with A. B. Ramsay). 1929.
Suffolk and Norfolk: A Perambulation of the Two Counties. 1930.
Forty Stories by Hans Christian Andersen (translator). 1930.
The Apocalypse in Art. 1931.
Collected Ghost Stories. 1931.
Two Ancient English Scholars: St. Aldhelm and William of Malmesbury. 1931.
The Woodwork of the Choir at St. George's Chapel, Windsor. 1933.
The New Testament (editor). 1934–35. 4 vols.
Letters to a Friend. Ed. Gwendolen McBryde. 1956.
Ghost Stories. Ed. Nigel Kneale. 1973.
M. R. James's Book of the Supernatural. Ed. Peter Haining. 1979.
Casting the Runes and Other Ghost Stories. Ed. Michael Cox. 1987.

H. P. Lovecraft
1890–1937

HOWARD PHILLIPS LOVECRAFT was born on August 20, 1890, in Providence, Rhode Island, the only son of Winfield Scott and Sarah Susan (Phillips) Lovecraft. When he was three his father, a traveling salesman, suffered a seizure and spent the rest of his life in an insane asylum, dying of syphilis in 1898. The boy's upbringing was left to his overprotective mother, his two aunts, and his grandfather, Whipple Phillips, a wealthy industrialist. A precocious boy, Lovecraft was reading at two, writing poems and stories at seven, and learning Latin and Greek at eight. As a teenager he started producing his own hectographed journals devoted to chemistry and astronomy.

The family's fortunes suffered a reversal in 1904 at the death of Whipple Phillips, and Lovecraft and his mother were forced to move into smaller quarters in Providence. His formal education was sporadic because of his chronic ill health, and in 1908 he suffered an apparent nervous breakdown that forced him to leave Hope Street High School without a diploma. The next five years were spent in virtual hermitry, as Lovecraft continued to amass an impressive self-education in literature, science, and philosophy.

In 1914 Lovecraft joined the amateur journalism movement, plunging into the literary and political activities of the United Amateur Press Association and, later, the National Amateur Press Association. He produced thirteen issues of his own journal, *The Conservative* (1915–23), filling it with poems, essays, and commentary. Gradually, at the urging of friends, Lovecraft recommenced the writing of fiction: "The Tomb" (1917) is the first story of his mature period.

For years Lovecraft had no thought of publishing his work professionally. In 1923, however, he was urged to contribute to the fledgling pulp magazine *Weird Tales*. Over the next fifteen years the bulk of his fiction appeared in the pages of that magazine; in 1924 he was even asked to be its editor, but he refused. Lovecraft's genteel upbringing rendered him persistently diffident about commercially marketing his writing, and several attempts by book publishers to issue his work came to nothing.

Lovecraft's mother died in 1921; two months later he met Sonia Haft Greene, a Ukrainian Jew several years his senior. In 1924 they married, and Lovecraft moved into Sonia's apartment in Brooklyn. Their marriage, however, was not a success: Lovecraft was unable to find regular work, a hat shop owned by Sonia went out of business, and later her health gave way; she was forced to take a job in the Midwest, leaving Lovecraft alone in a city he had come to loathe for its noise, overcrowding, and "foreigners." He wrote few stories during this period, but did the bulk of work on his study "Supernatural Horror in Literature" (first published in an amateur magazine, the *Recluse*, in 1927).

In April 1926 Lovecraft returned to Providence, essentially ending the marriage, and proceeded to write his greatest work—tales such as "The Call of Cthulhu" (1926), *The Case of Charles Dexter Ward* (1927), "The Colour out of Space" (1927), "The Whisperer in Darkness" (1930), "The Shadow over Innsmouth" (1931), *At the Mountains of Madness* (1931), and "The Shadow out of Time" (1934–35). These stories established Lovecraft as both the pinnacle of the Gothic tradition and the forger of a new form of weird fiction—closely linked with the developing genre of science fiction— in which Gothic conventions (the vampire, the ghost, the haunted house) are transmuted into the horrors to be found in the depths of space. Lovecraft, an articulate spokesman for his brand of weird writing and for his philosophy generally (he was a mechanistic materialist and atheist), described his work as "cosmic" in its orientation. Many of his tales are linked by plot and theme in their use of a fictional New England topography, pseudomythologi- cal "gods" from outer space, and a series of imagined books of magic and occult lore. This group of stories has been collectively called the "Cthulhu Mythos," although Lovecraft never used the term; it has been widely imitated by later writers.

During the last ten years of his life Lovecraft traveled widely on various antiquarian expeditions and became a stunningly voluminous letter writer, corresponding with fantasists such as August Derleth, Donald Wandrei, Clark Ashton Smith, Robert E. Howard, Frank Belknap Long, Robert Bloch, and many others. Although a towering figure in the realms of amateur journalism and pulp fiction, Lovecraft had only one book, *The Shadow over Innsmouth* (1936), issued by a small press before his death of intestinal cancer on March 15, 1937.

After his death Lovecraft's friends set about rescuing his work from oblivion. Derleth and Wandrei founded the firm of Arkham House for the express purpose of publishing his work in hardcover; their first volume, *The Outsider and Others* (1939), is a landmark. Lovecraft's stories, essays, and letters have subsequently appeared in many hardcover and paperback editions and have been translated into more than a dozen languages. His *Selected Letters* appeared in five volumes between 1965 and 1976, and his collected fiction was republished in a corrected text under the editorship of S. T. Joshi between 1984 and 1989. His *Miscellaneous Writings* was published in 1995.

Critical Extracts

W. PAUL COOK   Howard P. Lovecraft is widely and favorably known throughout the amateur journalistic world as a poet, and in a lesser degree as an editorial and essay writer. As a story-writer he is practically unknown, partly because of the scarcity of publications large enough to accommodate much prose, and partly because he does not consider himself a competent story-teller. His first story to appear in the amateur press was "The Alchemist," published in the *United Amateur*. This story was enough to stamp him as a pupil of Poe in its unnatural, mystical and actually morbid outlook, without a hint of the bright outdoors or of real life. His second story, "The Beast in the Cave," published in the *Vagrant*, was far inferior in every respect, even in being given a modern setting, which may be counted as against it in Mr. Lovecraft's case. The outstanding feature of this really slight effort was the skill with which an atmosphere was created.

In "Dagon," in this issue of the *Vagrant*, Mr. Lovecraft steps into his own as a writer of fiction. In reading this story, two or three names of short-story writers are immediately called to mind. First of all, of course, Poe; and Mr. Lovecraft, I believe, would be the first to acknowledge his allegiance to our American master. Second, Maupassant; and I am quite sure that Mr. Lovecraft would deny any kinship with the great Frenchman.

Mr. Lovecraft with "Dagon" is not through as a contributor of fiction to the amateur press. He will never be as voluminous a fiction writer as a poet, but we may confidently expect to see him advance even beyond the high mark he has set in "Dagon."

W. Paul Cook, "Howard P. Lovecraft's Fiction" (1919), *In Memoriam: Howard Phillips Lovecraft: Recollections, Appreciations, Estimates* (North Montpelier, VT: Driftwind Press, 1941), p. 61

H. P. LOVECRAFT   There is ⟨one⟩ phase of cosmic phantasy ⟨. . .⟩ whose foundations appear to me as better grounded than those of ordinary oneiroscopy; personal limitation regarding the *sense of outsideness*. I refer to the aesthetic crystallisation of that burning & inextinguishable feeling of mixed wonder & oppression which the sensitive imagination experiences upon scaling itself & its restrictions against the vast & provocative abyss of the unknown. This has always been the chief emotion in my psychology; & whilst it obviously figures less in the psychology of the majority, it is clearly a well-defined & permanent factor from which very few sensitive persons are wholly free. Here we have a natural biological phenomenon so untouched & untouchable by intellectual disillusion that it is difficult to envisage its total death as a factor in the most serious art. Reason as we may, we cannot destroy a normal perception of the highly limited & fragmentary nature of our visible world of perception & experience as scaled against the outside abyss of unthinkable galaxies & unplumbed dimensions—an abyss wherein our solar system is the merest dot (by the same *local* principle that makes a sand-grain a dot as compared with the whole planet earth) *no matter what relativistic system we may use in conceiving the cosmos as a whole*—& this perception cannot fail to act potently upon the natural physical instinct of *pure curiosity*; an instinct just as basic & primitive, & as impossible of destruction by any philosophy whatsoever, as the parallel instincts of hunger, sex, ego-expansion, & fear. ⟨. . .⟩ A great part of religion is merely a childish & diluted pseudo-gratification of this perpetual gnawing toward the ultimate illimitable void. Superadded to this simple curiosity is the galling sense of *intolerable restraint* which all sensitive people (except self-blinded earth-gazers like little Augie Derleth) feel as they survey their natural limitations in time & space as scaled against the freedoms & expansions & comprehensions & adventurous expectancies which the mind can formulate as abstract conceptions. ⟨. . .⟩ The time has come when the normal revolt against time, space, & matter must assume a form not overtly incompatible with what is known of reality—when it must be gratified by images forming *supplements* rather than *contradictions* of the visible & mensurable universe. And what, if not a form of *non-supernatural cosmic art*, is to pacify this sense of revolt— as well as gratify the cognate sense of curiosity?

H. P. Lovecraft, Letter to Frank Belknap Long (22 February 1931), *Selected Letters 1929–1931*, ed. August Derleth and Donald Wandrei (Sauk City, WI: Arkham House, 1971), pp. 293–96

FRITZ LEIBER   Howard Phillips Lovecraft was the Copernicus of the horror story. He shifted the focus of supernatural dread from man and his little world and his gods, to the stars and the black and unplumbed gulfs of intergalactic space. To do this effectively, he created a new kind of horror story and new methods for telling it. ⟨. . .⟩

The universe of modern science engendered a profounder horror in Lovecraft's writings than that stemming solely from its tremendous distances and its highly probable alien and powerful non-human inhabitants. For the chief reason that man fears the universe revealed by materialistic science is that it is a purposeless, soulless place. To quote Lovecraft's "The Silver Key," man can hardly bear the realization that "the blind cosmos grinds aimlessly on from nothing to something and from something back to nothing again, neither heeding nor knowing the wishes or existence of the minds that flicker for a second now and then in the darkness."

In his personal life Lovecraft met the challenge of this hideous realization by taking refuge in traditionalism, in the cultivation of mankind's time-honored manners and myths, not because they are true, but because man's mind is habituated to them and therefore finds in them some comfort and support. Recognizing that the only meaning in the cosmos is that which man dreams into it, Lovecraft treasured beautiful human dreams, all age-worn things, and the untainted memories of childhood. This is set forth clearly in "The Silver Key," the story in which Lovecraft presents his personal philosophy of life.

In the main current of Lovecraft's supernatural tales, horror of the mechanistic universe gave shape to that impressive hierarchy of alien creatures and gods generally referred to as "the Cthulhu mythos," an assemblage of beings whose weird attributes reflect the universe's multitudinous environments and whose fantastic names are suggestive renderings of non-human words and sounds. They include the Elder Gods or Gods of Earth, the Other Gods or Ultimate Gods, and a variety of entities from distant times, planets, and dimensions.

Although they stem from that period in which Lovecraft mixed black magic in his tales and was attracted to Dunsanian pantheons, I believe it is a mistake to regard the beings of the Cthulhu Mythos as sophisticated equivalents of the entities of Christian demonology, or to attempt to divide them into balancing Zoroastrian hierarchies of good and evil.

> Fritz Leiber, "A Literary Copernicus" (1949), H. P. Lovecraft: Four Decades of Criticism, ed. S. T. Joshi (Athens: Ohio University Press, 1980), pp. 50, 53

MAURICE LÉVY   What Lovecraft teaches us, and what he himself learned from Machen, is that the best fantasy is that which is rooted in folklore, tradition, and myth. Puritanism and the history of New England play the same role in our author's tales as medieval myth did in the Gothic novels of the end of the eighteenth century. Somehow, myth, in the superficial sense of the term, orients and localizes dream-activity, thereby assuring it an even greater intensity and benefic homogeneity.

On a personal level, myth gives depth and efficiency to the fantastic, precisely insofar as this return to the primordial it involves coincides with a quest for a cure, and also because it permits the irrational to be built on the foundations of the universal psyche. At the most, the idea would be defensible that anything truly fantastic implies a return to *archetypes*.

It will always be impossible to define the fantastic universally, which is too rich, too basic to be encompassed definitively by any discourse. Examples, complementary or contradictory, can but illustrate that Lovecraft's work is one, a very significant one, we believe, and particularly if we consider the time and place in which he lived.

He vehemently stood, in his letters, against the ravages of industrial civilization, which was attacking man at his deepest level: isolating him from the past, from the traditions of his race, tearing him from his native soil; in a word, alienating him. From this viewpoint, fantastic creation is a protest and a refusal. No; life is not as simple, rudimentary, and facile as the billboard advertisements might lead us to believe. No; the laws that rule the universe are not as well known as popular science—the only type of science possible in a "democratic" society, based on numbers—seems to indicate. No; space is not as certain, time is not as "chronological," the past is not as dead as some people declare. In truth, there are more things in heaven and *under the earth* than are dreamt of in our philosophies.

In a society that is becoming each day more anesthetized and repressive, the fantastic is at once an evasion and the mobilization of anguish. It restores man's sense of the sacred or the sacrilegious; it above all gives back to him his lost depth. For the myth of the automobile, the washing machine, and the vacuum cleaner, for the modern myths of the new world that are merely surface myths, Lovecraft substituted the Cthulhu Mythos.

> Maurice Lévy, *Lovecraft: A Study in the Fantastic* (1972), tr. S. T. Joshi (Detroit: Wayne State University Press, 1988), pp. 119–20

BARTON L. ST. ARMAND   It is my contention that Lovecraft would never have been Lovecraft without Providence—its history, its atmosphere, its legends, its peculiar and individual character—and that, genius that he was, it is not so much escape from but improvement on the rich native materials that lay in his own back yard that helps to make his tales so intriguing and so striking. Perhaps what I am really saying is that Lovecraft, like his Southern contemporary William Faulkner, is a great local color writer, who sometimes goes beyond the conventions of mere local color quaintness or picturesqueness in order to get at terrifying ambiguities having to do with the scope and status of human nature itself.

The city of Providence and the state of Rhode Island thus become for Lovecraft a kind of *prima materia*—a basic, irreducible substance—which he transmutes through the alchemy of his art into a rarefied and golden product. There was an almost symbiotic relationship between the author and his environment, and here ⟨Colin⟩ Wilson's categorization of Lovecraft as a romantic would seem to be truly valuable, though there were actually two Lovecrafts—one classic and one romantic, one an eighteenth-century mind and one a nineteenth-century Gothic sensibility. The eighteenth-century side of his personality manifested itself in Lovecraft's admiration for colonial times, his sardonic skepticism, his view of himself as a detached spectator of the world and its problems, and his intense interest in science and technology. This attitude could sometimes become both escapist and defensive, although it also led Lovecraft to become, like his eighteenth-century counterpart Horace Walpole, one of the great letter writers of the century. ⟨. . .⟩

The other dimension of his character, the romantic, balanced off the wit, urbanity, rationality, and cosmopolitan nature of the classic side which comes through the letters. Lovecraft was like a man poised between the end of the eighteenth and the beginning of the nineteenth century, and his choice of a Gothic form for writing reflects that literature which had developed at precisely this point in history. Thus Lovecraft chooses the mode of the "Gothic Novel," reminiscent of such thrilling and supernatural best-sellers of the 1790s and 1800s as *The Castle of Otranto, The Monk, The Mysteries of Udolpho,* and *Frankenstein.* His romantic dimension was embodied in that side of his personality which delighted in the weird, the ethereal, the remote, the shadowy, and the terrifying—a thrill for the sake of a thrill—though we have already noted that Lovecraft's science-fiction tales go beyond this toward Ann Radcliffe's shadowy "sublime." Closely connected with this predilection is what Wilson calls Lovecraft's "provinciality" and what I would call his sense of place—his love of the particular and peculiar atmosphere of a very definite and circumscribed locality, just as Wordsworth and the Lake Poets made the Lake District of England famous for its individual aura of beauty and picturesqueness. Lovecraft focuses on Providence and its outskirts so much that, like many romantics, he develops an almost mystical attachment to the place he has chosen to celebrate in art.

Barton L. St. Armand, "Facts in the Case of H. P. Lovecraft," *Rhode Island History* 31, No. 1 (February 1972): 10–11

DONALD R. BURLESON   By the time he wrote his book-length critical survey, *Supernatural Horror in Literature* (1925–27), Lovecraft had reread Hawthorne intensively and devoted considerable space to him in the survey, describing him—albeit in a tone of distaste for Hawthorne's allegorical didacticism—in terms of genius. This survey, far from being "a piece of frivolous self-indulgence" as remarked by L. Sprague de Camp in his *Lovecraft: A Biography* (1975), is an indispensably useful source for the student of Lovecraft's critical views, and it sheds light upon an important aspect of Lovecraft's interest in Hawthorne: the regional aspect. With his own love for the dark side of New England history and folklore, Lovecraft found endless fascination with Hawthorne's shadowy interest in and ancestral connection with New England Puritanism and witchcraft persecution. The inclination of Hawthorne to be led by this state of mind to plant his creations in his own native Novanglian soil is reflected in Lovecraft's developing preference for such settings. Prior to his serious study of Hawthorne, Lovecraft's tales show no particular tendency to concentrate upon New England; but as his style ascends to its maturity in the late 1920s and early 1930s, he weaves the byways and accumulated lore of his native region into the heart even of his most sweepingly cosmic conceptions. And so many are the thematic and imagistic echoes of Hawthorne in Lovecraft's work that the two writers, for all their differences in outlook and purpose, are remarkably similar in their use of New England terrain and culture as a canvas on which to try to suggest the hues of their respective personal visions.

Sometimes similarities are evident even with respect to Lovecraft's early writing. Hawthorne, with ever an eye on the past, was fond of darkly personifying old New England houses in his fiction, saying, for example, of the House of the Seven Gables: "The aspect of the venerable mansion has always affected me like a human countenance, bearing the traces not merely of outward storm and sunshine, but expressive, also, of the long lapse of mortal life, and accompanying vicissitudes that have passed within. . . . The deep projection of the second story gave the house such a meditative look that you could not pass it without the idea that it had secrets to keep, and an eventful history to meditate upon."

It would be difficult, for one familiar with Lovecraft's work, to read these passages without thinking of his story "The Picture in the House" (1920), in which the narrator says of certain old New England farmhouses remote from travelled roads: "Two hundred years and more they have leaned or squatted there, while the vines have crawled and the trees have swelled and spread. They are almost hidden now in lawless luxuriances of green and guardian shrouds of shadow; but the small-paned windows still stare shockingly, as if blinking through a lethal stupor which wards off madness by dulling the memory of unutterable things." This passage has an alliterative style not unlike Hawthorne, and a feeling for the sentient nature of *place*, a characteristic tendency in Lovecraft and one also shown by Hawthorne in such tales as "The Hollow of the Three Hills" and in such scenes as the forest meeting in *The Scarlet Letter* (1850).

Donald R. Burleson, "Lovecraft: The Hawthorne Influence," *Extrapolation* 22, No. 3 (Fall 1981): 262–64.

PETER CANNON   As with Poe, the French can claim the honor of having been first to appreciate Lovecraft's worth. Then again, to be classed with Poe is no guarantee of a place in the pantheon. Poe historically has been belittled by some of our most eminent critics and authors, from Henry James to T. S. Eliot. As Harold Bloom observes in a review dating to 1984, "Poe's survival raises perpetually the issue whether literary merit and canonical status necessarily go together. I can think of no other American writer, down to this moment, at once so inescapable and so dubious." By Bloom's standards Lovecraft would seem both escapable and dubious. If Henry James could think that to take Poe with more than a certain degree of seriousness is to lack seriousness oneself, then no doubt he would have regarded the master of *Weird Tales* as the mark of a stage of reflection so decidedly primitive as to be beneath notice. For many Lovecraft's is essentially an adolescent sensibility that appeals to other adolescents. When John Updike says that "I read Lovecraft with suitable chills and rapture when I was about fifteen and haven't much looked at him since," he in effect speaks for a majority of mature adults, for whom in literature as in life "ordinary events and feelings," as Lovecraft concedes in *Supernatural Horror in Literature*, "will always take first place."

Granted its "juvenile" quality, Lovecraft's fiction yet bears comparison with the best of such literature, in particular the Sherlock Holmes stories of Arthur Conan Doyle, a connection Edmund Wilson makes explicit at the conclusion of his attack: "But the Lovecraft cult, I fear, is on even a more infantile level than the Baker Street Irregulars and the cult of Sherlock Holmes." On a far more modest scale, Lovecraft has inspired the same sort of playful, affectionate response—the journals, the organizations, the rituals, the tongue-in-cheek quibbling over fine textual points—that characterizes the world of the greatest fictional detective. At this popular level he seems likely to continue to thrive.

As a subject of more serious critical consideration, Lovecraft can hold his own, as Brown University's Barton L. St. Armand has demonstrated, to single out one scholar who has placed him without apology in a larger literary context. Unlike his fellows in the *Weird Tales* triumvirate of the thirties, Clark Ashton Smith and Robert E. Howard, he has transcended his pulp origins. While the best work of M. R. James, Algernon Blackwood, and Arthur Machen may be technically superior to any one Lovecraft tale, theirs lacks the philosophical and psychological breadth that his possesses as a whole. In contrast to his successors, he stands as the last major figure in the field to have written exclusively in a literary tradition, uninfluenced by movies and television. While outside the genre he may be a pygmy beside such classical giants as Poe, Hawthorne, and Melville, Lovecraft in the darkness of his vision can be compared as their spiritual heir. (The doctoral candidate who might otherwise select one of our standard authors for a dissertation may well find Lovecraft a rewarding and relatively wide-open alternative.) As for twentieth-century writers, he belongs in a broad sense, as Darrell Schweitzer has suggested, "on a level with Borges and Franz Kafka."

Peter Cannon, H. P. Lovecraft (Boston: Twayne, 1989), pp. 124–25

S. T. JOSHI   The notion of decline enters Lovecraft's fiction at a very early stage. It is generally manifested in two discrete forms: individual or collective *regression* into a primitive state and a socio-political decline in the future. The ultimate effects are virtually identical, for in both states we find a barbarism and a loss of those aspects of civilisation—intellectual and aesthetic endeavour; racial purity; gentlemanliness of behaviour—that Lovecraft so valued. It is to his credit that in the end he chose to measure the progress or decline of a civilisation by the first of these aspects. ⟨. . .⟩

If the past has suddenly become problematical, the future is no less so. Here we must turn to the prose-poem "Nyarlathotep" (1920), which I see as a virtual parable for the decline of the West. In a letter describing the dream on which the story was based, Lovecraft recalls some of the details of Nyarlathotep's stage show: "These exhibitions consisted of two parts—first, a horrible—possibly *prophetic* [my italics]—cinema reel . . ." Already in the dream the notion of futurity is evident. In the tale we find ourselves in a "season of political and social upheaval" in which people "whispered warnings and prophecies which no one dared consciously repeat". And what does the narrator see "shadowed on a screen"?

> And I saw the world battling against blackness; against the waves
> of destruction from ultimate space; whirling, churning; struggling
> around the dimming, cooling sun.

The West's decline heralds the decline of the whole planet with the extinction of the sun. Later the world seems to be falling apart:

Once we looked at the pavement and found the blocks loose and
displaced by grass, with scarce a line of rusted metal to shew
where the tramways had run. And again we saw a tram-car, lone,
windowless, dilapidated, and almost on its side. When we gazed
around the horizon, we could not find the third tower by the
river, and noticed that the silhouette of the second tower was
ragged at the top.

People begin milling about irrationally; and when one group "filed down a
weed-choked subway entrance", I wonder whether we are to read some hint
that we have been doomed by our own technology. "Nyarlathotep" is one
of Lovecraft's most powerful vignettes—and the fact that he *dreamed* it
makes us realise how deeply rooted was his anxiety for civilisation.

S. T. Joshi, *H. P. Lovecraft: The Decline of the West* (Mercer Island, WA: Starmont
House, 1990), pp. 138, 140

STEFAN DZIEMIANOWICZ   The significance of "The Call of
Cthulhu" cannot be overemphasized. It is the first story to articulate clearly
the cosmic perspective he had only suggested in earlier stories and that would
henceforth dominate his fiction. There is perhaps no better explication of
this viewpoint than the well-known opening passage:

The most merciful thing in the world, I think, is the inability
of the human mind to correlate all its contents. We live on a
placid island of ignorance in the midst of black seas of infinity,
and it was not meant that we should voyage far. The sciences,
each straining in its own direction, have hitherto harmed us little;
but some day the piecing together of dissociated knowledge will
open up such terrifying vistas of reality, and of our frightful
position therein, that we shall either go mad from the revelation
or flee from the deadly light into the peace and safety of a new
dark age.

The island metaphor was an appropriate choice of images, considering
Lovecraft's earlier concentration on specific geographic locales and focuses
of "outside" forces. In his early New England stories Lovecraft had presented
towns like Arkham and Kingsport as small breaches in the fabric of our
world through which the terrors of the void occasionally vent themselves.
Here, though, the old perspective is inverted, and we are asked to consider

the incomprehensible void a sort of greater reality, a "sea" in which our small world of limited knowledge is but an island. This telescoped point of view presents an image of mankind as an isolated presence on the "black seas" of an infinite cosmos, a figure dwarfed into insignificance by the vastness of the universe.

The way Lovecraft intended to express this alienated viewpoint is implicit in his opening paragraph. By saying it is "merciful" that the human mind cannot correlate its contents, Francis Wayland Thurston, the narrator, implies that he himself has already made such a correlation. Something he has discovered has given him a burden of knowledge not shared by other men, and so he stands apart from the rest of mankind, just as Lovecraft's earliest narrators were outside their own society. Thurston describes his devastating, newly acquired knowledge as something "flashed out from the piecing together of separated things," echoing his remark about the inability of mankind to piece together the separate contents of its collected knowledge. By drawing a parallel between Thurston's personal experience and the fate of the human race, Lovecraft makes it clear that Thurston is not merely a character in a horror story. He is a symbol for mankind itself, alone in the void, piecing together random bits of information in an effort to find greater meaning. Thus, Thurston's internal alienation reflects humanity's greater external alienation as a consciousness aware of its own insignificance in the cosmic scheme of things.

Stefan Dziemianowicz, "Outsiders and Aliens: The Uses of Isolation in Lovecraft's Fiction," *An Epicure in the Terrible: A Centennial Anthology of Essays in Honor of H. P. Lovecraft*, ed. David E. Schultz and S. T. Joshi (Rutherford, NJ: Fairleigh Dickinson University Press, 1991), pp. 174–75

STEVEN J. MARICONDA   *At the Mountains of Madness* (1931) employs human artifacts (the work of Poe, Dunsany, and Nicholas Roerich), alien artifacts (the murals of the Old Ones), and even ultra-alien artifacts (the murals of the shoggoths) in its meditation on the nature of reality. The expedition's scientists must take continual recourse to analogies with the most fantastic human art, yet can convey only the merest hints of the strangeness of their discoveries. At first it is a case of life imitating art— that is, weird art. Only seven pages into the story, on the first leg of the voyage toward Antarctic peaks, the narrator notes that "something about the scene reminded me of the strange and disturbing Asian paintings of Nicholas Roerich". On the next page, a passage from Poe's "Ulalume" is quoted upon the sight of Mt. Erebus, with the narrator noting that the mountain "had undoubtedly been the source of Poe's image". The line between weird art and reality begins to blur: the locale evoked the writing of the poem and the quoting of the poem is evoked by the locale. Three pages later, objective reality blends into the vision of an artist "supreme in the creation of a gorgeous and languorous world of iridescently exotic vision" ("Supernatural Horror in Literature"), Lord Dunsany: "often the whole white world would dissolve into a gold, silver, and scarlet land of Dunsanian dreams". ⟨. . .⟩

The strangeness conveyed by these human artifacts, once again, pales in light of the art—"mature, accomplished, and aesthetically evolved to the highest degree of civilised mastery"—created by the Archaean race called the Old Ones. Most of the narrator's information about this race and their epoch is drawn from the mural sculptures which abound in their ruined city. ⟨. . .⟩ These alien artists possess a different set of sense-equipment than we do, and as a result their art tells us something about the cosmos we otherwise could not know. "In delicacy of execution", too, "no sculpture I have ever seen could approach it." This perhaps reflects the different physiognomies of the Old Ones—five arms each ending in twenty-five tentacles.

It is not, however, the physical differences alone of the alien sculptors that give their art such tremendous impact for the human observers. There is another element: "Their method of design . . . embodied an analytical psychology beyond that of any known race of antiquity." This calls to mind Lovecraft's famous pronouncement on his theory of aesthetics:

> To me beauty as we know it, consists of two elements; one absolute and objective, and based on rhythm and symmetry; and one relative and subjective, based on traditional associations with the hereditary culture-stream of the beholder. The second element is probably strongest with me . . .

At first it seems strange that humans could be so moved by art that is by definition lacking in the second, subjective element. We may conclude that there is enough of an overlap in the outlook of this particular alien race and the human race for the explorers to feel the great depth of the Old Ones' art. Thus the narrator's remark that the murals possessed "an artistic force that moved us profoundly" foreshadows the sympathy of his later exclamation: "whatever they had been, they were men!" The shoggoths, which supplant the Old Ones as the objects of our fear, certainly are not men. Art is used as a cue for the redirection of the explorers' terror, as the murals reflect a subtle change from the supreme artistic accomplishments in those murals first seen by the explorers: "This new and degenerate work was coarse, bold, and wholly lacking in delicacy of detail." It seemed "more like a parody than a perpetuation" of the Old Ones' work. Apparently, "some subtly but profoundly alien element had been added to the aesthetic feeling behind the technique". Unlike the Old Ones, the shoggoths are so antipodally alien that the explorers feel no empathy whatever for their "aesthetic feeling". These "multicellular protoplasmic masses" can have no art as we know it; as Lovecraft remarked in a 1933 letter, our art is "more intrinsically removed from the unevolved protoplasmic stage of organic creation than any other human manifestation except pure reason".

Steven J. Mariconda, "H. P. Lovecraft: Art, Artifact, and Reality," *Lovecraft Studies* No. 29 (Fall 1993): 9–11

◈ *Bibliography*

The Crime of Crimes. 1915.
United Amateur Press Association: Exponent of Amateur Journalism. c. 1916.
Looking Backward. 1920.
The Materialist Today. 1926.
The Shunned House. 1928 (printed but not distributed).
Further Criticism of Poetry. 1932.
The Battle That Ended the Century (with R. H. Barlow). 1934.
The Cats of Ulthar. 1935.
Charleston. 1936.
Some Current Motives and Practices. 1936.
The Shadow over Innsmouth. 1936.
HPL. 1937.
A History of the Necronomicon. 1938.
The Notes & Commonplace Book. [Ed. R. H. Barlow.] 1938.
The Outsider and Others. Ed. August Derleth and Donald Wandrei. 1939.
Fungi from Yuggoth. 1943.

Beyond the Wall of Sleep. Ed. August Derleth and Donald Wandrei. 1943.

Marginalia. Ed. August Derleth and Donald Wandrei. 1944.

Supernatural Horror in Literature. 1945.

Best Supernatural Stories. Ed. August Derleth. 1945.

Something about Cats and Other Pieces. Ed. August Derleth. 1949.

The Lovecraft Collectors Library. Ed. George Wetzel. 1952–55. 7 vols.

The Challenge from Beyond (with C. L. Moore, A. Merritt, Robert E. Howard, and Frank Belknap Long). 1954.

The Shuttered Room and Other Pieces. Ed. August Derleth. 1959.

Dreams and Fancies. [Ed. August Derleth.] 1962.

The Dunwich Horror and Others. Ed. August Derleth. 1963, 1984 (ed. S. T. Joshi).

Collected Poems. [Ed. August Derleth.] 1963.

At the Mountains of Madness and Other Novels. Ed. August Derleth. 1964, 1985 (ed. S. T. Joshi).

Selected Letters. Ed. August Derleth, Donald Wandrei, and James Turner. 1965–76. 5 vols.

Dagon and Other Macabre Tales. Ed. August Derleth. 1965, 1986 (ed. S. T. Joshi).

The Dark Brotherhood and Other Pieces. [Ed. August Derleth.] 1966.

Prose Poems. [Ed. Roy A. Squires.] 1969–70. 4 vols.

The Horror in the Museum and Other Revisions. Ed. August Derleth. 1970, 1989 (ed. S. T. Joshi).

Hail, Klarkash-Ton! Being Nine Missives Inscribed upon Postcards to Clark Ashton Smith. [Ed. Roy A. Squires.] 1971.

E'ch-Pi-El Speaks: An Autobiographical Sketch. 1972.

Lovecraft at Last (with Willis Conover). 1975.

The Occult Lovecraft. Ed. Anthony Raven. 1975.

First Writings: Pawtuxet Valley Gleaner 1906. Ed. Marc A. Michaud. 1976.

The Conservative. Ed. Marc A. Michaud. 1976, 1977.

Writings in The United Amateur *1915–1925*. Ed. Marc A. Michaud. 1976.

To Quebec and the Stars. Ed. L. Sprague de Camp. 1976.

The Californian 1934–1938. Ed. Marc A. Michaud. 1977.

Writings in The Tryout. Ed. Marc A. Michaud. 1977.

A Winter Wish. Ed. Tom Collins. 1977.

Uncollected Prose and Poetry. Ed. S. T. Joshi and Marc A. Michaud. 1978–82. 3 vols.

Science Versus Charlatanry: Essays on Astrology (with J. F. Hartmann). Ed. S. T. Joshi and Scott Connors. 1979.

Juvenilia 1897–1905. Ed. S. T. Joshi. 1984.

Saturnalia and Other Poems. Ed. S. T. Joshi. 1984.

In Defence of Dagon. Ed. S. T. Joshi. 1985.

Uncollected Letters. Ed. S. T. Joshi. 1986.

Medusa and Other Poems. Ed. S. T. Joshi. 1986.

Commonplace Book. Ed. David E. Schultz. 1987. 2 vols.

European Glimpses. Ed. S. T. Joshi. 1988.

Yr Obt Servt: Some Postcards Sent to Wilfred Blanch Talman. Ed. R. Alain Everts. 1988.

The Vivisector. Ed. S. T. Joshi. 1990.

Letters to Henry Kuttner. Ed. David E. Schultz and S. T. Joshi. 1990.

The Fantastic Poetry. Ed. S. T. Joshi. 1990, 1993.

Letters to Richard F. Searight. Ed. David E. Schultz and S. T. Joshi. 1992.

Autobiographical Writings. Ed. S. T. Joshi. 1992.

Letters to Robert Bloch. Ed. David E. Schultz and S. T. Joshi. 1993.

Miscellaneous Writings. Ed. S. T. Joshi. 1995.

◈ ◈ ◈

Arthur Machen
1863–1947

ARTHUR MACHEN was born Arthur Llewelyn Jones at Caerleon-on-Usk, Wales, on March 3, 1863; he adopted his mother's maiden name in grade school. Fascinated from youth by the Roman ruins of Isca Silurum near his birthplace, Machen would later give them an important place in his novels and tales. He attended Hereford Cathedral School but failed the examination for the Royal College of Surgeons in 1880 and went to London as a tutor, cataloguer, and editor. Just before leaving Wales he privately printed the poem *Eleusinia* (1881) in an edition of one hundred copies; he later claimed that his systematic destruction of this early work left only two copies of the pamphlet in existence. In addition to translating the *Heptameron* of Marguerite of Narvarre (1886), Machen wrote the curious pseudophilosophi-cal treatise *The Anatomy of Tobacco* (1884) and the picaresque novel *The Chronicle of Clemendy* (1888). He married Amelia Hogg in 1887; she died in 1899. In 1903 he married Dorothie Purefoy Hudleston; they had a son, Hilary, and a daughter, Janet.

The death of his father in 1887 ensured Machen economic independence for the next decade and a half, and it was during this time that he not only produced the standard translation of Casanova's *Memoirs* (1894) but wrote the supernatural tales that would bring him immediate notoriety and ultimate fame: *The Great God Pan and The Inmost Light* (1894), *The Three Impostors* (1895), and *The House of Souls* (1906). These works—as well as the heavily autobiographical novels *The Hill of Dreams* (written 1895–97; published 1907) and *The Secret Glory* (written 1907; published 1922)—were con-demned as the outpourings of a diseased imagination; Machen gathered the early, and largely unfavorable, reviews of these works in *Precious Balms* (1924).

In 1901, his inheritance depleted, Machen was forced to seek employment. He worked as a bit player in Frank Benson's Repertory Company (1901–09) and wrote voluminously for newspapers and literary journals—including *Academy, London Evening News, T.P.'s Weekly, John O'London's Weekly,*

Independent, Daily Mail, and many others. He wrote relatively little fiction during this period, but one story, "The Bowmen" (1914)—about the ghosts of medieval English soldiers who rescue a beleaguered unit during World War I—was taken as a true account despite Machen's repeated protests to the contrary, gaining the author great but unwanted celebrity. Machen wrote three autobiographies during this period, *Far Off Things* (1922), *Things Near and Far* (1923), and *The London Adventure* (1924). A small amount of his journalism was collected in *Dog and Duck* (1924), *Notes and Queries* (1926), and in two olumes edited by Vincent Starrett, *The Shining Pyramid* (1923) and *The Glorious Mystery* (1924). Starrett played an influential role in introducing Machen to American readers, and Machen's work was very popular in the 1920s, thanks largely to the many reissues of his early volumes by Alfred A. Knopf.

By the late 1920s Machen had again fallen into poverty, but efforts by his friends secured him a Civil List pension of £100 a year. In 1929 Machen finally left the London that had exercised his imagination for fifty years, moving to Old Amersham in Buckinghamshire. He produced few notable works in his later years: the poorly received novel *The Green Round* (1933) and two collections of tales, *The Cosy Room* (1936) and *The Children of the Pool* (1936). Purefoy Machen died on March 30, 1947, and Arthur Machen died on December 15, 1947.

▨ *Critical Extracts*

UNSIGNED   If a man has a turn for carving gurgoyles one cannot fairly blame him for failing to produce pet lambs. We should be the last to dispute such a sound canon of criticism and have thoroughly enjoyed the brisk yet subtle shower of satire which Mr. Machen descends (in the preface to this collection of fantastic tales ⟨*The House of Souls*⟩) upon the shoulders of those who demand a pet lamb, as a serious, moral rallying point, and a profitable asset to boot, in the corner of every work of fiction. For all that, we cannot help feeling that he has put powers of imagination, on which he justly prides himself, to somewhat sinister uses. He is, in fact, more often than not obsessed by the gurgoylesque. He speaks somewhere of ages in which man lived in a world of mystery and love and adoration, when sacraments stood about all his ways, when the veil of the Temple grew there before his gaze and he saw the great sacrifice offered in the Holy Place; yet the atmosphere of the tales themselves is, except in one instance, wholly different, and the sacrifices therein are offered in the most unholy places. If "almost every page contains a hint (under varied images and symbols) of a belief in a world that is not of ordinary every-day experience, that in a measure transcends the experience of Bethel and the Bank," one is left with the impression that the world behind the veil, as dimly imagined here, is indescribably hideous and appalling.

Unsigned, [Review of *The House of Souls*], *Academy*, 11 August 1906, p. 136

JOSEPH WOOD KRUTCH   The horror which ⟨Machen⟩ would present is the horror of that unseen world which, for the mystic, surrounds the little spot of seeming light and seeming reality in which we dwell; it is the dissolving of the solid wall of actuality and the direct presence of the ultimate mystery; something so profoundly unnatural that, as one of the characters says, its evil affects one as a mathematician would be affected if he were brought suddenly face to face with a two-sided triangle—there is nothing left to do but go mad. All his villains are Fausts, taking supernal knowledge by storm; all his heroes Blakes, gazing mildly at the tree full of angels and harkening to the chant of the morning sun.

The Terror, though interesting in theme, is very markedly inferior to the other books ⟨*The House of Souls* and *The Secret Glory*⟩ in manner, for they reveal the fact that Mr. Machen is gifted with a very remarkable style, rich and colorful but always simple and clear. Yet though he is unmistakably an artist he has never enjoyed anything like popularity—except once when the unusual conditions at the time of the war gave a factitious interest to his tale, "The Bowmen"—his best work having been done in the nineties and he being as he has said "a past-master in the Lodge of Disappointment." Now, however, John Masefield, James Branch Cabell, and Carl Van Vechten are crying him from the housetops and Mr. Knopf is reprinting some of his works. Withal they are making something of a mystery out of his failure to win popularity, but actually there is no mystery at all, for by no possibility could the peculiar temperament which not merely underlies but is the very texture of his work win any wide acceptance. He belongs to the always small company of genuine mystics, and though his creed is superficially similar to that of Chesterton and Belloc he uses his position not primarily as a vantage point from which to shoot paradoxes but as a world into which to retire. He has only one theme, the Mystic Vision, and only one plot, the Rending of the Veil. In "The Great God Pan," one of the stories of *The House of Souls,* he does the Faust side of the theme so well that it renders the other stories of the volume unnecessary, and in *The Secret Glory* he does the other side even better; but beautifully as they are done they remain a thing of fairly limited appeal—stories by a mystic and for mystics.

Joseph Wood Krutch, "Tales of a Mystic," *Nation,* 13 September 1922, pp. 258–59

ARTHUR MACHEN   ⟨. . .⟩ I can now turn to the matter in hand: the writing of *Eleusinia.*

I was seventeen at the time; the year, 1880. I had left Hereford Cathedral School at the end of the Easter Term. I had spent most of the summer at Wandsworth and had seen London, then a rare and wonderful town. I had failed by reason of defective elementary arithmetic to pass the preliminary examination of the Royal College of Surgeons, and here I was at Llanddewi Rectory with nothing particular to do, and less to expect. I loafed about, wandering all over the country round Llanddewi, taking peculiar delight in turning into bridle-paths—narrow ways, with high hedges on each side— and following them till they brought me out into unknown country. I would go walking on and walking on, and the dusk fell and it grew dark, and I, with the vaguest notions of the lie of the land, would somehow find my way back to the Rectory and tell the story of my traffics and discoveries. And I wandered also in and out of the books in that unselected library which I have described elsewhere; and on the whole, I suppose, got the education, apart from the Humanities, which was most to my purpose.

I believe it was in November of that Autumn of 1880 that I set out one morning to walk to Newport; for no particular reason that I can remember. Probably, there had been a slight frost in the night; the day was shining and splendid, and there was a briskness in the air that made the walk—it would kill me now—go very well. I had climbed up the long hill from Llantarnam, and was on my way towards Malpas when I saw the mountain, from Twyn Barlwm to the heights above Pontypool, all a pure, radiant blue under a paler blue sky; and the sun shone on the farm houses and cottages of the mountain side, and made the whitewashed walls shine gloriously as if they were marble. I experienced an indescribable emotion; and I always attribute to that moment and to that emotion my impulse towards literature. For literature, as I see it, is the art of describing the indescribable; the art of exhibiting symbols which may hint at the ineffable mysteries behind them; the art of the veil, which reveals what it conceals. So, in the eighteenth century phrase, I commenced author; and began, with little delay, to write *Eleusinia*.

Arthur Machen, "Beneath the Barley: An Essay on the Origins of *Eleusinia*" (1931), *Eleusinia and Beneath the Barley* (West Warwick, RI: Necronomicon Press, 1991), n.p.

H. P. LOVECRAFT   I'd a great deal rather have Machen as he is than not have him at all! What Machen probably likes about perverted and forbidden things is their departure from and hostility to the commonplace. To him—whose imagination is not cosmic—they represent what Pegana and the River Yann represent to Dunsany, whose imagination *is* cosmic. People whose minds are—like Machen's—steeped in the orthodox myths of religion, naturally find a poignant fascination in the conception of things which religion brands with outlawry and horror. Such people take the artificial and obsolete concept of "sin" seriously, and find it full of dark allurement. On the other hand, people like myself, with a realistic and scientific point of view, see no charm or mystery whatever in things banned by religious mythology. We recognise the primitiveness and meaninglessness of the religious attitude, and in consequence find no element of attractive defiance or significant escape in those things which happen to contravene it. The whole idea of "sin", with its overtones of unholy fascination, is in 1932 simply a curiosity of intellectual history. The filth and perversion which to Machen's obsoletely orthodox mind meant profound defiances of the universe's foundations, mean to us only a rather prosaic and unfortunate species of organic maladjustment—no more frightful, and no more interest-ing, than a headache, a fit of colic, or an ulcer on the big toe. Now that the veil of mystery and the hokum of spiritual significance have been stripped away from such things, they are no longer adequate motivations for phantasy or fear-literature.

H. P. Lovecraft, Letter to Bernard Austin Dwyer (1932), *Selected Letters 1932–1934*, ed. August Derleth and James Turner (Sauk City, WI: Arkham House, 1976), p. 4

ROBERT HILLYER   On the surface, one might say that Machen's life was a failure. He never escaped from the poverty that had dogged him since his birth as the son of a High Church clergyman in Wales. The magic which he found in the Roman ruins and prehistoric mounds, the domed hills and strange forests, of his homeland, and all the mystery of the Holy Grail, he summoned into words with as much devotion and skill and industry as an artist could muster, but the profits of an uncongenial age eluded him. He attempted to compromise, to write potboilers, but only succeeded in mystifying his audience. In some cases he was the victim of plain bad luck. For example, some years ago he published an account of Elizabeth Canning, the heroine of a famous kidnaping (or else a tremendous hoax) of the eighteenth century. The work fell flat. Yet in 1945 a book on Elizabeth Canning (and a very good book) by another author was among the season's successes. And so it went with him even during that brief period when collectors were paying hundreds of dollars for his first editions—from which he derived nothing.

But he was never daunted. He regarded life with a mixture of awe and high good humor, and had a penetrating sense of proportion. After describing a strange and mystical experience that had happened to him and changed the whole current of his life, he broke off suddenly: "Of course, that was important, but I consider an act of mercy to a homeless kitten far more so."

He had the power of investing his world with excitement and of communicating it. One day we were passing a large field which was public land—or, as the expression is, "Crown land." "This tract," said Machen, gesturing expansively with his pipe, "belongs to our dread Sovereign Lord, the King." One expected Majesty to make an appearance in person,—not the then reigning monarch, George V, clad in country tweeds, but some magnificent personage out of the Middle Ages, in ermines and silks and with a golden crown on his head.

In Machen's presence one saw the landscape under the enchanted light of another age. The ruins of St. Margaret's and Manorbier Castle rekindled with the glories of their ancient pride. One eagerly explored St. David's Cathedral in search of the little altar which, according to Machen, was in truth the Holy Grail. Perhaps he did fail to summon all this into his pages for the benefit of the common reader, but he lived in it, and when I was with him I lived in it, too. He could change ginger beer into nectar, and Australian Burgundy into Château d'Yquem.

Robert Hillyer, "Arthur Machen," *Atlantic Monthly* 179, No. 5 (May 1947): 139

ROBERT L. TYLER   What makes Machen a minor writer was his inability to transcend his own situation, either artistically or intellectually. This judgment can be sustained by examining his mysticism and by observing how it actually weakened his fiction. Ironically, Machen was as much of a "message" novelist as the non-ecstatic sort he excoriated in his essay on criticism ⟨Hieroglyphics⟩. However hard he tried to weave his charged symbols and his "style" into an autonomous work of art, he never really succeeded. The stories and The Hill of Dreams remain curious machines to lead the reader to Machen's metaphysical position. At best his works become covert, but nonetheless, discursive arguments. Moreover, when the argument becomes explicit, as in Hieroglyphics, it ends with a frank admission of failure, an admission all mystics in an argument must honestly make. After all, ineffable means inexpressible. Machen accepted more than he knew the "rationalist" or "materialist" culture he so railed against, accepted it in a deeper sense than was easily recognizable. He accepted, for example, the form of its semantic, its conviction that words and symbols were tools with simple referents. So, for Machen, Art with its difficult reference to the immediate and unique inner life of man had perforce to refer either to the road and the street or to some other form of reality.

What makes Machen an interesting and significant writer, even though minor, are his near misses. He did at least resist the "positivism" of his age, that intellectual pride which would have lost art completely in the evolution of the species, the class struggle, economic progress, or some equally abstract and non-existential criterion of value. In his stubbornness he produced several curious, individual books worth the sampling of the inveterate book lover. Machen is a poignant figure, a writer of great dedication who held his lantern up boldly in the dark, though in slightly the wrong place.

Robert L. Tyler, "Arthur Machen: The Minor Writer and His Function," Approach No. 35 (Spring 1960): 25—26

WESLEY D. SWEETSER   The most typical of the weird facets of his work and the most distinctive are the constantly recurring themes which he obtained from the living folklore of Wales: dwarfish, wizened, and malignant fairies; the unintelligible languages and speaking with tongues; transformations and transmigrations; and the hint of cannibalistic rites among the Little People. This aspect of Machen's work is most uniquely his own. He has turned local color into symbols of universal meaning and application. His work in this field differed in two respects from that of his predecessors: first, in the use of Celtic legend; second, in the de-emphasizing of physical manifestations of terror in favor of the psychical. The real impact of his tales of horror and the supernatural lies not in their sensational effect but in their transcendental significance. The net result is a humanistic study of the nature of good and evil.

Commenting on *Brave New World*, Machen said that a world without evil would be an unspeakably awful place. His early studies of diabolism and Black Magic suggest that he believed evil to be latent in man and to be held in check only by the moral force; but his evil is always something more vague and terrible than mere earthly transgression. Evil he considered to be that which is completely contrary to the natural order of things, such as a talking dog or animate furniture. Sanctity he considered as the realization of the perfection that was before the Fall, the recovery of the Lost World, the attainment of the Graal. Certainly he believed that evil is a necessary concomitant to good and that life offers only intimations and hints as to the true nature of both. In other words, Machen was not concerned with the acts of giving candy to children or of cohabiting with prostitutes. His purpose both as an artist and a humanist was to discover, behind the ordinary, the extraordinary and transcendental meaning. Primarily, he was concerned with matters of the soul, with the essence of man, with the paradise lost and never regained, and with the great errantry.

Wesley D. Sweetser, *Arthur Machen* (New York: Twayne, 1964), pp. 131–32

PATRICIA MERIVALE   Stripped of its two dozen supernumerary characters, and with the mystery pursued through eight chapters at last elucidated, the story 〈"The Great God Pan"〉 is simply of the conception, birth, life, and death of a female creature who is the daughter of the God Pan and is his embodiment upon earth. The activities of her life, and thus the events of the story, consist largely of leading others to their death of terror, by forcing or persuading them to look upon Pan; at last her own death restores the normal balance of life.

The plot depends for its horror upon two basic themes. One is that the sight of Pan is so terrifying that it must result in death, or, at best, insanity. 〈. . .〉 The other theme is that of an unholy rape: "I was shown a small square pillar of white stone, which had been recently discovered in the wood [where Helen's childhood had been spent] . . . The inscription is as follows: 'To the great god Nodens (the god of the Great Deep or Abyss) Flavius Senilis has erected this pillar on account of the marriage which he saw beneath the shade.' " The "marriage," it is implied, is the unholy and enforced union of the goat-god and a human woman, which took place in Roman Britain even as in modern Wales. ⟨. . .⟩

Vaguely described as are Pan's two "actions" of rape and murder (Machen's probable sources give more concrete details than he does), Machen is vaguer yet about Pan's physical attributes, leaving the reader to supply them from his own knowledge. There is, however, a felicitous contrast of habitat in which Pan may be worshiped: "the vineyards and the olive gardens," and the "dim London streets"; and the Welsh countryside blurs into a Greek landscape for Clarke's vision of Pan: "The beech alley was transformed to a path beneath ilex-trees."

Like several later writers, Machen is determined that Pan should not only "be but mean," and Pan means "all things mingled, the form of all things but devoid of all form." Machen may well have had available many more occultly neo-Platonic sources than the works of Emerson for this Pan, but the "eternal Pan / Who . . . Halteth never in one shape" of "Woodnotes II" provides one possible analogue, and "The Natural History of Intellect" provides another: "he was only seen under disguises, and was not represented by any outward image." Machen invites the comparison by calling the branch of science that makes possible Mary's vision "transcendental medicine."

A visible world which is only "dreams and shadows," hiding the real world somewhere beyond, does not lend itself to the description of a solid and visualized Pan; like Emerson's, Machen's Pan is too Protean, and the effect of terror is diminished accordingly. When "Human flesh may become the veil of a horror one dare not express," the inexpressible is likely to remain the unconveyed; when "that which is without form [takes] to itself a form," its incarnation should be more memorably appropriate than is "Helen."

We have seen that the consequences of such a mystic vision are disastrous to the mortal soul and frame, and whatever the moral status of the "real world" may be, the vision of it is purely evil. If Machen's notion of Pan as transcendental resembles Emerson's, his notion of the horror of Pan is more like Swinburne's in "A Nympholept": "If I live, and the life that may look on him drop not dead . . . / Yet man should fear lest he see what of old

men saw / And withered." He was, like Machen, shudderingly vague, though
more succinct, about what happened when one saw Pan. Machen's answer,
or that of his characters, to Swinburne's question "Is it rapture or terror
that circles me round?" is that first there is rapture, which is swiftly glossed
over, and then there is terror, which matters far more. Swinburne is concerned with the paradox of apparently contradictory emotions, the rapture
of terror; Machen uses the other emotions simply to counterpoint terror.
> Patricia Merivale, *Pan the Goat-God: His Myth in Modern Times* (Cambridge, MA:
> Harvard University Press, 1969), pp. 161–62, 164–66

ANDY SAWYER   *The Hill of Dreams* is not fantasy as such, although
it is possible to read it so. Machen's prose shifts from one order of reality
to another; Lucian's self-created garden of Avallaunius is shown as real, as
tangible as the ordinary world he inhabits. ⟨. . .⟩

The last chapter of the book, as powerful and mysterious a piece of prose
as anything Machen ever wrote, is full of dark Satanic images which weave
in and out from Lucian's consciousness. Yet the book's real power doesn't
lie in its imagery but in the picture it gives of the problem of the artist in
the last few years of the nineteenth century when the decadents revolted
against the self-satisfied bourgeoisie. (I must stress that these labels depict
tendencies merely: many artists who themselves would have strenuously
denied any connection with the movement dubbed "the decadents" were
well aware of a gulf between themselves and a society whose values they
could not accept.) Art was something far from the common round of making
a living. "Art and Life are two different spheres," wrote Machen (*Hieroglyphics*). Lucian Taylor concludes "books should not be written with the object
of gaining the goodwill of the landed and commercial interests."

If the mundane world was not a fit subject for art, what was? Significantly,
many artists turned to fantasy to resolve this conflict; at least in fantasy
values could be portrayed as they *should* be. In practice, different artists
resolved the problem (or failed to do so) in different ways. We all know
the fate of Oscar Wilde. William Morris allied himself to Socialism, and
focused on the future rather than the past—although anyone taking a cursory
glance at his novels would perhaps be forgiven for thinking otherwise. The
fantasy of Lord Dunsany, perhaps the best fantasist of the period, is shot
through and through with a melancholy alienation, cushioned, though, by

his aristocratic background and conventional Etonian unconventionality—
hence, perhaps, his reservations about the "unwholesome" side of Machen
(introduction to The Hill of Dreams, The Richards Press, 1954).

Machen himself, forced to struggle against poverty, against artistic neglect,
against an easy ability to write, clung as so many from his kind of shabby-
genteel background would to high aristocratic values—Catholicism, anti-
democracy, mysticism—as his lifeline. I do not share these values, yet like
so many avowedly "reactionary" writers—Thomas Nashe in Elizabethan
times, George Borrow in the mid-nineteenth century—his writing attracts
me. It is as if, like these other writers, the whole current of Machen's time
and circumstances rubbed up against him, keeping him throwing off literature
like sparks from amber.

The Hill of Dreams is for me an extremely painful book to read. Whereas
much of Machen's work is flawed, and much of his literary theory is gloriously
(I used the word deliberately) wrong-headed, The Hill of Dreams distils the
best part of his writing—that sense of the numinous on the other side of
the veil—and fuses it with a deeply personal tragedy. A minor classic? Yes,
I think so.

Andy Sawyer, "The Court of Avallaunius," Arthur Machen: Apostle of Wonder, ed.
Mark Valentine and Roger Dobson (Oxford: Caermaen Books, 1985), pp. 50–52

ROGER DOBSON   As Wilde might have observed, Ornaments in
Jade, following a biblical precedent, begins in a garden and ends with
revelations. Surely it was no accident that Machen designed the collection
to conclude with "The Holy Things", that splendid encapsulation of everything he strove to express in his sixty-year literary odyssey. Besides being
an affirmation of his beliefs, "The Holy Things" strikes a curiously prophetic
note. It seems to predict the annus mirabilis which, paradoxically, Machen
experienced after the great sorrow caused by the death of his first wife Amy
in 1899. Inexplicable phenomena confronted him in the most mundane of
London streets: the pavement of Rosebery Avenue seemed transmuted into
air; "the odours of rare gums . . . seemed to fume before invisible altars in
Holborn, in Claremont Square, in grey streets of Clerkenwell" (Things Near
and Far); the walls of 4 Verulam Buildings, Gray's Inn, trembled before
his eyes; and certain people began to resemble characters from The Three
Impostors. Life, Machen found, had taken a very mysterious turn indeed.

When we meet him, the protagonist of "The Holy Things"—an artist of some kind, though Machen is intentionally vague about the works which issue from his hand—is sick at heart. Life seems arid and without purpose. Even the beauty of existence, represented by the summer light playing on the houses in the distance, transmuting the commonplace vista of a London street into "a rich tabernacle, mysterious, the carven house of holy things", fails to move him.

The uplifting of his spirit is masterfully foreshadowed: the music of the barrel organ, the costermonger's shout, the jangling bell of a bicycle, the smoke of the lamplighter's ribbon, and the golden sunlight are harbingers of the grace to come, heralding, in turn, the church organ, the choir's anthem, the holy bell, the fragrant incense, and the angelic shapes. At first the artist is blind to all this: "He had viewed the scene hundreds of times, and for a long while had found it a nuisance and a weariness." Thus do we see daily the miraculous procession of life—the Grail carried before us, Machen would say—and account it nothing.

Yet in the depth of the man's despair the world assumes new meaning, for he experiences a supernal vision. He hears the notes of a triumphant organ, an invisible choir begins to sing, and commercial and prosaic Holborn becomes as the nave of a mighty church. He is summoned to participate in a solemn and awesome ceremony. ⟨. . .⟩ Like Edward Darnell in *A Fragment of Life*, the artist realises that "man is made a mystery for mysteries and visions", that ineffable glory surrounds him if he but lift his head. Yet is the revelation granted to the artist merely illusory, just as Lucian Taylor's golden city of Isca Silurum in *The Hill of Dreams* is an illusion created from misery and loneliness (an imaginary fantasy which gives Lucian kinship with Machen's beloved Don Quixote)? Is there a hint of irony in the words "He could not be mistaken, he was sure now"? The matter is not pursued, perhaps because Machen is hinting that although under a sensory delusion the artist has gained understanding of the true nature of the universe. "The Holy Things" may be a fantastic tale, but its symbolism, insofar as Machen was concerned, represents the truth; for the author the "Shining Mysteries" were no fable.

Roger Dobson, "Chronicles of Secret Lives," *Machenalia*, ed. R. B. Russell (Lewes, UK: Tartarus Press, 1990), Vol. 2, pp. 11–13

S. T. JOSHI   It is worth discussing the short novel *A Fragment of Life* here since, although it was written after *The Hill of Dreams*, it carries on the sense of ecstasy in common things that typifies *Ornaments in Jade*. Some passages in the autobiographies are helpful in showing Machen's change of direction from horror to awe and wonder. Of "The Great God Pan" he remarks: "Here . . . was my real failure; I translated awe, at worst awfulness, into evil" (*Far Off Things*). Elsewhere we find what is the real heart of the story: "And it is utterly true that he who cannot find wonder, mystery, awe, the sense of a new world and an undiscovered realm in the places by the Gray's Inn Road will never find those secrets elsewhere, not in the heart of Africa, not in the fabled hidden cities of Tibet." This remark is important not only because it relieves Machen of the charge of empty escapism in his notion of ecstasy as a "withdrawal from the common life" (which, it is now evident, really means a penetration through the ordinariness of daily existence to the spiritual realities beyond), but because it captures the essence of Machen's whole world view. And yet this would scarcely seem to be what is going on in the novel as we read its opening pages. In this story of Edward Darnell, an ordinary city clerk, and his wife we might—but for the British setting—imagine that we have stumbled into a social novel by Edith Wharton or Louis Auchincloss. But the very ordinariness of their lives—spent discussing the furnishing of the spare room, the reception of guests, the monotonous coming and going to and from work—is vital to establish the fact that, "day after day, [Darnell] lived in the grey phantasmal world, akin to death, that has, somehow, with most of us, made good its claim to be called life." To be sure, Darnell—and still more his wife—are (as we must call them in our post-Freudian age) repressed. Not merely sexually repressed, they are repressed in their very inability to communicate to each other—or even to realize clearly to themselves—their love, their awe, their ecstasy. The material world has crushed them—socially, financially, emotionally; as Machen says poignantly in another context, "It was all a very small life."

But as the novel progresses Darnell imperceptibly begins to step back and realize the vacuity of this stolid material existence; he hears the call of his Welsh heritage, and at the end he and his wife return to a fuller life in Wales. But the alteration is more than that of mere scenery: through his new vision of the world even prosy London is transformed:

> London seemed a city of the Arabian Nights, and its labyrinths of streets an enchanted maze; its long avenues of lighted lamps were as starry systems, and its immensity became for him an image of

the endless universe. He could well imagine how pleasant it might be to linger in such a world as this, to sit apart and dream, beholding the strange pageant played before him, but the Sacred Well was not for common use, it was for the cleansing of the soul, and the healing of the grievous wounds of the spirit. There must be yet another transformation: London had become Bagdad; it must at last be transmuted to Syon, or in the phrase of one of his old documents, the City of the Cup.

But the miracle of this novel is its absolute seamlessness: it is impossible to tell when or how this transition in Darnell has occurred; he can simply conclude that he was "filled with the thought of that far-off summer day, when some enchantment had informed all common things, transmuting them into a great sacrament, causing earthly works to glow with the fire and the glory of the everlasting light." This is the Machen we love and admire: the writer who can invest the ordinary with a sense of numinous wonder. We know that the material world was for Machen only the crude symbol for something greater; and he has never more flawlessly realized that conception than in A Fragment of Life. Without the least violence in diction or incident, it is as violent a condemnation of late Victorian social constraints as The Way of All Flesh; and I suspect, too, that Machen with this work was wanting to show his contemporaries how a real "social novel" should be written. But, more than mere social satire or literary polemic, A Fragment of Life strives to awaken us all to the beauty and mystery of things. It is Machen's most finished and satisfying work.

S. T. Joshi, "Arthur Machen: The Mystery of the Universe," The Weird Tale (Austin: University of Texas Press, 1990), pp. 27–29

Bibliography

Eleusinia. 1881.

The Anatomy of Tobacco; or, Smoking Methodised, Divided, and Considered After a New Fashion. 1884.

The Heptameron or Tales and Novels of Marguerite Queen of Navarre (translator). 1886.

A Chapter from the Book Called The Ingenious Gentleman Don Quijote de la Mancha Which by Some Chance Has Not Till Now Been Printed. 1887.

The Chronicle of Clemendy. 1888.

Thesaurus Incantatus. 1888.

Fantastic Tales or the Way to Attain by Beroalde de Verville (translator). 1889,
      1890.

The Memoirs of Jacques Casanova (translator). 1894. 12 vols.

The Great God Pan and The Inmost Light. 1894.

The Three Impostors; or, The Transmutations. 1895.

Hieroglyphics: A Note upon Ecstasy in Literature. 1902.

The House of the Hidden Light (with A. E. Waite). 1904.

The House of Souls. 1906.

Dr. Stiggins: His Views and Principles. 1906.

The Hill of Dreams. 1907.

"Parsifal": The Story of the Holy Graal. c. 1913.

The Angels of Mons: The Bowmen and Other Legends of the War. 1915.

The Great Return. 1915.

The Terror. 1917.

War and the Christian Faith. 1918.

The Pantomime of the Year. 1921.

The Secret Glory. 1922.

Far Off Things. 1922.

Things Near and Far. 1923.

The Grand Trouvaille: A Legend of Pentonville. 1923.

The Shining Pyramid. Ed. Vincent Starrett. 1923.

The Collector's Craft. 1923.

Works (Caerleon Edition). 1923. 9 vols.

Strange Roads ⟨and With the Gods in Spring⟩. 1923.

Dog and Duck. 1924.

The London Adventure; or, The Art of Wandering. 1924.

The Glorious Mystery. Ed. Vincent Starrett. 1924.

Precious Balms. 1924.

Ornaments in Jade. 1924.

The Shining Pyramid. 1925.

A Preface to Casanova's Escape from the Leads. 1925.

The Canning Wonder. 1925.

Dreads and Drolls. 1926.

Notes and Queries. 1926.

A Souvenir of Cadby Hall. 1927.

A Fragment of Life. 1928.

Parish of Amersham. 1930.

Tom O'Bedlam and His Song. 1930.

Beneath the Barley: A Note on the Origins of Eleusinia. 1931.

In the 'Eighties: A Reminiscence of the Silurist. 1931.

An Introduction to John Gawsworth's Above the River. 1931.

A Few Letters. 1932.

The Glitter of the Brook. 1932.

Remarks upon Hermodactylus by Lady Hester Lucy Stanhope (translator). 1933.

The Green Round. 1933.

The Cosy Room and Other Stories. 1936.

The Children of the Pool and Other Stories. 1936.

The Awful Conjunction. 1938.

The Great God Pan and Other Weird Tales. 1943.

Holy Terrors. 1946.

Tales of Horror and the Supernatural. 1948.

Bridles and Spurs. 1951.

A Critical Essay: His Thoughts on A Bookman's Diary *by Sir J. A. Hammerton*. 1953.

A.L.S.: An Unimportant Exchange of Letters between Arthur Machen and J. H. Stewart, Jr. 1956.

A Receipt for Fine Prose. 1956.

A Note on Poetry. 1959.

From the London Evening News. 1959.

The Strange World of Arthur Machen. 1960.

Guinevere and Lancelot and Others. Ed. Michael T. Shoemaker and Cuyler W. Brooks, Jr. 1986.

Selected Letters. Ed. Roger Dobson, Godfrey Brangham, and R. A. Gilbert. 1988.

Chapters Five and Six of The Secret Glory. Ed. R. B. Russell. 1992.

Ritual and Other Stories. Ed. R. B. Russell. 1992.

Rus in Urbe and Other Pieces. Ed. R. B. Russell. 1992.

Arthur Machen & Montgomery Evans: Letters of a Literary Friendship 1923–1947. Ed. Sue Strong Hassler and Donald M. Hassler. 1994.

The Secret of the Sangraal. Ed. R. B. Russell. 1995.

Richard Matheson
b. 1926

RICHARD BURTON MATHESON was born on February 20, 1926, in Allendale, New Jersey. His family moved to Brooklyn when he was three, where his parents, Bertolf and Fanny (Mathiesen) Matheson, eventually separated; he was raised by his mother and older sister. The insularity of his family—a close-knit group of Norwegian immigrants—and the Christian Science faith embraced by his mother made him a withdrawn and introspective child.

Matheson began reading at an early age and discovered fantasy through books and films when he was eight. By the time he was nine he had stories and poems published in local newspapers. He studied structural engineering at Brooklyn Technical High School and upon graduating in 1943 enlisted in an army training program in engineering. When the program ended in 1944 he was put in the infantry and saw action during World War II. Wounded in combat, he was discharged and upon returning to the United States enrolled at the University of Missouri, where he graduated with a B.A. in journalism in 1949.

While still trying to decide whether to pursue a career in writing or music, Matheson sold his first story, "Born of Man and Woman," to the *Magazine of Fantasy and Science Fiction* in 1950. Although he had not consciously tailored the story to fit the science fiction market, it was hailed by readers as a science fiction classic that captured the anxieties of the dawning nuclear age. Eventually it became the title story of his first collection, published in 1954. Stories that followed earned Matheson the reputation of a writer whose spare, natural style lent itself to explorations of the dark side of the ordinary and everyday.

Shortly afterward Matheson moved to California, where he wrote short fiction during his spare time while working as a machine operator at Douglas Aircraft and trying to break into screenwriting for the movies. Through his friend William Campbell Gault he was introduced to the Fictioneers, a group composed primarily of mystery writers, and began writing mystery novels of his own.

Matheson also made the acquaintance of Ray Bradbury, Charles Beaumont, William F. Nolan, and George Clayton Johnson, all of whom strongly influenced his decision to concentrate on writing fantasy and horror fiction. *I Am Legend*, a tale of the last mortal in a postapocalyptic world ruled by vampires, appeared in 1954; it was filmed as *The Omega Man* in 1971. In 1956 Matheson published *The Shrinking Man*, about a man who begins shrinking following a toxic exposure. In their portrayal of men alone struggling to survive in a hostile world, these novels crystallized a theme that underlies all his writing. *A Stir of Echoes* (1958), the story of a man endowed with psychic powers he is ill-equipped to handle, introduced another of Matheson's favorite motifs, the paranormal; in later books such as *Hell House* (1971), *What Dreams May Come* (1978), and *Earthbound* (1989), this theme yielded metaphysical speculations on the afterlife.

Matheson's screen adaptation of *The Shrinking Man* (as *The Incredible Shrinking Man*) in 1957 gave him his entrée to Hollywood. He began writing teleplays for Western, detective, and military series, and in 1959 he became one of the major scriptwriters for Rod Serling's "The Twilight Zone." To support his wife Ruth Ann Woodson, whom he had married in 1952, and his four children, Matheson concentrated on screenwriting and adapting his short stories to television and film throughout the 1960s and 1970s. His best short stories were collected in *Shock!* (1961), *Shock II* (1964), *Shock III* (1966), and *Shock Waves* (1970), but in 1970 he ceased writing short fiction and, except for an occasional effort such as the World Fantasy Award–winning *Bid Time Return* (1975), his output as a novelist slowed to a trickle until the 1990s, when he returned to writing fiction regularly with a series of Western novels based on undeveloped screen treatments.

Matheson's *Collected Stories* appeared in 1989. He is a recipient of lifetime achievement awards from the World Fantasy Convention and the Horror Writers of America. His literary and extraliterary efforts have been acknowledged as important influences on Stephen King, George Romero, and other leaders of the contemporary horror movement. His son Richard Christian Matheson has also become an accomplished writer of short stories and novels in the horror and science fiction fields.

◈ Critical Extracts

ROBERT BLOCH   Whether writing in the first person, as a child
in "Dress of White Silk," or in the third, as in "Third from the Sun,"
Matheson gets *closer* to his characters than anyone in the field of fantasy
today.

The result is important from the reader's point of view. You don't *read* a
Matheson story—you *experience* it. You get inside those tortured, tormented,
twisted people and writhe with them and for them. Try "Madhouse," for
example, and see if you don't feel the mounting tension, the rage born of
frustration, the hallucinatory horror of a persecution complex *in extremis*.
This, I submit, is a considerable achievement.

"Dear Diary," in a few short pages, utilizes this ability to adopt another's
viewpoint and deftly encapsulate a volume of psycho-sociological commentary; a feat of compression apparently denied the current school of "realistic"
writers who must perforce drag their readers for hundreds of pages through
a neon wilderness in order to hint at what Matheson reveals in less than
1500 words.

But Matheson is not a "trick" writer. Pick up "Lover When You're Near
Me" and read it through. That's not as easy as it sounds. It can be a shattering
emotional experience. Matheson is utterly ruthless; he does not spare his
characters, nor himself, nor the reader. All three go through hell—and he
has created a genuine hell in this story.

"Genuine" is probably a key word to remember in dealing with his work.
It's the absolute honesty that comes through and makes his stories believable.
A theme generally considered "taboo" takes on stature and significance in
the hands of a creative artist, and Matheson has worked with such themes
not once but a number of times. Always the result is a tale that transcends
the routine products of the genre. "The Traveller" is such a story. It is my
belief that the average reader will either ecstatically embrace or violently
reject it—but it is my further belief that *no* reader will ever *forget* this tale.

Robert Bloch, "The Art of Richard Matheson," *Born of Man and Woman* by Richard
Matheson (Philadelphia: Chamberlain Press, 1954), pp. 12–13

ROBERT FRAZIER   Matheson's unusual empathy enables him to
create a wide range of characters all the way from humdrum, frustrated

humans to the wildest monsters of interplanetary nightmares. His style is
versatile. He writes delightfully in the simple narration of an innocent child
or deftly in the second person. Constantly he strives to deviate from the
orthodox. Sometimes he attempts to repeat his most successful ideas from
a new angle. That is why, as a rule, one would prefer not to read too many
of Matheson's stories at one sitting. Matheson is definitely en route, swiftly
and surely, but he has not arrived quite yet. He is certainly a recognized
talent with a little more punch and finish and originality than most in the
field.

> Robert Frazier, [Review of *Born of Man and Woman*], *Fantastic Universe* 2, No. 2
> (September 1954): 126–27

GROFF CONKLIN   For what I think is Gold Medal's first venture
into the field of original science fantasies, it has chosen a weird, and I fear
rather slow-moving first novel by a man heretofore known for his excellent
short horror tales.

I Am Legend tells of a disease that almost completely wipes out the human
race, leaving behind only a handful of hideously changed creatures to attempt
to revive civilization.

It is "supernatural" science fiction, a horrid, violent, sometimes exciting
but often too overdone tour de force.

> Groff Conklin, [Review of *I Am Legend*], *Galaxy* 9, No. 4 (January 1955): 121

DAMON KNIGHT   Richard Matheson is a prim young man whose
talent is usually submerged in an indiscriminate creative gush. Like most
of his generation (as Algis Budrys points out in a recent article), he has no
sense of plot; in each story he puts together a situation, carries it around
in circles until he gets tired, then introduces some small variation and
hopefully carries it around some more, like a man bemused in a revolving
door. His stories sometimes reach their goal by this process, but only, as a
rule, when there is no other possible direction for the story to take; more
often they wind up nowhere, and Matheson has to patch on irrelevant
endings to get rid of them. "Blood Son," "Trespass" and "The Curious
Child" are botches of this kind. Other, slighter stories such as "The Funeral,"

"Clothes Make the Man" and "The Doll That Does Everything" are almost as weak, but are saved by Matheson's impudence.

Except for whimsy, Matheson's dramas are all domestic, not to say banal, and their hero is almost always Matheson himself. He has a profound interest in the trivia of his daily life and in his own uninspired conversation, which he reproduces without irony. (" 'Oh, my God, it's hot. . . . It's your imagination . . . It's not hot . . . It's cool. As a cucumber.' 'Ha . . . What a month for driving . . . I'm done on one side. Turn me,' " and so on, and so on.) At its best, by sheer honesty and intensity of emotion, this kind of thing turns into art, as in "The Test," Matheson's harrowing story of an old man losing his grip on life. "Steel," although it is built on a creaking sports-pulp plot and an even creakier set of robots, achieves tragic stature.

At its worst, Matheson's bare natural style, with its corner-drugstore vocabulary and inflections, is thin and dull. Apparently realizing this, he makes frequent efforts to jazz it up; I would lay odds that he owns and uses a thesaurus. He cultivates George Meredith's "he said" avoidances: "the little man asided," "Marion sotto voiced," "he dulceted." He has a sure touch for the gaudy solecism ("Another right concaved his stomach"; "The Count bicarbonated"), for the unnecessary word ("unwanted garbage"), and for unconscious anatomical humor ⟨. . .⟩

Like many another talented writer, Matheson got into this field more or less by accident, found that it paid, and never bothered to learn its basic techniques. It's hard to know whether to be more grateful to him for minor masterpieces like "The Test" and "The Last Day," or more annoyed by the piles of trash he has left us to wade in.

Damon Knight, [Review of *The Shores of Space*], *Infinity* 2, No. 4 (July 1957): 97–98

P. SCHUYLER MILLER   The author's macabre sense of humor and his ability to twist familiar situations into grim parodies of themselves have probably helped keep him busy scripting Hollywood shiver-shows like the alleged version of Poe's "The Pit and the Pendulum." Most of the stories in this lot ⟨*Shock!*⟩ come from *Playboy*, *Fantasy & Science Fiction*, and *Galaxy*—which had one out-and-out weirdy, "Long Distance Call," under the name "Sorry, Right Number."

The one really outstanding story in the book is "Dance of the Dead." We see a somewhat sheltered teen-age girl out with more sophisticated friends, watching a "loopy" dance—one of the living undead who have survived the next annihilation. Look around you for the seeds and feel your bowels crawl: this is, in a way, the counterpart of "sick" humor. So are two or three other stories, which can be taken as a "straight" portrayal of psychopathic distortion, very much like Ray Bradbury but more brutal. "The Distributor," for example, is the little man who deliberately goads a quiet neighborhood into murderous, insane frenzy. It's his job. In "Legion of Plotters" a paranoid goes over the edge and strikes back at the persecutors all around him. And haven't you longed to do just as he does? Then there's "The Holiday Man" who experiences every death and maiming in the holiday traffic toll, so that the morning's reports will be accurate.

There are comedies here, too, but comedy with a death's head behind the clown mask. "The Creeping Terror"—in which Los Angeles becomes openly alive and engulfs the world. "One for the Books," in which a janitor suddenly finds himself absorbing all sorts of knowledge—for someone else. "Montage"—fantasy, if you like—in which a man lives like a screen treatment. "The Splendid Source"—not grim, for a change—which explains where the great dirty jokes come from.

What else? "The Children of Noah", if it's set in our time, is just growing horror; if it's supposed to be in the future, call it a kind of technical S-F. "Lemmings," very brief, very effective, totally unexplained, brings mankind to its end. "Long Distance Call" is straight horror with a supernatural ending; "Death Ship" has an interplanetary setting but is also supernatural. "The Edge" is the *doppelgänger* theme again, professional but minor.

P. Schuyler Miller, [Review of *Shock!*], *Analog Science Fact/Science Fiction* 69, No. 1 (March 1962): 168–69

JAMES BLISH   Malignancy is not only present in the Matheson novel, but its subject, for the Hell House of the title is haunted by its dead owner, an entirely evil man who had used the place during his lifetime as a Hell Fire Club. The leading character, a physicist who thinks all psychological phenomena are essentially electromagnetic (this appears to be Matheson's theory too, though there is massive evidence against it), has been hired to spend a week in the house by a millionaire who is hoping for evidence that there is an afterlife. Other members of the party are the physicist's wife, a

Spiritualist medium, and a man who is the sole survivor of a previous nine-man investigating team.

Subsequent events are suitably spooky, not to say bloody, and fatal to two of the four. This is a Gothic novel in the old-fashioned, *Castle of Otranto* sense, in which terror is piled upon marvel upon terror until the reader, depending upon his degree of susceptibility to such goings-on, is either paralyzed with fright or bursts out laughing. I found myself suspended somewhere in the middle: I didn't believe a word of it, but the story is in its way quite as well crafted as del Rey's ⟨*Pstalemate*⟩, and has imbedded in it an intellectual puzzle of considerable complexity, the well-concealed answer to which simultaneously involves several other major mysteries. The characters don't run very deep, but in this kind of story there's no special reason why they need to, and at least they're all clear-cut individuals. Even the ghosts have an interesting psychological twist.

James Blish, [Review of *Hell House*], *Magazine of Fantasy and Science Fiction* 45, No. 1 (July 1972): 61–62

STEPHEN KING   Horror fiction, as we've said before, is one small circular area in the larger circle of fantasy, and what is fantasy fiction but tales of magic? And what are tales of magic but stories of power? One word nearly defines the other. Power is magic; power is potency. The opposite of potency is impotence, and impotence is the loss of magic. There is no impotence in the stories of the sword and sorcery genre, nor in those stories of Batman and Superman and Captain Marvel which we read as children and then—hopefully—which we gave up as we moved on to more challenging literature and wider views of what the life experience really is. The great theme of fantasy fiction is not holding the magic and wielding it (if so Sauron, not Frodo, would have been the hero of Tolkien's Rings cycle); it is—or so it seems to me—finding the magic and discovering how it works.

And getting back to the Matheson novel ⟨*The Shrinking Man*⟩, shrinking itself is an oddly arresting concept, isn't it? Tons of symbolism come immediately to mind, most of it revolving around the potency/impotency thing . . . sexual and otherwise. In Matheson's book, shrinking is most important because Scott Carey begins by perceiving size as power, as potency . . . size as magic. When he begins to shrink, he begins to lose all three—or so he believes until his perceptions change. His reaction to his loss of power, potency, and magic is most commonly a blind, bellowing rage:

> "What do you think I'm going to do?" he burst out. "Go on letting them *play* with me? Oh, you haven't *been* there, you haven't *seen*. They're like kids with a new toy. A shrinking man. Godawmighty, a shrinking man! It makes their damn eyes light up . . ."

Like Thomas Covenant's cries of "By hell!" in the Donaldson trilogy, Scott's rage does not hide his impotency but highlights it, and it is Scott's fury which in a large part makes him an interesting, believable character. He is not Conan or Superman (Scott bleeds plenty before escaping his cellar prison, and as we watch him go ever more frantically about the task of trying to escape, we suspect at times that he is more than half mad) or Doc Savage. Scott doesn't always know what to do. He fumbles the ball frequently, and when he does he goes on to do what most of us would probably do under the circumstances: he has the adult equivalent of a tantrum.

In fact, if we regard Scott's shrinking as a symbol for any incurable disease (and the progress of any incurable disease entails a kind of powerlessness which is analogous to shrinking), we see a pattern which psychologists would outline pretty much as Matheson wrote it . . . only the outline came years later. Scott follows this course from disbelief to rage to depression to final acceptance, almost exactly. As with cancer patients, the final trick seems to be to accept the inevitable, perhaps to find fresh lines of power leading back to the magic. In Scott's case, in the case of many terminal patients, the final outward sign of this is an admission of the inevitable, followed by a kind of euphoria.

Stephen King, *Danse Macabre* (New York: Everest House, 1981), pp. 325–26

TED KRULIK   Although author Damon Knight seemed to frown on Matheson's homespun technique when he wrote: "He has a profound interest in the trivia of his daily life," it is Matheson's ability to capture a sense of realism in a few lines of scenery which allows the reader to take the imaginative leap necessary. The author's detailed method makes plausible the nightmare thoughts that many people share, at least as children. The process of seeking some credible scientific excuse for the mythologies and superstitions of the human imagination is an important part of Matheson's writings. If vampires really could exist, how could they be explained? If shrinking were a genuine possibility, how could science explain the phenomenon? Can the workings of fantasy be explained in rational terms? Another author could have shrouded the causes of vampirism or shrinking in mystery, or made veiled implications about their conditions. But Matheson, much to his credit, presents the science behind the fantasy.

In *I Am Legend*, the reader learns with Neville that the vampire state develops from a germ like any other disease. With his discovery of the *bacillus vampirus* on a microscope, Neville wipes away all the superstitious fears of centuries. Although Matheson's pseudoscientific explanations may not stand up to informed scrutiny, it is remarkable how much his bacillus can explain. In one part, Neville tells another normal human how a stake kills a vampire without the need to be driven through the heart. He explains that the bacillus supplies energy to the "undead" as long as it is not exposed to oxygen. If, however, the germ is exposed, it becomes parasitic and feeds upon the body that had acted as its host. Thus, any deep wound in the body, no matter where, allows air in, and the vampire is destroyed. Even if this seems like pseudoscientific gibberish, we can enjoy digesting this highly interpretive theory that rationalizes the existence of the vampire.

Matheson uses similar medical terminology to describe the reasons for Scott Carey's condition in *The Shrinking Man*. The immediate biological cause of his shrinking is an irreversible and persistent loss of specific bodily elements, such as nitrogen, creatinine, phosphorous, and calcium; these elements are associated with development of tissue and muscle, and bone. Matheson is attempting to deal with one of the basic considerations of the SF genre, the "what if—" question. What if a person could shrink? How might it happen? What experiences might he have? By using medical jargon that sounds half-reasonable to answer some of these questions, the author shows a high regard for the science behind the unknown.

Ted Krulik, "Reaching for Immortality: Two Novels of Richard Matheson," *Critical Encounters II: Writers and Themes in Science Fiction*, ed. Tom Staicar (New York: Frederick Ungar Publishing Co., 1982), pp. 4–5

RICHARD MATHESON   The leitmotif of all my work—and certainly this collection of short stories—is as follows: *The individual isolated in a threatening world, attempting to survive.*

Strange to reduce hundreds of thousands of words to this one statement. Yet, with obvious exceptions, it is accurate. ⟨. . .⟩

I trust it is a good sign that, from the very beginning of my work in short stories, an attempt to survive is part and parcel of the recurring theme. However the main character—usually (predictably) a male of whatever age—is afflicted, however he fails to "fit in" or is harassed by outside forces, he attempts to survive. The protagonist in "Third from the Sun" (my second published story) tries to survive and help his family survive. The protagonist in "When the Sleeper Wakes" (my third published story) tries to survive if more involuntarily and with the aid of a larger survival mechanism, society itself.

These survival attempts rarely succeed, of course; my initial cynicism on display. Outside menace most often overcame the isolated individual despite any attempt to survive. ("Dress of White Silk," "Blood Son," "Through Channels," "Lover When You're Near Me.") The apogee of these early paranoiac flights was surely reached in the story "Legion of Plotters." Can any title better express the paranoiac point of view? Still, there was always that thread of attempted survival—for which I am gratified. Nice to note that Mr. Paranoia did have his positive side from the start of his creative appearance. ⟨. . .⟩

During this period my stories were deeply imbued with a sense of anxiety, a fear of the unknown, of a world too complicated which expected too much of individual males, sometimes humorously ("Clothes Make the Man," "SRL Ad," "The Wedding"), more often grimly ("Mad House," "Trespass," "Shipshape Home," "The Last Day"). "We are beset by a host of dangers," says my male protagonist in "The Wedding." I believed it.

Add to this another aspect of my paranoiac leitmotif: the inability of others to understand the male protagonist, to give him proper recognition. Their inclination (virtually insistence) on victimizing him with ignorance, stupidity, cliché thinking and unwitting power. ("Return," "Mad House," "Legion of Plotters," "The Test.") That I, sometimes, gave alternate emphasis to the possibility that the male protagonist might be partially responsible for his own problems—that his real adversary was his own mind—does not alter the fact that he is, in the end, threatened by actual outside forces. Or, to paraphrase the old joke, just because he's paranoid doesn't mean someone isn't out to get him.

So I dealt with my personal anxieties, my own fear of the unknown, relieving my angst by exteriorizing it in the form of characters in my short

stories. Even "objects" could be used to represent outside menace—clothes
in "Clothes Make the Man," household items in "Mad House," a television
set in "Through Channels," a bed in "Wet Straw." The world is a scary
place, I was saying in my stories. If I'd said it aloud as myself, I would have
gotten uncomfortable looks. Saying it in the form of "fantasy" stories not
only was acceptable, it was *recompensed*. That menacing world out there
actually began to pat my little paranoiac head and say "Well done. Here's
some money for your trouble."

> Richard Matheson, "Introduction," *Collected Stories* (Los Angeles: Dream/Press,
> 1989), pp. xix–xx

TERENCE HOLT   Richard Matheson's 1950 story, "Born of Man
and Woman," engages in just such an ambiguous display, demonstrating
some of the mechanisms implicating us in the nuclear dilemma. The title
asserts a parentage, but asserts it in order to deny: another mutant, the child
identified by the title is yet another putative child of the bomb. The slimy,
misshapen, powerful creature is kept chained by its parents in a sealed room,
from which it continually tries to escape. After each attempt, it is beaten
and chained more tightly, while its mother laments (in the classic formula
of scapegoating), "Why have you *done* this to me?" As the beatings become
more savage and the chains tighten, the child becomes enraged. "I have a
bad anger with mother and father," it concludes. "I will show them. I will
do what I did that once . . . If they try to beat me again I'll hurt them. I
will." In promising to hurt his parents, the child promises no more than
what the parents have done to him: parent and child mirror each other in
violence, suggesting that what we fear in the bomb is only a distorted image
of ourselves.

The story acknowledges this mirroring through a self-reflexiveness that
comments on its own implication in this drama of projection and denial.
The parents' greatest fear about the child's attempts to escape is that the
neighbors might see. Whatever the parents' feelings on this subject, however,
for the story itself the point is plainly that they (or we) *should* see—the
basic tactic of the strategy of nuclear deterrence, in which the display of a
nation's possession of the bomb stands in the place of its use. The tension
between concealment and revelation takes on a new meaning in the child's
final threat, where "show" means both "reveal" and "punish"—"I'll *show*

them." Both meanings are implicit in the passage's historical allusion: if the child stands for the bomb, then "what I did once" is the previous "showing" of the bomb's power, its use on Japan. The strategy *says* that since we used it once, we no longer have to use it again—the display is sufficient. But this story exposes another logic as well. In its obsessive focus on the child, the story exposes its own desire not just to display but also to "show"—to use the bomb again as we did "that once."

In a ritual of mutual punishment and justification, the child provides the parents with the opportunity to punish it, and the child in turn threatens to punish the parents. Both are punished, because both are guilty. And we, as audience, participate in the punishment as well, as victim through our identification with either child or the parents he promises to "show"—*and* as punisher through our identification with parents, child and the implied narrator "showing" these events. Matheson's story, by speaking from so many positions, and reducing all of them to the common desire to "show," points to our own desires for such a display even as it demonstrates the tactics of denial that make such wishes tolerable. By locating its display of power in a locked room, the story does not merely show us what goes on in there: while locking the room suggests that we, like the characters within, are trapped in a drama of mutual assured destruction, as readers we are in fact free to leave this particular locked room whenever we wish. The story localizes what is usually a pervasive and inescapable prison. And the point of the story is that we do not really *want* to leave anyway: the story compels us to read it, to follow its logic, but as readers we are complicit in that compulsion. In that room, we are not merely witness to, we *enjoy* the power to mutate, to beat and chain, to "show": the power we have achieved to destroy ourselves, and the strategies we use to allow us to do it. The point of the story, as in all exercises of power, especially the power latent in the bomb, is to draw attention to that power, to set it up as if it were an independent agency, and, hence, as something for which we are not responsible, something we might be able to escape. Yet, by eliciting our enjoyment, by enlisting us through our spectatorship as willing participants, the story also implicates us within the structure of power relations that needs the bomb to uphold itself.

Terence Holt, "The Bomb and the Baby Boom," *Triquarterly* No. 80 (Winter 1990–91): 210–12

STEFAN DZIEMIANOWICZ   In some ways, *The Shrinking Man* can be read as a response to the novel that immediately precedes it in the

Matheson oeuvre, *I Am Legend* (1954). Where the former tells the story of a man who finds that the "normal" world has become alien to him, the latter tells of a man who seeks refuge in the mundane remnants of a world that has lost normality for him.

In the first chapter, Matheson introduces Robert Neville as a diligent homeowner embarked upon an apparently daily ritual of inspecting damage to his property by an undefined "they". Some details that come to light in the course of this process seem a little unusual—Neville has completely boarded over his windows, he cultivates garlic in a greenhouse behind his living quarters, and he has converted half of his bedroom into a workshop where he fashions dowling material into pointed stakes—yet the whole operation is carried out to the rhythm of a comfortable routine. Matheson describes every banal detail of Neville's tasks, down to the minutiae of his preparations of a dinner of frozen lamb chops, frozen string beans, and bread. When a commotion begins outside his house after dinner, he drowns out the noise through a combination of reading, drinking, and playing classical music on his stereo.

As Matheson describes him, Neville could be the average suburbanite winding down at the end of an exhausting day. In fact, he is the last human being on earth. Three years earlier, a mutated virus, possibly the result of germ warfare (here again, Matheson is sketchy on the origins of his extraordinary phenomena, concentrating instead on how his characters accommodate them), gradually wiped out the world's population, including his wife and child, and turned the rest into vampires. Every night, Neville's vampirized neighbors besiege his house in the hopes of catching him off-guard. Every day, he seeks out their resting places and stakes as many as he can find.

Like a latter-day Robinson Crusoe, Neville tries to gain control of the chaos around him by maintaining as much of his former life as circumstances will permit. Where the intrusion of the extraordinary becomes unavoidable, he displays an admirable resourcefulness, finding scientific explanations for why these accidents of a biological mishap are subject to the limitations of the vampires of myth and legend. Certain characteristics of the virus cause its host to crave blood and shun sunlight. Psychological factors account for the vampire's reaction to the cross and mirrors. Garlic has a natural chemical toxin repellent to the vampire's metabolism. Metabolic changes stimulate the rapid regeneration of tissue immediately after wounding by a bullet or knife. Even death and dissolution by staking have an explanation: the virus is an anaerobe that becomes parasitic once air enters into the closed system of its host. In contrast to most Matheson characters, who usually find the most reassuring details of life transforming before their eyes into things with a sinister side, Neville systematically demythologizes the individual details of the vampire legend, reclaiming them as fragments of the normal world he desperately hopes to salvage.

But there is no more "normal" world, at least as Neville knows it. The last mortal in a world of vampires, it is *he* who is the anomaly. Neville's relationship to the world outside his door has been irrevocably altered, and thus so has his role in it. Just how is related in the novel's closing paragraphs, as Neville is led to his public execution by leaders of the vampire populace:

> They all stood looking up at him with their white faces. He stared back. And suddenly he thought, I'm the abnormal one now. Normalcy was a majority concept, the standard of many and not the standard of just one man.
>
> Abruptly that realization joined with what he saw on their faces—awe, fear, shrinking horror—and he knew that they *were* afraid of him. To them, he was some terrible scourge they had never seen, a scourge even worse than the disease they had come to live with. He was an invisible specter who had left for evidence of his existence the bloodless bodies of their loved ones. And he understood what they felt and did not hate them.

Neville goes to his death savoring the irony of his situation: for all his efforts to preserve the ordinary world of the past, he has become "a new superstition entering the unassailable fortress of forever", an agent of disorder in a world turned upside down.

Stefan Dziemianowicz, "Horror Begins at Home: Richard Matheson's Fear of the Familiar," *Studies in Weird Fiction* No. 14 (Winter 1994): 33–34

▣ *Bibliography*

Someone Is Bleeding. 1953.
Fury on Sunday. 1953.
I Am Legend ⟨*The Omega Man*⟩. 1954.

Born of Man and Woman: Tales of Science Fiction and Fantasy. 1954, 1954
  (abridged; as *Third from the Sun*).
The Shrinking Man. 1956.
The Shores of Space. 1957.
A Stir of Echoes. 1958.
Ride the Nightmare. 1959.
The Beardless Warriors. 1960.
Shock! 1961.
Shock II. 1964.
Shock III. 1966.
Shock Waves. 1970.
Hell House. 1971.
Bid Time Return ⟨Somewhere in Time⟩. 1975.
What Dreams May Come. 1978.
Shocks 4. 1980.
The Twilight Zone: The Original Stories (editor; with Martin Harry Greenberg
  and Charles G. Waugh). 1985.
Collected Stories. 1989.
Earthbound. 1989.
Through Channels. 1989.
Journal of the Gun Years. 1991.
The Gun Fight. 1993.
By the Gun. 1993.
7 Steps to Midnight. 1993.
The Path: Metaphysics for the '90s. 1993.
Shadow on the Sun. 1994.
Now You See It—. 1995.